# THE
# CHILD
# OF
# GOD

JENIFER BANNISTER

Ordering Information:

Prime Seven Media
518 Landmann St.
Tomah City, WI 54660

Printed in the United States of America

# TABLE OF CONTENTS

Chapter 1    Meeting With My Devine Father ................................. 1

Chapter 2    First Time I Met My Ancestral Family ...................... 6

Chapter 3    A Woman Entity Attacking My Aura ....................... 11

Chapter 4    Karma Bites Back ................................................ 14

Chapter 5    Resting Underneath A Big Single Tree ................... 18

Chapter 6    Being Attacked by the Black Entities ..................... 21

Chapter 7    The Emperor Husband ....................................... 24

Chapter 8    The Black Shadow ............................................. 28

Chapter 9    My White Angel Wings ...................................... 38

Chapter 10   Why I Can't See Your Face .................................. 43

Chapter 11   An Asian Looking Face Inside My Stomach ........... 47

Chapter 12   An Angel Warriour ............................................ 54

Chapter 13   Spiritual Contract ............................................. 61

Chapter 14   Royal Blue Colour Man ...................................... 67

Chapter 15   Matrix Web ...................................................... 71

Chapter 16   War Zone Battle ............................................... 75

Chapter 17   Little Square Blue ............................................. 79

Chapter 18   Angel Hermii .................................................... 80

Chapter 19   Floating Map .................................................... 88

Chapter 20   I Don't Feel Normal ........................................... 91

Chapter 21   Who Is My Mother? ........................................... 95

Chapter 22   What if I Go Blind? ..................... 98

Chapter 23   Finding My Magical Music Box ............... 101

Chapter 24   What Is My Purpose? .................... 107

Chapter 25   Seeing the Purgatory .................... 112

Chapter 26   Tame That Wings .................... 117

Chapter 27   Volcano Ready to Erupt ................ 120

Chapter 28   The 6th Dimensions ................. 126

Chapter 29   Healing the World .................... 129

Chapter 30   American Indian the Shaman ................ 133

Chapter 31   They Are Asking For Their Lives ............ 135

Chapter 32   My Black Outfit for the Battle ................. 138

Chapter 33   Big White Book .................... 145

Chapter 34   A Long Metal Weapon .................... 150

Chapter 35   "Feel It" .................... 155

Chapter 36   My Devine Father Is Furious ................ 157

Chapter 37   Meeting Papa God Near the Stream ............ 159

Chapter 38   Stalkers Invading My Space .................... 164

Chapter 39   Messaged From Above "Paralysed" ............ 167

Chapter 40   Time to Reflect .................... 168

Chapter 41   Purple Bubble Inside .................... 171

Chapter 42   "I Am Missing Sky" .................... 174

Chapter 43   My Ancestral Kingdom .................... 178

Chapter 44   "Whip" the New Weapon .................... 183

Chapter 45   Golden Key In My Music Box .................... 187

Chapter 46   Green Lady Motherly Being .................... 190

Chapter 47   A Ball of Fire in Papa God's Hands .................... 193

Chapter 48   Solomon and a Big Book .................... 195

Chapter 49   A Big Heart Shape of a Balloon .................... 197

Chapter 50   Lady Entity Got Burnt During the Journey ............ 200

Chapter 51   Word Sacrifice .................... 202

Chapter 52    "City of Angels" ............................................. 205

Chapter 53    Black Entity Came to Collect.....................211

Chapter 54    A Bait..it Was a Sacrifice..................................215

Chapter 55    No Termination Contract ......................... 220

Chapter 56    The Day I Was Created ............................. 224

Chapter 57    My Birthday!! :)...................................................227

Chapter 58    The Queen of England Died.............................228

Chapter 59    The Black Canvas of My Life............................ 231

Chapter 60    11th Dimension Travels.................................... 234

Chapter 61    The Queen Elizabeth Funeral ...................... 238

Chapter 62    The Green Little Being....................................242

Chapter 63    Soul Connection............................................. 245

Chapter 64    The White Sword ........................................ 247

Chapter 65    The Earth Is Black...........................................251

Chapter 66    "Orion" and Angels in the Dungeons........... ......... 253

Chapter 67    Feel the Rhythms............................................260

Chapter 68    Equator Healing ..........................................264

Chapter 69    Ginger Blue.................................................... 267

Chapter 70    Business or Healing......................................... 270

Chapter 71    The Black Book.............................................. 274

Chapter 72    Royal Blue Grandfather Angel Metatron............... 279

Chapter 73    Square White Light Energy............................. 282

Chapter 74    The Dark City ............................................ 285

Chapter 75    Golden Cross Bow ...................................... 293

Chapter 76    The World Is Mine ........................................ 297

Chapter 77    The Battle Field ............................................ 299

Chapter 78    Crystal Weapon ............................................ 302

Chapter 79    Vertigo............................................................. 307

Chapter 80    Healing the Jungle and the Animals.........................311

Chapter 81    Sleeping in a Cocoon.......................................316

Chapter 82    The Shooting Star ...................................................318

Chapter 83    New Weapon Presented ............................... 320

Chapter 84    Between Us "Ours"...................................................... 322

Chapter 85    The Vatican Church ............................................. 325

Chapter 86    Go Back to "Nature" ...........................................331

Chapter 87    The Vatican Church and the Tombs........................ 333

Chapter 88    Two Airport Blasted?? ......................................... 339

Chapter 89    Descending Down to Meet Solomon ....................... 342

Chapter 90    Meeting Abraham.................................................. 347

Chapter 91    Christmas Day Surprise Coronation ...................... 350

Chapter 92    Arizona.................................................................. 358

Chapter 93    Sunami in South East Asia................................... 362

Chapter 94    Japanese Battle Warriour...................................... 364

Chapter 95    Big Storm on the Way Home................................. 370

Chapter 96    "Trust" Your Feelings During the Battle.............. 375

Chapter 97    Annoying Bug ...................................................... 379

Chapter 98    Black Heart .......................................................... 383

Chapter 99    God of Thunder ................................................... 388

Chapter 100   Back to My Ancestral Home................................. 394

Chapter 101   No Mercy During the Battle................................... 398

Chapter 102   Where My Personalities Came From...................... 402

Chapter 103   Valentines Day With My Devine Father................. 406

Chapter 104   Mirror Mirror on the Wall .................................410

Chapter 105   Another Battle With an Evil Entity......................... 412

Chapter 106   Spiritual Battle Preparations.................................. 416

Chapter 107   Portal to a Different Dimension ............................. 422

Chapter 108   Horrible Looking Beings Falling From the Sky ..... 428

Chapter 109   Aligning With the White Being and
              My Devine Father.................................................. 432

Chapter 110   A Download While in the Shower ........................... 435

Chapter 111 The Devil Walking Accross My Path......................439

Chapter 112 Extra Protection Vortex Machine ...........................443

Chapter 113 7 Disasters Represents....................................................446

Chapter 114 To Shift My Writing........................................................450

Chapter 115 Everything Is Angelicl Colour the Bow and

Arrow and Round White and Glittery Ball............452

Chapter 116 The Spiritual Warfare Battle .......................................454

Chapter 117 Pitch Black.........................................................................458

# MY SPIRITUAL JOURNAL

# CHAPTER 1

# MEETING WITH MY DEVINE FATHER

JOURNAL

5TH MARCH 2022

This book is all about the reality of my life and the connections to my spiritual world. I wish this book will give you a special peek to your own spiritual beliefs, and most of all to have more FAITH IN OUR DEVINE CREATOR. YES, GOD IS REAL, JESUS is REAL, Heaven and Hell are real, and the Dimensions and Galaxies are real.

My connections to my DEVINE FATHER is not so unfamiliar, i grew up with it. So it is not hard for me to connect with him spiritually. Although, he doesn't makes it easy for me the way i want for my life. He always said..LIFE is all about learning to reach your own destination. Other words, he wants me to do the hard way and learn about my life on the way towards my destiny. Sometimes in my life i almost gave up..but for some reason somebody from nowhere came to rescue me.

Then one day i am feeing the overwhelming tiredness of what's going on arround me, i wish life is not that too complicated. last night there was a messages about the number 30. Papa God showed me this number. A big problem or disaster coming into our world.. number 30 was given to me from the above last night. I'm not sure if it's the month of March 30 has a significant to what might be going to happen to our world. I will pray hard and i will be praying tonight. I don't like this premonition.

Last night i meditated..i knocked on my Devine FATHER's door to see if i can talk to him. I said..Father can you please let me in? Then the door started to open slowly. I can see him waiting for me..and i can see his right hand was on his face, and the left hand holding a pen. Somehow he is writing on a piece of old paper.. ancient looking light brown square piece of paper, just one piece. And When he saw me coming, he put the pen down and asked me to come in.

His room is full of clouds..he's wearing a light brown robe, but i couldn't see his face..i never see his face. He asked me to sit down, the chair just a normal chair sorrounded by the clouds..we are sorrounded by the clouds. He asked me why it took me so long?..i then innocently said..i was pre occupied with something else. He then smiled..then i asked him about what is the meaning of number 30 that you have given me Papa GOD from previous night? What is it FATHER? i asked curiously.

He looked at me calmly straight into my eyes and stated..you will know when it comes. I feel no threatening feelings about it or what he just said, so i didn't persist. I asked him for forgiveness of what's happening and what's going on arround the world..i asked him to stop the WAR! PAPA GOD in response was STILL..no words came out from him..but only "neutral", neutral feeling he made me feel, then conversations was over.

My lovely journal, let me take you back 20 years ago the beginning of my curiousity of my spirituality. I always dream..sometimes good, but sometimes bad and something scary and mostly annoying. Some specific dreams always happens the next day. One day i dreamed about the SEPTEMBER 11 in america..the flooding..the plane disasters, train disasters, cities gone and went under water and many more. Sometimes, i'm watching the news about a person being shot.. then suddenly i felt like i have been shot on my head. All that i have written in my journals and destroyed..i burnt it all!!

I didn't know what to do with my visions at that time..i was scared to death of what will be the consequences and what might happen to me if i tell anybody? So i decided to kept it to myself and started journaling. Everyday my visions and intuitions becoming more and more apparent and clear. I even see entities that other people can't see and this is really freaking me out. Sometimes it does caused so much chaos arround me, and sometimes almost causing an accidents many times while driving my car..and i am always feeling exhausted.

The best things that i could say and admitted of what's happening to me when i was in that trance of my spirituality..that it was my hands..my hands can heal anything..just one touched and it changed everything. Everytime i touched a patient or anyone with physical problems, there are something good has happened to them..or maybe cured??? I was puzzled and very confused at that time.

Then again, i thought that would only just a coincidence?..i don't know i thought, so i made up my mind not to believe it. I didn't want to believe that this is happening to me. And At that time i was even more confused and feeling scared and uneasy. One day i took a photo of my hands from my camera by accident..i was puzzled??? the colour of my hands are golden colour..i thought it can't be, it has to be some camera exposures. So i took it again, and this time, the colour gold it's all the way up towards my shoulders.

I have shown this towards my colleague as i was confused and puzzled. When she saw it she said..OMG!!! you have healing hands. Shhhh..i said to her. I quickly took away my hands from her while she was looking at it. I was petrified and hid my hands into my pockets. Everyday and everyday i was becoming more isolated and anxious.. yes..i solated myself a lot, and as my dreams becoming more apparent and clear.

I asked for help spiritually..but nothing or nobody can explained what i have experiencing. I was so desperate to find out more about myself. Then suddenly i was connected to the meditation group workshop, and that was the time i have found out the reality of my curiousity. During the guided meditation session..when i closed my eyes, i felt like i was plugged in into an electrical current straightaway!

Everything was moving in a slow motions..i saw myself walking through the clouds and feeling confident trusting that the clouds will support me. During my walk..somehow i was looking for somebody to guide me. The first person i have encountered was an old man, and i asked him, are you my guide? he said no. Then i kept walking and saw another old man just walking opposite me, and then i stopped and asked him too, are you my guide? and again he said, No..i'm not your guide. So i continued walking..then when i reached to the small and narrow lane with full of clouds, suddenly..i fell over on the ground! Then I looked what i have fallen to..i have tripped over on a very big boulder and faced down, didn't hurt myself.

Then when i was about to get up and looked up straight to the west horizon, and here it is, my eyes caught an amazing bright light from above and directly facing to me. I thought it was a sun..but it's not a sun because it's not irritating my eyes. The lights almost absorbing into my whole body without getting burnt..and a matter fact it was soothing..i was drawn ot it..i feel like i have being hypnotised with the white light. Then suddenly the figure of a MAN suddenly appeared.. and it looks like an old man..it's a silhouette..or spirit. I couldn't take my eyes off him..the whole figure of this old man looking at me from the distance..but i noticed, i can't see his face!

I have felt some overwhelming gratitudes and sense of peace during the encounter, and then he spoke to me in my head.."DON'T LOOK ANY MORE FURTHER, I'M HERE FOR YOU". I then saw Arch Angel Michael wearing a blue cape on my left side and Mother Mary in my right side, then Jesus standing closer to the image infront of me. Then in my head this is "GOD". He then told me..i have some message for you to spread. Then this 3 words appeared infront of me. LOVE..CARE..HEAL. Now, spread this to the world with a gentle and soothing voice. I said, i will. lately, i understand now of what he wants me to do..spread it to the world, he said..to give LOVE..to show CARE..and to HEAL the world. That is the words of GOD.. so simple and profound.

# CHAPTER 2

# FIRST TIME I MET MY ANCESTRAL FAMILY

JOURNAL

14th MARCH 2022

I seek counselling with Papa GOD again last night, I can see a little smile on his face..but still..i can't and i don't see his whole face again. I sat down sat in my little chair and told him what has happened recently. I told him i'm feeling low and feeling insignificant at this moment..as i am crying..he looked at me and touched my chin up, and wiped my tears in my face with his thumb. He didn't say anything.. although i want to hug him, but instead he put his right hand on my head, and that instant i felt a lot better, and feeling loved again sorrounded by golden aura. He then said something in my head.. my girl..the word GIRL is always he called me ever since i could remember when i was a child.

Remembering that time when i was growing up, my grandmother used to say, i have always been talking to someone especially when i was sick. You have grown up now he said..that's what the free will is all about. I never understood the free will when i was a kid. You are protected he said, and do not worry i'm always here for you.

Remember when we first met? And what did i say to you? He asked me with a very comforting voice..Yes, i remember with a smile on my face..yeahh..you tripped me over, and he laughed!!..and you said don't look anymore further "I'm here for you". PAPA GOD has a very funny sense of humour. He knows how to make me laugh and makes me feel better. And i think i do that to him too. :)

He reassured me..keep going my child, no one can harm you, I'm always here and your ANGEL..Arch Angel Michael. Where ever you are going he is with you. And that's explains everything..sometimes i don't have fears going travelling on my own. I felt like i always have company, Yes..papa GOD said. Because you always have..not just one..many.

Another thing i have asked him in my head. PAPA GOD who am i? I felt different from everybody else..feel weird sometimes..who am I father? I can see things that people cannot see..i have premonitions in my head and my dreams that has happened. I can hear things or people whispering, I can feel someone's and somebody's energy. I can see Angels sometimes. I thought i was going crazy..but now i started to understands the spirituality sides of it. It is sometimes scary..and the other thing is, i find it so hard to process in my head and get very tired, and papa GOD you know that. U humm..he agreed. You are the only one who can make me sleep, i said.

PAPA GOD one night i had a dream..remember i asked who am i? One night somebody visited me in my dream..a very kind man looking like a KING. He was wearing a white robe..has a beard and very well and soft spoken. I saw myself getting up from my bed and with my dressing gown. I took this Emperor looking into my back verandah and offered him some water. During that time there, was not much conversations going on..instead he asked me to come home. I said with curiousity in my head..come home? where is home? take my hand and close your eyes..which his right hand extended to me.. and i will take you there, he said.

At that moment i took his hand then suddenly, we are both in a magnificent place..just like that in a blink of my eyes.The place i am feeling i have been here and belong to. We were standing infront of this magneficent verandah looking at the open space of water the ocean, and on the right side..the waterfalls. We were also moved to the right and standing infront of a magnificent waterfalls. The waterfalls are connected to the very high wall mountain rock, and almost sorrounding the palace.

Then i can see trees, flowers..the birds are singing, the breeze of the wind almost caressing my face. The serenity of the place makes me feel so enchanted, and i felt like this sorrounding is just so familiar to me.. and i felt like..i miss it. I looked at myself..my clothes i was wearing has changed into a long white and silky dress. My hair is very long and almost touching the ground..and i felt taller and slim, very petit looking. I felt like i'm different and a feeling of i have experienced this before.

Then suddenly, i heard a very faint foot steps behind me, and when i slowly turned arround, i saw this beautiful lady..looks a little bit older..and she looks like me??? Before i could say something..she's your mother..the Emperor said. She's also wearing a beautiful white silky gown or a dress, and her cape is a beautiful baby pink colour cape. The colour i always love..baby pink colour..

She welcomed and hugged me..i can smell her beautiful perfume a very familiar scent..i am feeling home in my mother's arms. The scent of sweetness and pure love. She too has a long hair..a beautiful dark straight long hair. Her hair is almost looks like dancing when she walks. So beautiful..she said come back home while she have her both hands on my face. She's looking at me lovingly.

They took me to their long verandah looking at the waterfalls.. and on that table there was a lot fruit, fruits that i have never seen in earth and there was some kind of vegetables too that never seen before. That's the only thing they eat. I didn't eat any of them as i was pre-occupied just looking at the sorroundings. Fascinated with the waterfalls! I spent my time with them just walking arround, then i asked my Emperor Father..where are we? He said..you would not believe or understand if i tell you. I'm willing to listen, i said. We are in a different world which no one can harm you, he said.

I felt so relaxed and loved again..i was in between with my father and my mother..they are hugging me:), i saw beautiful energies arround the area. I tried to touched them, but they just disappeared. I then saw little kids energies..and animals playing arround. What a beautiful and wonderful and very enchanting place..i feel like i'm home. THIS IS ALL MAKES SENSE NOW TO ME!!!

My mother took me to my bed and tucked me in..then i wake up suddenly with the scratching sounds on my door. Oh it's my dog kelly trying to open my bedroom door, while my cat staring at me looking really puzzled with his one eye and looking at my messed up hair..then i realized i am back to my reality. Darn that was quick! My 2 furry babies are hungry. Got to get up and feed them. Arghh..:(

Now i understand the way of my curiousity i have been feeling.. searching for something that was missing from my life..and i didn't know what it is. A feeling of looking for my home..a home of natures and now i truely understand why i am always fascinated with natures, and the destinations of water, waterfalls, mountains, trees, beautiful flowers, and the animals.

NOw i know where i came from..and will be there at the end of my time with my mother and father open arms. I remember my mother now..my real mother in a spiritual realm. She sounds like me sometimes, she has this comforting..love..and never ending sense of reassurance. My father is an Emperor and his name is king Artheru, and My mother is an Empress, Empress Glydica..i am the only child with them in a spiritual realm. My name is Empress Shinarea..and my father called me SHINAE..and my mother called me SHINE. My father told me..i am always with you..now this is so reassuring to me. They told me i am stubborn always wants to explore..very curious child.

# CHAPTER 3

# A WOMAN ENTITY ATTACKING MY AURA

JOURNAL
16th MARCH 2022

Our conversations last night was cut off short, and i was little bit disappointed. You know, i'm always looking forward to talk to you.. but last night it was something that scared me..but i shouldn't get scared because you were there papa GOD. Well..i think my lovely journal wants to know what has happened to me last night. Well..i was in the middle of my counselling with papa GOD dear journal.. and i poured out about my deep concerns lately, as i have no one i can tell in my own little world..here right now where we are.

During my conversations with him, there was an entity that appeared on top of me while i was laying down on my bed. A woman..and that woman i have never seen before. And what she was doing to me, she was clearly sucking my energy out of my mouth. I can see my energy.. beautiful colour pink sparkling energy, and she's sucking it up slowly. But before my energy reaches her mouth, i suddenly realised that she will be harming me. I asked again this time to stop in my mind..but she's persistingly continued, suddenly, i realised my devine enternal weapon that papa GOD gave me recently to use if necessary.

This entity kept going and continueing engulfing my energy. I started to feel lethargic and going down to my unconsciousness. And that moment someone wake me up and encouraged to use my internal weapon. I have no choice at that moment, i was disperately trying to fight back and get my conciousness back together..so i pulled my dagger looking very bright with golden colour and somehow there is a force that lead my hands to this woman's face..and the second times of my strikes, her head changed into a skull..a very black skull, she then disappeared.

In a few seconds, another 2 entities trying to attacked me, a man and a woman wearing the black hoods. Suddenly, Michael Arch Angel appeared behind me. I saw his sword protecting me and trying to fight with this 2 entities. Then the 2 faces of the entities became so aggressive and changes into a scary faces. The faces with skull and red eyes. During that time of the battle with this entities, Arch Angel Michael told me to pray, the latin words of prayers came out from my mouth while fighting back, while i was signing cross and hitting them at the same time.

After the scary moments, I don't know how long it lasted..the entities disappeared. My internal weapon looks very black. I raised my internal weapon with my two hands up and suddenly the lights from above "Golden lights" washes and dissolved the black colour of my internal weapon and became clean again with golden colour.

I returned my internal weapon into my chest again, then i thanked Arch Angel Michael for rescuing me. Then i fall asleep..the next morning i wake up with different energy..a good energy sorrounded my body. Sometimes i asked Papa GOD, am i crazy? Although i was tested by the priest when i was a kid with his spirituality healing. He said to my grandma, it's too early to tell, as she's only a child.

My grandma knew what i was going through with this scary gifts. SHe said, it's a gift from GOD. But i then said, i don't want it because it scares me. But why? my grandma asked. well..maybe people will take me away from you and everyone else in here. This things kept going until i was in high school. That time i want to fit in with my school friends. I didn't tell anyone or anybody about this at that time. Would you imagine if they knew..i'm sure they will put me in a mental institution or give me some blue pills.

I asked my grandmother..is it possible not to have this grandma? How can i get rid of it? I get very tired and i don't feel happy and feeling isolated. My grandma responded, well..if you don't want it at this time, all you need to do is block it. Block it? How? i asked curiously. Well..just like this..Do some prayers, and ask Papa GOD nicely not to have it. OK..i said, then what? i asked persistently. Well.. everytime you have experiencing some kind of sipiritual happening to you, just don't believe. DON'T "BELIEVE" it. It's the only way to stop them from coming to you and from harming you.

Well from that moment, i felt so really relieved that there is an answers for my problem. I exercised and tried to block everything that comes to me at that time and for long time. I enjoyed my normal life now then..and until 20 years ago it has been opened again. I think my contract has been expired! Then now it plays havoc in my life again, but this time i have more understanding about it and how it is impacting my lifestyles including my family life.

# CHAPTER 4

# KARMA BITES BACK

JOURNAL
20th March 2022

I asked Papa GOD if i could talk to you first, he waved his hand and said to my head..it's ok, you can reach me anytime. Although he's so busy looking down..he's watching..i asked him Papa GOD what are you watching? he looked at me and smile..people..he said. I saw papa GOD sittinig on a BIG chair made a marble stone..although shiny and colour beige with gray light sparkling beside the chair. Papa God is wearing a white long clothes with his half robe with colour red from the chest long way down..papa GOD I'll say to you good night this time before my curfew time from is 3 am in the morning..i don't know why it's 3..??? i never asked him.

Well my journal i must admit i never understood the person says to me you have put a spell on me, to me if you ask me why? why would i do that for? I don't even know how to do that, and a matter of fact i don't even believe in that..rather i believe in karma.

Let me take you back when i was just started with my carreer, i was young..naive and full of life and excitedly looking forward to starting my job as a young Registered Nurse. I really worked hard to obtained my Science Degree related in Nursing. From the department i have started, there was a person who hated me with passion, ever since the day i have started in that department. There was an actual harrassment always happened from this person towards me. But i thought there is no point to be engaged in such a none sense bigotry. And also i was trying not to ruin my first job, so i kept ignoring the harrassment.

The problem was, the more i ignored the more this person got agitated..and i always thought..what is this person's problem? but kept pushing my button. Sometimes i get home miserable and feels like not coming back the next day just to avoid any harrassment. The harrassment kept going, and then one day i informed the manager of the department, and i was shocked of what the manager responsed to me about my report. Oh..i't's just the personality..you just have to get used to it. This person has been here longer than you.

I was shocked! in this modern day, my claimed was just kicked under the table and shoved it in the bin..i couldn't believe i have just heard. So, I left the manager's office and i was in tears. I ran to the bathroom, took a deep breathed and fixed myself and faced again the daily rituals from this person. The next day, i was doing the ward rounds with the Surgeon and other doctors..and then suddenly the lady doctor intern told me that the nurse as she pointed out who.. spat on my back!! I said what? I thought..wow..i went straight to the bathroom and cleaned my back and reported the incident.

At that time, i was very upset..i could not contained my emotion..i went back to the toilet and cried. Then i asked Papa GOD, why? why this person continuing harrassing me? and this time have gone far to upset me! what have i done to this person to have such vengeance towards me? What is my wrong doing? I could not even remember one, A matter of fact i have always been so friendly to this person. I cried..and cried in the bathroom. And i thought this time is not acceptable..I wept my tears and came out from the bathroom and continued my work until i finished that afternoon.

I avoided and didn't confronted this person, because i thought there is no use..also i just started my job and don't want to loss it just like that. I went home home that day feeling miserable, i didn't feel like going back to work next day, and mattter of fact i was thinking a day off..but i didn't. Anyway, i decided to go back the next day, and luckily this person was not working the same shift with me..instead this person has been rotated to night shift. I thanked Papa GOD.

After couple of days, we recieved a shocking news that this person had an accident and in a critical condition but stable in ICU. Car accident..this person T-Boned the tree, and the damaged was extensive. Multipled fractures, face and ribs, FIB'S and TIB's and the most shockingly i heard was this person's tongue! Yes, you heard me.. This person's tongue was shockingly cut off half way, and only some small piece of the tongue connected was intact and able to hold, the remaining tongue was hanging down!!

I was shocked and recovered quickly, so i went to the bathroom and reached for PApa GOd, and i said to him..you know i didn't asked for this. He then said to me in my head..yes..i know my child. Now, that's what i called BAD KARMA!! and i'll it say again..i never ever wish to anybody's harm when i cried and speak to my Devine Father. when he's consoling me, he always touches my head and after that i always feels better. My head became clearer, and ready to face the reality again. This scenarios always have a comeback to some people who mistreated me, and that time i have no idea why? when they mistreated me, the next day BANG!! There's always happened to that person or people. It wasn't me..it's the UNIVERSE! Papa "GOD" is watching YOU!

Goodnight my dear journal got to go now before my curfew time. I glimpsed on my DEVINE FATHER again before i closed my eyes..i can see he still sitting on his big marble chair looking down..and i asked..Father, is there any messages i need to know? He then showed me a glimpsed of a storm in the horizon..and there are some black colour in the middle of the storm??? or is it looks like a sand storm?! He then said..good night my child, don't forget to pray. I won't forget FATHER..and goodnite my journal.

# CHAPTER 5

# RESTING UNDERNEATH A BIG SINGLE TREE

JOURNAL

21ST MARCH 2022

The next day back to the reality of course, and today i'm just sitting in my office and just finished my lunch. I meditated in my room and just suddenly i was connected to the stairways going up. When i reached the top, i saw the place full of clouds and pillars arround the area. This moment i am looking for my DEVINE FATHER as i couldn't find him during my meditation.

During my walks through the clouds..i saw little angels playing with some instruments..beautiful music that i have never heard before.. vey deep loving sound and very soothing..and every notes they are playing it's absorbing into my body and my soul. This angels are so beautiful looking, but so giglly. They makes me feel happy. I then continued looking for Papa GOD, but i couldn't find him. So i sat down on the edge of the stairs, and suddenly i saw Papa GOd just looking down again while sitting on the clouds.

He asked me to come with him, and then he showed me the WORLD.. yes looking down and showing me the area with green valley,and big high mountains. He didn't say why we are looking at this..and then he shifted the scenery,this time the North pole. I said to myself why North pole? But i didn't ask him again, because the sceneries kept changing so quick, and i didn't want to miss anything of this beautiful sceneries, it looks like a slow motion movie.

Then suddenly he asked me to come with him, i will show you more he said, but don't asks so many questions. Ok i said, i feel like i'm a child again to him. He extended his right hand to me and i placed my left hand to his hand,and then we began our journey. We travelled beyond..and more up higher to the horizon and beautiful stars.

Then we slowly descending to the ground and in the middle of the big open field. Then we decided to sit underneath the big tree, just one tree itself in the middle of ther field. Then i saw the west horizon full of golden colour. We are sorrounded by the golden colour lights and i can see myself as a child again, a little girl and almost about 5 years old with a short hair to the neck length.

Then i saw papa GOD sitting comfortably underneath the tree with 2 fruits. He said which one do you want? i said, that one on your right hand, he said why? a smile on Papa GOD's face. Well..i said innocently, because that one on your left hand has mould! Then papa GOD LAUGHED!! You are a smart child! At that time i started seeing so many butterflies..then i started walking barefooted on the grass and started chasing the butterflies..i kept chasing them..Then i suddenly woke up from my journey, someone came in into my office room.

I Asked my DEVINE FATHER one day..Father why do you always call me a child? I'm an adult now you know..well..you are always a child to me, he said. No matter how grown up you are..to me you are still my child. Why? i asked again..well, because i see your heart is always a "child". OH OK..i said, and thank you. Got to go now..catch up later papa GOD..he then waved at me, and when i was waving back to him..i noticed he was holding a long "solid stick". I thought..i have never seen that on him before..but i continued running and he said this time..don't tripped over. I won't papa GOD.

# CHAPTER 6

# BEING ATTACKED BY THE BLACK ENTITIES

JOURNAL

23RD MARCH 2022

Dear journal, last night i was very tired mentally..i got home from work and had a power nap, but still too tired. While i was resting in my bed after had a shower, i was falling asleep again..then suddenly i felt like someone touching my right face..a very gentle touched. I guess i feel asleep again..then suddenly i saw myself again being attacked by the entities. Before they get closer to me, there was some kind of energy sorrounded my body quickly as a protection. I felt like i was inside the bubble with the colour purple energy. The black entities were so vicious and trying to attacked my face from the outside the bubble, and several times trying to penetrated into my protection bubble, and of course tyhey could't get through!

I was very scared and i was screaming!!!then suddenly Arch Angel Michael came suddenly and came to the rescue, and with his sword trying to eliminate this very vicious entities..sooo many of them..it kept comimg and coming..then Arch Angel Michael asked me to use my internal weapon, but somehow i couldn't get it out!..he then, he asked me again with very sterned voice, but very Angelic and not intimidating voice."Try again now", he said.

Finally i pulled it out, and then i started to strike, and trying to protect myself from this aggressive entitiies who's trying to attacked me. And at the same time, i tried the sign of the cross again and again every time they attacked me. I saw Arch Angel Michael behind me..he was outside my bubble and finally, he slowly eliminated the whole entities whose trying to hurt me. Thank you my Angel.

Arch Angel Michael is a very tall, handsome Angel with beautiful blue eyes. He's also been with me since i can remember, and sometimes he appeared to me wearing a blue cape..and sometimes red. His sword looks magnificent, and it looks very light. I meant to say, it looks heavy but when he strikes the entities..there is this sounds..a very light and flawlessly sounds in the air. His strikes are always horizontal always horizontal..and that's i have always noticed every time i saw him during the battle.

Then after the attacked and we eliminated the entities, i always say sorry and asked forgiveness to my DEVINE FATHER..and HE always said to me..You know your enemies..never say sorry when it comes in protecting yourself. Yes, FATHER, i answered.

My dear journal, i will continue this tomorrow.. i am very tired and i need to sleep, goodnite..i have more to tell.

This morning i woke up very early morning to prepared myself to work. I asked Papa GOD, how do i know that they are my enemies? He then showed me a "wrinkled" face. I said, who is it? i asked curiously..and then he said..it's "YOU"! Your face will be definitely will be wrinkled if you always think who's after you. Oh..i see..i smiled at him. Just "TRUST" and use your "INTUITION". Papa GOD always used his funny sense of humour..then he laughed..it's so funny! I LOVE my DEVINE FATHER:)

CHAPTER 7
# THE EMPEROR HUSBAND

JOURNAL
27TH MARCH 2022

MY dear journal, i know it is very early in the morning to write my dreams and my interaction with Papa GOD. This specific person who's been visiting me in my dreams have visited me again. He was inside my aura field last night. I am trying to figured out what was our connections before? somewhere in time? as i am very curious. This person is very familiar to me..it's a kind of feeling of De Javu? I know the face very well and the voice. It has been inprinted into my head and my soul. It's becoming my biggest thoughts and mystery. I know i have so many past lives connections, some i have already meet for short time as i recognised thier souls buty this recent one now is somehow persistent. It kept flashing back and fort in my AURA..a feeling of and saying heyy..remember me? So it became a curiousity mindset to me, and i want to know more who is this person? it's really bugging me.

I asked my DEVINE FATHER to give me a glimpse of my previous lifetime in relation to this person. Papa GOD then asked me to close my eyes, and then we went for a journey..an incredible and interesting journey.

Papa GOD showed me that he was an Emperor sitting on a throne looking at the open space..i would say Enermous kingdom with an open yard of the palace. I can see him looking at the south Horizon and the ocean. The sea is extended so far away..the white birds flying on sky and there was no clouds in the horizon. It's beautiful and then i can see myself standing beside him, and i was wearing a long beautiful silky white gown..a dress of an EMpress. Again my hair is so long and straight.

The Emperor is holding my left hand, and i can feel the connections between me and him during my journey with papa GOD. It's bizzare and a matter of fact i am little bit emotional. I miss this Emperor when he holds my hands..i can feel his energy and the connections. It heals him emotionally, and gave him comfort..i feel like crying papa GOD. why? Then papa GOd said, because your life with him have never been finished. There was no closure from the time when you died. Oh ok..i said, i wiped my tears slowly. shall we continue he said?

I had a good look of my Emperor..he looks tough, good looking, and inside of him..he is very loving and have a good beautiful heart,and mostly very intelligent and have very funny sense of humour. He makes me laughed. At that time we had 2 children, a boy and a girl, twins. The boy was very close to his father Emperor..and my girl lili.. she was just beautiful. I loved my little girl so dearly and so does my little boy, and that was our happy family in our KINGDOM.

Then one day, our little boy suddenly died..and this is when the Emperor my husband, have suddenly changed his behaviour and personality. He went away for longest period of time, and he only came back in our palace once in a while. His absence became unbearable to me and to the palace. I managed most of the engagements in our KINGdom without his presence. I was trying to console him, but refuses to be consoled. I left on my own to carry my responsibilities,and then one day i beccame ill..and died.

The Emperor even more became solemn, but he didn't stop there.. he asked to investigates my death, and later on he found out i was poisoned, slowly.. I saw my body laying on the Marble BED, covered with a beautiful silky pink materials cloth, but my head still exposed and not covered. I saw my husband the Emperor mourning so deeply, even now i can feel his deep emotions..i can see my daughter lili infront of the door standing but she didn't come near me.

Papa GOD showed me the number 7, I then asked him.. what is the meaning of the number 7? He said, after i died, the Emperor had severals women and it was 7, and tried to have more and had 7 boys. Now, my past life husband Emperor from my other lifetime, we build an Empire..built with LOVE for humanity, but humanity brokes our hearts, but we didn't seek revenge. Instead, we taught the humanity that can be improved in the next lifetime, if we continue and capable in giving LOVE. That makes sense now when my DEVINE FATHER told me to spread the LOVE...to show CARE... and to HEAL the humankind.

DEVINE FATHER showed me number 2, an of course i asked again..what is number 2 FATHER? Number 2 is your remaining life cycle in earth before your ascensions..and that was it..my DEVINE FATHER stopped the journey. And then when i wake up, i heard kelly my dearest dog crying in the other room. I thought about of what's my Devine Father just have said. I have 2 lifetime left in earth..hmm..how exciting but a little bit sad, then i heard a word from above..don't be sad..then the voice disappeared.

Thank you my dearest journal, i feel much better now..i thought i have to tell you this before it will disappeared from my thoughts. I guess another lifetime memories has been solved, and i have more understanding about myself, and now with this particular person. THANK YOU FATHER.

## CHAPTER 8

# THE BLACK SHADOW

JOURNAL

31ST MARCH 2022

Good morning my dearest journal, i must apologise that i haven't been updating you lately. I have been very busy with my work. Well, i must tell you there is something that has been bugging my head lately. The night before, i was very tired and i went to bed very exhausted. I think i fell asleep quickly that i didn't even talked to papa GOD. I thought..i will talk to him later. When i was sleeping, subconsciously my body started to become paralysed.. sleep paralysis..i couldn't move, but my subconscious is awake. Then suddenly i saw my body..or should i say, my spirirt started to rise up, and then i saw my self walking out from my bedroom. I looked at my whole body still in bed.

Then suddenly, i felt like somebody have their hands on my neck..I couldn't move..i can see black shadow arround my neck. Then i can feel the pressure getting tighter, and i was feeling going into a state of unconsciousness. Then suddenly, Arch Angel Michael came to the rescue! Descending from above very quickly and with his sword attacking the evil entities. Again, I saw the bad entities attacking me, and it was just thier faces..no forms of whole bodies..it's only thier heads.

I was very scared..i have never been attacked like this in my entire life before. It feels like i have opened the pandora box of my life. But this time i have regained my courage, and i remembered my internal weapons it was given to me by my Devine Father. This weapons are just new, i am reluctant to use it as I don't know really know how to fight! and don't want to hurt anyone.

But suddenly, there was an energy in my body hovering, and feeling like it is altering and recovering my whole system, making me feel not to be scared of. You must protect yourself!! A voice came from above shook my senses! So i pulled out my internal weapons, and then started to protect myself from the incoming of so many ugly heads and trying to attacked me with their sharp teeths. Nasty..nasty looking heads! While i was protecting and retaliating back to them, i was praying at the same time and eradicating them all..eventually. After that, i lifted up my devine weapons to my DEVINE FATHER and washed it away with the golden lights, Then i slowly tucked it away.

I thanked Arch Angel Michael, and he gave me a beautiful smile. He is so handsome..and yes his eyes really fascinated me..blue eyes. Ohh..i love my Angel. And then when he was about to go..I asked him..where are you going? can i come with you and with your battle? but he said "no", not yet..but why? i asked. because you are not ready yet, then he disappeared from my sight.

I then reached to my DEVINE FATHER and had a talk to him. I said, papa GOD why me? I mean..why did you choose me? He then said you are choosen for your responsibility here in reality and especially spiritually. At first just close your eyes he said, which i did, then i can see myself as a child again..up there sorrounding by the clouds, with lots and lots of flowers arround the open fields, looks like a high valley on the west horizon.

I saw myself kneeling infront of this mysterious old looking man. I couldn't see his face again, and with his right hand on top of my head, and then my whole body suddenly covered with golden colour, and radiating out towards the sorroundings and extending to the whole area of the horizon. I was looking down..and then i can see him lifting my chin up, and he said you are going to be alright. Spread the love and you will be protected. Then i saw Arch Angel Michael again, and he took my right hand then we both walked away slowly then left the area. Then suddenly i heard a word..remember your wings..then i woke up.

Remember my wings? I don't have wings, i was kind of puzzled then..but then again if i can make it sense, i am always drawn to an Angel wings even when i was a kid and of course until now. I even considering a little tattoo wings on my back, i don't know why i thought about this lately..and yes, it does makes sense now some of the questions in my head..it's getting clearer.

Then i asked Papa GOD again..how is it possible to have wings, if i am here in an existing reality? He said, my child, everytime you are experiencing this attacked from the bad entities is really happening.. and everytime you are experiencing this attacked, you must imagine that your wings are being opened to protect yourself. The same thing as i have told you before..when you are feeling sad, you must get your wings out and wrap yourself arround with it as a protection. Imaginary wings papa GOD? i asked. Imaginary in reality, but real in spirituality, that's why your work is here in the spiritual realm, Papa God said.

Let me ask you something, papa GOD said. Do you feel sometimes on your back that something brushing off your back with the fearthers? I feel yesss...I felt it many times especially when i'm feeling vulnerable. Well now you know..it is reminding you that you have it on your back, papa GOD said. I thought great..more weight to carry..so how do i use it FATHER? well, you just need to know how to extend it in your thoughts..as your thoughts is powerful, he said. But your vulnerability still in you, because you are in a human form still existing in the physical world. Oh FATHER this is so new to me, i feel like i'm protesting..it's going to take me times to digest this new informations.

Oh yes, it is slowly making sense now my DEVINE FATHER. As i remember when i was in a primary school, I had an assignments and it was about something that we have to find something for ourselves. So i wrote..it was all about wings..i was looking for my wings. Then my teacher didn't acknowledge my assignment because it doesn't makes sense she said. She laughed and ridiculed me instead, and sort of failed my assignment. SHe said, what are you talking about? what wings? witchy wings perhaps? she said it sarcastically. After that, I didn't talk about wings or Angel's wings anymore.

Anyway Father, how do i use it? i mean in a spiritual realm? well.. when you are in a battle with Arch Angel Michael with this nasty entities..you have to imagine that you are extending your wings.. Once you do that, it will slowly open up, and with your entenal "GIFt" weapon i have given you. You "MUST" use it!

The "MUST" word is highlighted. No more hesitation, you must protect yourself. There are so many battles you are going to face with Arch Angel Michael. And soon more Angels will be joining you.

Who are they papa GOD? Earth Angels, reincarnated earth Angels, and Most of this angels are hidden from earth people, so their souls doesn't get manipulated and including "you" he said. Oh wow.. that is a big responsibility papa GOD. Yes it is my child. You are chosen before you have been created.

Oh my Dear DEVINE FATHER..i didn't know that this does exists. Yes it does exists in the spiritual realm, he said. So now you know your responsibility..and starts meditating and more in a daily basis. During the journey of your battle, i will be with you, and a matter of fact, i am here always, but sometimes you need to learn something in protecting yourself, Papa GOD can i ask again? Yes my child..but i know your questions, and the answer is "NO", you are not going to refuse this because this is your destiny. And if you don't, your life will be different mostly miserable and will be very difficult.

So i get punished then? But papa GOD didn't answer, instead he gave me half of a smile look..Gosh..i always dislikes it when he does this to me, then he went..and i heard the voice again, and said.. remember, open your wings, then he disappeared completely. Then suddenly i have an itchy back, i thought it must be triggered with my subconscious, hmm..if i tell somebody about this, they will difinitely think i am crazy! Then i heard a voice up there..no..you are not crazy.. remember you have been tested by the priest, then he laughed!! yeahh right i didn't like that priest anyway. Bye papa GOD..can i talk to you again tonight? Yes my child, and you know how to find me. Ok thank you my DEVINE FATHER.

My DEVINE FATHER is my sanctuary and my biggest comfort. He is always my companion at least in my thoughts, and i didn't know that I am overly protected from my heavenly DEVINE FATHER.

It does make sense now with all my previous experience..weird or i would call it's just a coincedence. During the time i was travelling alone, we were in the 4 wheel drive car. We travelled almost 8 hours to find the place of our destinations and places that i really wanted to see. I was sitting in tne middle of the back passenger seats, and with 2 ladies sitting besides me.The car didn't have seat belts at the back that we were sitting, and i was in between with this 2 ladies, no seat belts attached, i had no choice. while the driver driving in the express way, we heard a sudden impact!! And our 4 wheel drive car just hit the front car and invloved another one.

During the impact, i saw the slow motion of the impact..and then quickly BANG!! we collided between 2 cars and our front car massively damaged including the other cars. When the impact stopped, i saw myself tucked into the small gap between my feet. My bottom was tucked in into that small area, my legs and upper extremities were up and pointing towards the ceiling of the car! I was shoot down or tucked in into the very small space. The car wreckaged company said i should be dead after the impact. Well..i thought..i'm here and still alive with only small scratches, and my thumb and little finger were sore. The car company stated, in reality with sudden impact, my body would have been thrown infront of the car window, and your face should have been smashed. And if i'm unlucky you would have been dead lady, he said to me and that's the theory, the man said. Count your blessing lady, you are so lucky!

Well that was an experience, and my injury was my right hand, and my thumb, and little finger. No fractured injury, and it was only a ligament..but i think my right little finger has been twisted during the impact. I did heal myself for couple of days with my energy healing, and it worked! The rest of the passengers had some injuries, but mine was minor.

Another experience i had when i was travelling in Asia. During the night travelling in an Aircon bus, it was a very pleasant night. The bus only stopped in a particular places and in certain hours. So we have no choices as passengers to do the same as with the drivers. When the bus stop, the drivers will eat thier dinner, go to the toilet and passengers will do the same. During that night, the bus was determined to get on time for the destination, 12 to 16 hours travelling in a comfortable big aircon bus. I love my travels during that time, It was my freedom..my curiousity of Natures different places, cultures and people. But sometimes during treavelling, it has never been easy, it's always have some challenging issues and dangers always there. But this doesn't stop me from exploring another places.

During that night of travelling in the bus, i heard a sudden stopped! Our bus was stopped by the the military car, almost scretching infront of the bus. Infront of us, there was a private car with passengers, and looks like it's a family passengers. The driver of the car infront was being checked, i saw the man handed in his drivers licence and some kind of paper works to the military army. Then we saw from our bus window, there were some people coming out from nowhere and from the side of the road.

Before the bus driver can go ahead, he was suddenly stopped by the army guys and came accross to the front of the bus, and waved the hand to stop. The guys were not friendly, they were kind of very intimidating. I was nervous and the same as eveyone else in the Bus, and the BUS driver trying to talked to this guys nicely and calmly. I hugged my backpack infront of my chest and suddenly prayed for protection and everyone in the bus. And somehow, Arch Angel Michael came into my AURA when i closed my eyes, and with his sword standing infront of me. The army guys asking some money, and of course we gave them. They were not interested with our things or belongings.

Once they have collected some money from everyone including me.. then one of the army guy have noticed me, he turned arround and was facing at me. I was sitting near the ailes, and he asked if i have company while i'm travelling. I thought to myself, even if i do, i will not say it to you and for what? to compromise the safety of my companion..i said no..i have no company and i am travelling alone. But for some reason he didn't believe me, he asked me to stand up, but i said NO!! He then said again to me with his forceful voice, STAND UP!! I said NO!!! on his face. He was becoming frustrated and then he attempted to grab my right arm..but interestingly, before he could reached my arm..he pulled his hand away from me so quickly!..as if somebody intercepted him before he can touched me.

He looked at me puzzled!..and he tried to comprehend of what has just happened to him? He was holding his hand while walking away backwards staring at me as he looks like he had seen a ghost on me. I saw him from the window, still holding his hand and walking away from the bus while his mate kept calling him. The army guy didn't turned arround but instead he kept walking really fast and away from the bus. Then the other army guy let us go..the driver proceeded and i saw him making a sign of the cross on his body..and thanking up there.

I didn't really know what to think of what has happened then during that incident inside the bus with me. During that journey, an old lady sitting beside me asked some questions. Who was that man infront of you? I looked at her with disbelief..she saw somebody intercepted, i thought to myself..i then said, which man? I didn't see anybody infront of me..oh you saw it..tall..handsome man with blue eyes. I have never seen that person in this area before, she said.

I was surprised with her statements, but deep in my heart it was Arch Angel Michael who intercepted. Anyway, i said to the old lady, i'm sorry i really don't know what are you talking about. But the old lady said..of course you don't know..with a smile on her face. Then i said to her..do you? and she nodded with a smile on her face, and that time i knew it was my Angel, and i said to the old lady, thank you. I thought, i'm not going to have any more unnecessary conversations with the old lady, so i kept quite and gave the old lady a warm smile. I hugged my backpack tightly to make sure my passport stays with me, then we continued travelling for 16 hours that night with no more problems.

During the night, i closed my eyes alternately, and sometimes i can see Arch Angel Michael on top of the bus almost looking like he's protecting us..sometimes in a driving seat driving the BUS!!! whoahh!!! YES! you heard me! i shook my head i thought i was going crazy! I can see his body and his back wearing a blue cape. I can tell it's him because our driver is a small guy and looks Asian. But somehow i am looking at a EUROPEAN driver!..tall guy..handsome looking!..i thought there has to be 2 drivers in the bus. So i stood up and looked arround..and looking from the front direction and back everyone were sleeping..and it's only me and the driver were awake. Then suddenly i saw his reflections on the glass front window.. OHHH its you!:)i said. He gave me a smile, and that's enoughed for me to validate that it's him..my Angel :)then i made myself comfortable in my seat and fall asleep until 5 o clock in the morning.

I looked at my wrist watch, it's 5 am and we reached the destination. We all got out the bus..and infront of us..there was a church across the street. The church name was ARCH ANGEL PARISH CHURCH!! whoaahhh!! i said to myself. Is it a coincidence or what??..i went inside the little church..and here he is..my Angel statue staring at me. I took a photo of it..and when the film was processed, i a have a beautiful orbs on top of my head! :) I thought..wow...

Then i saw the driver of the bus eating breakfast from the cafe area, i approached him nicely, but he looks at me uninterested, but i went ahead and asked him anyway. I asked if he does have another driver with him tall..white man looks European? yes it's him..pointing the old man beside him, but he is not tall or white or European..and Why? he asked. Oh nothing just curious..i said. The second driver is a 60 years old asian little man and doesn't look European..then I thanked both of the drivers, then i ordered my own breakfast from the cafe away from their table, then i continued my own journey.

# CHAPTER 9

# MY WHITE ANGEL WINGS

JOURNAL

2nd April 2022

Good morning my dearest journal I must thank you my DEVINE FATHER for another 2 weeks work clinical placement. It was exhausting though, i think i need a break..i mean i really need a break. I can't wait to travel again, and i do really miss my travelling..i feel like i'm being called again somewhere.

I like travelling on my own..no one there to bother you..it's just me with NATURE..bare footed walking arround the beach and watching the ocean that really seems so mysterious. I like to sit on the sand while looking up the stars. Now that's what i called magnificent nature. I'm having an itchy feet again, and that means i am due for my travelling. When i travel overseas this time, i will not try to have any technology. I will throw away my phone and just enjoy the scenery.

This morning i meditated, once i wake up i sat in my favourite rocking chair in my verandah looking at my backyard garden. I spoke to papa GOD about my personal concerns that i could not tell anyone, and about weird people lingering in my personal space. It became very frustrating to me because this people operates behind the scenes..stalking.

I am in the presence with my DEVINE FATHER at the moment and he's just listening to me..and then he showed me how to open my wings. But he showed me first a light brown wall, and then a very large wings started to manifest into a wide open Wings. The colour of the wings are light gray. Then papa God asked me if i could do the same thing as he showed me how.

Then i saw myself sitting on the chair and imagining slowly growing my wings..and then finally i have it..i said to papa GOD excitedly, i have it out! Then suddenly the wing hit my face!..as my body bent forward the right wing hit my face! But then i noticed..my wings are not that big, and the colour is white. I asked papa GOD..why the other wings you just have showed was gray? and my one is pure white? it's white as a cotton and smells new. Ohh..how can i explain it?..it's like when you buy a brand new t-shirt, there is a pure clean smell on it. Hmm..i love the smells of it..and that was the smells like a brand new t-shirt.

I asked papa GOD why do i have this very white wings? and little bit of a curly feathers arround the edges? Papa God said, the curls are your signature for your wings, he said it with a smile..i know you like curls..oh..thank you and that would make me a beautiful angel then:) and papa GOD laughed! I said, what about white? The one you showed me was light gray. He said, i know you are not going to stop questioning until you got some answers. Well.. he said, the white feathers or your wings now signifies pureness or haven't used it yet. It will grow once you started using. Ok..the gray wings? i asked again..it means maturity, and has been in the battle. Ohh..that wings colour i have seen on Arch Angel Michael sometime, yes he said. Papa GOD please one more question? He looked at me lovingly with a smile..yes go on..but i know what it is, he said, but say it anyway. Would i die? i mean die from the battle? His answered is.."NO". Not in a spiritual realm. Oh thank you Papa GOD.

Papa God last night i had my first encountered with entities. They were invading my protected aura field. I did what i have to do, and you told me to open my wings..but i couldn't open it quickly..so i quickly pulled out my internal weapon instead. I started hitting them back, and the more i hit them the more intitiess are coming. But i feel more stronger and bravier and more aggressive towards them. I have never felt this aggresiveness before on me..then finally with a long hard battle, i eradicated them.

They were nasty and black looking heads! And everytime i hit them, it turns into a skull, and then exploded! I didn't see Arch Angel Michael with me..why? papa GOD. Then papa GOD said..that battle was yours, and your very first time battle. Then my FATHER showed Arch Angel Michael to me standing in the far right side corner, and with his sword holding down, he was watching me all along during my battle with the entities. Do you mean You and Arch Angel michael watching me last night during my battle? Yes he said.. with a smile on his face, but one thing you need to remember is, you must say your prayers that i have given you at the same time you were hitting the entities.

Ohh yess..i have forgotten..yes..i kind of panicked at the same time when i saw the entities trying to penetrated into my protective aura. I panicked, because they have sharp teeth you know..and red eyes too, it was very scary but i did it! Yes you did it on your own, and this is the same thing you will be doing in the reality world. What do you mean papa GOD? well he said.. When you are feeling attacked in reality just close your eyes and put yourself in a spiritual realm. Then do the same thing whatever i have taught you before.

I think you are right my FAther..last week when i was at work..doing my work on my laptop, suddenly there was a man who sat in the same room but slightly a metre away from me. Then suddenly. i started having a headaches and feeling intimidated and mostly he's making me feel uncomfrotable. I don't normally have that kind of feelings in the morning, and if i know what i am writing. Then suddenly i closed my eyes, i focussed on this person..i can feel he is sending me some nasty vibes while he is sitting on that chair opposite me.

I didn't waste any minute because obviously he was intentionally hurting me with his bad energy! So i pulled out my internal weapons and i can see myself going towards him..i looked back, i still can see my whole body sitting in that chair with my laptop..and when i got closer to him..i attacked this person with my daggers. I then saw his body changed into a skeleton..and then he quickly got up and left the room.

I suddenly wake up..then the man disappeared from that room..i was looking for him as for my own curiousity, but i could'nt find him anywhere from that building. Papa GOD i must admit, it was a bizzare experienced. My question is why did i approach that man in a spiritual realm and attacked him? Papa GOD said..because your spirit knew he was attacking you silently.

I felt bad because i was the first who attacked him, this is not me.. yes..you are right, this is not who you are in a physical body, but in a spiritual realm you knew, and you know "who you are", and what exactly what you need to do. So papa GOD, to my understanding now, i just have to close my eyes and my thoughts will do the works? YES my CHILD! now you finally understood! You can do this during your meditation, you can go to the battle and protect the unfortunate ones with your Angel..Arch Angel Michael.

Arch Angel Michael was there for you since you were born, until now and forever. Thank you FATHER for our conversations..and thank you for hiding me from everyone who's trying to harm me. Now i know my purpose and with more clarity. Thank you papa GOD, i love you..bye for now and i must check on my little kelly if she's feeling alright.

She was bad last night and i can feel her pain..she didn't want to leave my chest when i was holding her. I will talk to you again papa GOD..bye for now. Then i saw my FATHER up there waving at me with a smile on his face. I still can't see his whole face, just the smile. Hmmm..he then said, get up and say hello to the sun shine..i made it sunny for you today as you asked me yesterday so you can dry your uniform. Oh thank you, you read my thoughts..of course my child, he smiled.

He always called me child..papa GOD, i am a grown up woman now..i shouted at him. He then laughed!!!so loud!!..just like a thunder!..i didn't know what's funny of that..but certainly i made him laughed. Papa GOD i will meditate tonight to see where it takes me...yes my child.. you must start now. You have everything..and all the protections.. and you have me..just remember your prayers i have given you..Yes FATHER i will never forget my prayers. Thank you. :)

# CHAPTER 10

# WHY I CAN'T SEE YOUR FACE

JOURNAL
9TH APRIL 2022

My dearest journal, sorry i have been very busy lately and haven't been updating you with my everyday's life. Work..work..work..my job is chasing me. although. It is good in some way, at least i can organise things ahead. Lately, i have been taken advantaged of my generosity with my work company. I have taken some steps and it's up to them to realised of what they are doing. As i said before..i will leave it to my Devine Father, it's out of my hands now. I talked to my DEVINE FATHER last night and apologised to him lately. He said to me..did you find what you wanted? I gave you a choice didn't I? Yeahh..i said solemnly. So what's that face my child? he asked, i saw him lifting up my face again slowly..and he looked at my eyes and said..are you ready now with your tasks? Your devine tasks, he said. It's time to align with me..come on, cheer up.

Papa GOD can you tell me something? Yes my child, he said. why so many people are trying to hurt me? :(:( what have i done to them? I am crying.. My Devine Father sat down infront of me and looked at me in my eyes..but i still can't see his face..and it's stranged because i can see his eyes looking at my face lovingly, but i cannot see his face. It doesn't make sense to me. Then i asked him, why i can't see your face papa GOD? Why aren't you showing me your face? Although i can see your whole body, but not your face why? then i cried..cried.. Then slowly, i can see myself turned into a child..he picked me up and sat me in my little chair. My chair is little and colour pink, with butterflies painted on it..oh, some dragon flies too and red bugs with black dots on its back. Anyway, he sat me down and talked to me in my level.

He then said, do you know your papa GOD is not human like you?.. ok, i said..so what are you papa GOD? i innocently asked him. Well..i am everywhere..it's like a wind papa GOD? and he laughed so loudly again!!..oh i love you my child, i have so much pleasure talking with you. I LOVE your innocence that's why i always revert you back as a child everytime we have our conversations...but when you say you are fully grown up woman now, you even makes me laugh harder. My child, i always love our conversations even you are older, but you are always a child to me.

Well papa GOD why i can't see your face? please..oh..i know you are not going to stop until you got an answer. Well thanks GOD for that at least he heard my question, i said it to myself. Then he said..i heard your thoughts you know. OH so sorry..hehehe..i forgotten you can read my mind:) he then gave me a little smile with his left eyebrow slightly lifted. Papa GOD please tell me, why i can't see your face? well my child..i am a form of a spirit..and when i said i'm everywhere..i'm everywhere, he said. So do you really see what everybody does to anybody and including their thoughts? i asked again. Yes my child..i know everything..oh ok thank you FATHER, i said.

It's complicated for me to understand as yet but i will listen to your thoughts and stories FATHER. You know i love stories..i know, he said. that's why you love comics when you were a child until you were growing up. Hehehe..we both giggled:) So papa GOD what do you want me to do this time? You said it's time for me to align with you..how do i do that? Well, remember i have always teach you when someone is trying to hurt you..always close your eyes and everything you want to manifest to fight back it will happen during your meditation in the spiritual realm.

You can protect yourself, but i am always here..and ARCH Angel Michael is always in your side and nobody can harm you. If they do, they will face their own KARMA. I know papa GOD i have noticed that all the time..and sometimes KARMA is so quick to hit back! PAPA GOD, i have a stalker, i guess you know this person or people. Yes i know my child, so this person or people won't leave me alone? Well my child this specific person is full of hatred, his soul is so consumed with bad energies, that's why this person is attracted to your light. Can you stop this person papa GOD, and please this person using a lot of people to follow me everywhere, and i don't really know this person's purpose.

Well my child don't be afraid, this person cannot touch you, if any attempt of wrong doing..this person is asking for his very own life, and including to those people who obeyed him..They will get their own KARMA and i will promise you that. They cannot escape from me, you know that, he said. Yes i know FATHER. It's not time for him to go yet, because i'm giving him a chance to find peace, if he listens to his inner self, he will find the way to go back to spirituality. So papa GOD he still is a good person? Yes, still have some goodness in his heart.

If he doesn't listen and make some changes of what he is currently doing especially to you..well, it's his choice and he knows the consequences. But Papa GOD he can't touch me or can he? I mean harm me? No my child, my FATHER said and i felt his great reassurance..if he does..he is asking for his own life.

Well my child, are you ready for your journey? Yes Papa GOD i am now. OK..when you feel my presence it's time for our journey starting tomorrow..and make time..and no more maniana..yes FATHER no more maniana..this time i will align with you..i can't wait. So go to sleep now my DEVINE FATHER said, and have a good rest. Goodnite PAPA GOD i love you. I saw papa GOD closed the door half way..but still have a bright light infront of the door. He waved at me with his right hand. I then said..your door still open..he said, i know..i did that in purpose just incase if you come back. THen i saw the clouds infront of me, and then suddenly i'm back again in reality. Thank you Papa GOD, I'm feeling better now. GO to sleep before your curfew time he said. Yess..i said.

Good morning Papa GOD. I'm still in bed because it's raining outside.. but can i ask for sunny day please? I have to wash my uniform..then in a few hours, i started to see the sun. Yes:) thank my DEVINE FATHER. iloveu :) :) no more onog onog..he said hehehe.:) this is our little secret language. Don't forget today, we have some tasks to do. Yes FATHER, i will wait for your sign. I'll get up now as i can see the sun through my bay window.

# CHAPTER 11

# AN ASIAN LOOKING FACE INSIDE MY STOMACH

JOURNAL

10TH APRIL

At last we made a journey, and it was little bit scary for me, but before i start, this morning before i got up, i have pain in my belly. I tried to massage my stomach because i thought it must be gas..i prepared my breakfast but i still can feel the pain. I went to sit on my throne while rubbing my tummy..then suddenly i saw inside my stomach. There is a face inside of me!!or i would say..it's a face!!! Yes you heard me my dear journal.The head of the face is a male person with Asian appearance. Then i called Papa GOD, and straight away he came and ripped that head inside of me, and threw it away up the sky and exploded. Then papa GOD touched my stomach and healed me instantly. He then said drink some water. I got up quickly and went to the kitchen and drank a glass of water. I felt better then. Then papa GOD asked me if i'm ready..but i asked him first..what was that all about papa GOD? He said to me..my child somebody is trying to stop you from going with me, our journey today. They tried but this time they are not going to be successful..can i see who it was? please papa GOD..i just want to know.

Ok then he said, close your eyes and don't open your eyes until i say so. OK papa GOD, i won't open your eyes and then..whoaahh..It's a woman..and this person is very connected to the famous and very influencial person, and another 3 men which they didn't want to show their faces to me. Papa GOD then eradicated the three men by just pointing his finger to them then it exploded into small pieces..but the woman didn't. I asked papa GOD why you spared this woman's life? He said i will give her a chance to live this time..and next time you will confront her in the spiritual realm, if she still exist. Well..i could not believe it was her! Amazing how this people can go to that extent just to have an immortality if that what she thinks..and then makes havoc to people's life and for what?

Papa GOD what about those 3 men? He said don't worry about them they were just evil, they're just bad entities they sold their souls to the devil. OHHH..ok..I said. Papa God can i open my eyes now? Yes you can my child. I did open my eyes and yes..my pain is not there anymore. Thank you Papa GOD. OK then let me know when you are ready he said. I will finish my breakfast first and play my cp and then we go for our journey, I said that to him. He didn't say anything then..but somehow i read his thoughts..he made me read his thoughts i guess..hmm he said..my child still a child..with a smile on his face. After several minutes from scrolling my cp, i decided to put it down and decided to call papa GOD.

Papa GOD i'm ready now, i said to him..he then suddenly appeared and without any saying he extended his right arm and asked me to take his hand. We begun to travel, and with ARCH ANGEL MICHAEL behind us. It's funny during the travel, i saw myself of course with my Devine FATHER, on top of this earth..i can see high mountains..big trees..valleys..large water, just like a lake in a zigzag formations..forests. I didn't see any animals though, either any clouds at all. Then suddenly we went up higher and i saw this very dark clouds, with some kind of fire behind the dark clouds.Then there was some thundering image and lighting but didn't hear the sounds of it..i was puzzled..this is all new to me..but i wasn't scared at all, because in reality i'm scared of thunders and lightnings.

We then suddenly stopped..somewhere that i'm not familiar with..i didn't know if we are still in earth or somewhere else out of this planet. Then i saw myself became a young teenager, and this time i have my wings!!! MY wings are both pure white and the curls arround the edges, the size it's just medium and not overwhelming. And then i looked down to my legs, there were white cloth wrapped arround both of my legs. OK..how can i explain it..my legs has been wrapped with pieces of white materials clothing.

My top is just a white sleeveless shirt and, somehow, i'm wearing white colour short pants, but this clothing i am wearing is somehow fitted tight to my body but somehow it's comfortable. Then i saw Arch Angel Michael wearing a blue cape..he looks so handsome tall with blue eyes neck length hair and always appears to me with colour blonde hair.

His hair looks wavy..and Papa GOD is wearing a long robe with a big red colour stripe infront of his clothes, although, sometimes i saw him wearing colour brown and light brown materials. So Papa GOD showed me the troubled area..i was little bit scared though, but my Angel touched my back and i felt the reassurance in my whole body. So my FATHER asked, are you ready?. I guess so, i said. Well, can you pull out your internal weapon? OH..?? why? i said. Well my child this is it! i will show you the reality in the spiritual realm..and this is your DEVINE tasks. So get your internal weapon then, he said. I was reluctant but just for curiousity, i felt my chest..but i didn't feel it there..i said to papa God! it's not here!! Papa God laughed so hard and loud!! do you mean you lost your weapon? where did you put it the last time you've used it? he asked. I felt it again..but nothing it isn't here! Try again arround you body, my FATHER said. Then suddenly..i felt a small bumped on my right side of my hip. OHH..here you go..i said to the weapon. I found it! papa GOD! i found it! that's my girl, he said, with a smile on his face.

When I pulled it out and saw this magnificent golden dagger in my hand..i looked at it so carefully..my beautiful weapon has a zigzag sign on the metal and cross sign before it reaches the handle! the dagger is pure devine with carvings of the clouds..moon..stars..and the sun.. and it's sorrounded by the different types of small and different colours of crystal precious stones. I would say it's colour green..blue.. sparkling white..yellow and red. i didn't see any pink colour in it.. and my weapon is colour gold..then papa GOD told me not to get scared no matter what is coming towards me during this journey.

I asked papa GOD again, are we going to the battle? he then said yes. This is your very important task to do..but no fear my child..i'm here and Arch Angel Michael beside you. Ok i said, just remember.. every attack you make, you must say the prayers i have given you.. and the formation of defence is the signing of a CROSS. So, can you remember that my child? Yes i said. Then i saw being wrapped arround with the bubble of some kind..and it's colour purple and the outside is golden colour..2 colours this time..but Papa GOd and Arch Angel Michael didn't have any bubble arround them..it's only me.

Then suddenly, we were standing on top of the black clouds..and behind that clouds, it was like..red fire! Then quickly we saw this black entities are coming towards us..so many of them..but only HEADS!!! No whole bodies formed but just heads!!! And with evil and red eyes!! Then they were starting to attacked us!! Arch Angel Michael was at the front and i was behind him, then papa GOd was on my right side. My FATHER has no weapon, just his hands and fingers..one pointed finger to the entities, then it exloded!! crumbled into pieces.

Michael Arch Angel was so good in fighting..his sword was just amazing, executing this entities with no problem..and then more coming towards me. and i SCREAMED!!! but suddenly i remembered my weapons i am holding, and i know this must to use to protect myself. It's so intense!!! This entities wants to eat my face!!! So scary looking!! the more we eradicated them the more it's coming! Until, suddenly it stopped..The whole entities were gone. Then after we eradicated them all..we then travelled down..anmd before we could touched our feet to the ground..some entities with just heads are starting to attacked us again. We were in the forest, the trees looks dead and the sorroundings was not very familiar to me, i have never been in this place before.

In the forests, this entities are coming towards us..and to my surprised!!!i don't know if you "my" dear jurnal would believe this that what i'm about to tell you..even me i don't really like saying it.. but i'm must as well..but i swear, i know Papa God would not like it if i swear infront of him..now my journal..are you ready to hear this? call me i'm crazy.. and i'm not making it up..and this is what i saw that made me fell off on the ground..It's "PUTIN'S HEAD"!!! Yes you heard me!!!..it's his head!! leading the other entities attacking us so aggressively!! So i'm confused here to what i saw from this very moment.

Arch Angel Michael trying to eradicated a lot of them..but papa GOD wasn't in the scene! it was only me and my ANGEL! PUTIN's HEAD got away..as he was attacking me..i was surprised and startled when i saw his head and his face very close to mine. So it got away.. then papa God suddenly appeared and the sorroundings became clearer, i looked up the sky and i can see som many souls going up to heaven including children and animals leading by the the beautiful white lights beaming from above. I saw a lady wearing a hat and has a black and white trimming arround her hat, i don't really know the significance of that hat..and saying thank you to me..and she mentioned my name..ohh..i almost cried..she said my name.

I feel like i want to go with them because i'm feeling their happiness of eternity..then papa GOD touched my shoulder..didn't say anything.. but just a look of reassurance and love towards me and to thier souls. They were waving at me..and that instant i am puzzled..why they are not sad? instead they are all happy. Then suddenly we were not in that area anymore..we are somehow..somewhere..and the feelings of lovingly familiar sorroundings with so many clouds sorrounding us. then i raised my devine weapon to heaven, and then saw this golden light washing off the dark colour of my internal weapon. Then i slowly put it back again into my chest.

I asked papa GOD, why my chest? why my weapon kept in my chest? i asked. Well, it's because it is close to your heart..your loving heart.. papa GOD said. And that's the biggest weapon you can have..it's your HEART..your LOVE. Oh ok..now i understand. So FATHER, what do i do now? Well, your life goes on..and back to normal..but if you have some calling or feelings of being called from me..you must come with me in the spiritual realm. Yes papa GOD..and what about my wings? what do i do with it? well..it's like an umbrella he said..you close it whenever you finished using with it.

Ok..how? i asked, well..feel it in your back, slowly folding it and tuck it down. Then i slowly doing it as my FATHER said..and finally..i did It!! Ok he said..did you hear it click? he asked. click? NO, i said. I was quite puzzled of what he just said. If you don't feel or heard the click it might open suddenly..and he laughed!!! but how and where do i click it papa GOD? well my child, use your beautiful imagination. Oh ok then..i smiled:) i tried to click..then finally i heard this very faint click sound, just the same as when you close the door so gently.. very..very slowly, and i did. After that i opened my eyes and back to myself again, i got up from my bed and feeling rejuvenated again. Thank you papa GOD and to my Angel, and then they both waved at me and with their beautiful smiles. I love you both. :) :)

# CHAPTER 12

# AN ANGEL WARRIOUR

JOURNAL
11TH APRIL 2022

Today when i came home from work, i went to bed and had a quick nap. I was very tired mentally and physically, but then i recovered after. It's amazing the power nap can do to my body. After i had my dinner, i sat infront of the TV and started watching the environmental program which relaxes me and de stressed. Few minutes after, i started to feel uncomfortable in my head. I quickly picked up intuitively that someone is playing with my head as i can feel some sharp pain. So i got up, and went to my room and sat on my bed and closed my eyes and to my surprised, someone is really hurting my head. Sharp needles penetrating into my head, then without any hesitation, i pulled out my internal weapon and started attacking this person.

Yes! it's a WOMAN! At that moment there was another person then followed with another one. Black entities were about to attacked me, but before they can get closer, i sorrounded myself with my protected bubble and instantly it has protected me. While i was in my protective aura, i was the one who's attacking them and myself a lot bravier.

I didn't see my Angel this time, but when i eradicated all the entities, i saw my Angel standing not too far away from me on my right side. I guess he watched me during my battle. When i finished eradicating this entities i felt braver. This time i didn't open my my wings, i have forgotten again!!..but i didn't need it anyway. After that i fall asleep.

During my sleep, i saw this woman came out from the black car, she's wearing a very tight and with tinted brown colour dress, and somehow looking like a leopard patterns black dots on her clothes. She's wearing a high heels shoes and looks very confident when she approached me. To my surprised, she have big wings! and its almost colour gray.

I saw myself as a teenager with my white wings, but this time it's little bit bigger than before. I thought..well..well..my wings are growing:) I asked this lady who she is, but she responded..there are "more coming like me", she then disappeared! At that moment, i consulted my DEVINE FATHER..and before i could ask some questions, he asked me to close my eyes, and don't open until i say so, he said. Ok Father, i will do that.

While my eyes closed..i felt like we were both travelling..i can feel the smooth transitions of our traveling..and somehow, i feel like it's far away. I felt bored while my eyes were both closed. So i started counting from 1 2 3 4....then until when i was about to get to number 59, PAPA GOD said now open your eyes and don't be afraid, what ever you see i am here for you.

Once i opened my eyes....WHOAHHHH!!!...i was confronted with this HUGE being towering me! He was sitting on a single big stone chair, and behind him there was a fire looking and with black shadows, and so many black entities sorrounding him. I saw myself looking up at this BIG scary entity, and he's looking at me down with intimidation! Then suddenly the black little entities who's sorrounding him starting to attacked me, and then my ANGEL, ARCH ANGEL MICHAEL quickly appeared infront of me and started protecting me with his own sword! And every strikes he made towards the entities, it's exploding and turned into dusts!

Then the BIG black entity started attacking me, and aggressively trying to grabbed my back. I quickly pulled out my internal weapon and started defending myself, i have my wings out this time and i didn't know how it came out! I saw myself attacking back this black and huge evil entity..but my weapon is not enough!!! And then suddenly another internal devine weapon quickly appeared in my left hand and it's identical to my other one!! I thanked my DEVINE FATHER, and he said Now USE IT! A command with great force and it gave me a sense of confidence and determination instantly. That moment i became bravier and my hands became so familiar to this weapons. It's strange..i feel like i have done this before. Now i have 2 weapons in both hands, and the power i have in my body i can feel..it's strangely amazing and BRAVE!

The black entity starting to attack me..but i saw myself bravely enough forging ahead and started attacking back this black entity strategically. And with my weapons, i finally went straight up on top of his head and with the assistance of my wings lifting my whole body up. I aimed my weapons and then i striked from the top of his head then down so quickly while slicing his body to the lower extremities, then back to the middle and where his chest and heart, then separated my arms towards his shoulders, and it looks like a sign of a cross. That moment, i saw the entity's body cut opened with a sign of the cross. I saw his heart slowly falling..then i quickly catches it with my right hand before it touches the ground. I noticed my dagger in my right hand automatically disappeared before i caught this heart's entity.

Then i saw the entity's body dropped on the ground, then i turned arround to face my DEVINE FATHER and showed him the heart of the entity while still holding it in my right hand. My DEVINE FATHER said, open the heart, slice it open my child..i said why? Just do it and i will tell you later. So i sliced the heart with my dagger.. then to my surprise..a small coloured rock..it's a metal looking silver rock. YES!!!! it's silver metal rock inside the entity's heart. What do i do with this now papa GOD? i asked. My DEVINE FATHER took it from my hand and threw it up higher to the sky, and then i saw it slowly melting with the sun shinning onto it!

Then Papa GOD said..that was your BIG mission accomplished my child, he then actually hugged me this time. When he hugged me.. there's an enermous power he released from his body, injecting my whole body and soul with enermous power of energy...love energy. My child, you have accomplished a very dangerous being..you are the one i have been waiting for this devine mission. Why me Papa GOD? i asked curiously. Because my child, you have a pure heart and before you were born you are already destined to this task, this is your destiny. YOU ARE AN ANGEL WARRIOR!! my ANGEL WARRIOUR! he said. WHOAHHH..really? more task to do? yes my child..you cannot stop now.. You have started it, now you must finish it. This is the same thing of what you are doing in the reality world, you have determination my child and that's what who you are. I made you that way! Oh thank FATHER.

My reality is always connected to my spirituality. I wish i have done this earlier in life..why? WHY didn't you push and forced me to do it? Why didn't you changed my path? Then my DEVINE FAHER said, because you my child weren't ready. You have to be ready and learn something about the real world before you commit to your destiny in the spirituality realm.

Everything what has happened to you good and bad in the reality world has purpose, whether you like it or not, i purposely orchaestrated it so you stay in your own path. Think about your past and recent.. you were wondering why and how? so many questions in your head, and you always said to yourself..it has to have a purpose. I cannot see it now..but i will see it later. You have learnt from that now my child. Yes, i must admit i learnt from my mistakes, and i think everyone does makes mistakes, after all we're all only human. I don't carry any grudges, i just moved on and forget the things of what has happened, and learned.

In the reality world, there is no such things are perfect. The word perfect is an illusion, papa GOD said. I must admit, i agree with that, i said to him. So what now papa GOD? You must continue your journey and fulfill your destiny. The more battle you encountered, the more you become stronger, just like in the real world. The more problems and obstacle you tackled, the more you bacome stronger. It's the same in the spiritual world. Your wings will grow and will get bigger as my DEVINE FATHER said with a smile on his face.

Papa GOD, do you think people who has bad intentions on me will come and hurt me? Yes!! that's definite! It has been going on since you were born until now. But they never succeeded and never will..i promise you that my child. You are protected, they might hurt you and they did..but what happens to their souls now? huh??..he said..but my child DO NOT WORRY, they will not succeed and their lives and souls will be compromised.

I have hidden you from the people who really wants to hurt you since the beginning of your life. I have hidden you from the prying eyes of bad influences in this reality world. Yes i must admit i didn't make you perfect physically..but it is to protect you from so many evil eyes. Your innocence remained with you, and that's the one i didn't change..but physically, i altered it. Yeah..i know and i am litttle bit disappointed..i always want to be a lot taller. Hahaha..:)

In your past life you were not an ordinary person. You belong to a higher level of DYNASTY and EMPERIAL status of ANCESTORS, papa GOD said..you were petit, tall and had a very long hair, almost touching your legs. Your past life belongs in a Royal blood. You were the daughter of the ROYAL EMPEROR from another WORLD. Yes..i miss them especially my father EMPEROR. Then you married the Powerful Emperor from another life time which is now in a reality world. Your other lives you have spent your lifetime in earth has been a great healing for them and the other people that you were connected with, it is your pure heart and kindness. I have been recycled many times then:)i said. :)

Oh wow..everything is making sense now..i thought i was going crazy. This time i have more clarifications, and now especially about my life previously and the present time. By the way, i can see the people now who's intentionally hurting me while doing something behind the door, and invading my privacy. It's amazing that i can just close my eyes and then suddenly i can see thier faces..i even can draw it. One day i will see an artist to draw their faces. Ok my child go to sleep now and tucked your internal weapons with you. Oh by the way, papa GOD said..you can always use your hands or fingers by pointing at them directly and you will explode their faces.

WHoahh really?..i said. Yes, you did that before to those people who's trying to hurt you remember?..and just by your fingers pointing at them, and they have been threwn far meters away, remember that? he said. They didn't leave you alone and they kept trying to hurt you..and finally you asked my assitance..so i gave you this internal weapon, and you were very reluctant to use it, you didn't want to hurt anyone or anybody. Luckily, you didn't use it to them, but you gave them a fright instead..until now, they have never done it again, papa GOD said. Yes, i noticed FATHER.

But this time papa GOD it's different..i saw people trying to hurt me. It's ok my child don't cry..i'm here with you..remember when you found me? I said to you..DON't look further, i'm here for you Always..so cheer up and always "TRUST" your instinct. My child go to sleep before your curfew. Ok goodnight my DEVINE FATHER. I LOVE YOU :)

# CHAPTER 13

# SPIRITUAL CONTRACT

JOURNAL

12TH APRIL

Tonight during my sleep and my meditated phase, i recieved a piece of paper, white paper rolled and holding by this man. He looks like an Emperor or spiritual messenger? and he has a BEARD, rough looking in man in a 60's. I only see his right hand handed the rolled white paper to me. I took it and asked him what is it? But suddently, he disappeared quickly. I asked and consulted my Devine FATHER, what is it? i asked. I didn't open the letter, and papa GOD said it's your contract VALIDATED. I still didn't open the letter, but papa GOD did open the letter..and i saw the writings wasn't in English format. I didn't understand it, but my DEVINE FATHER said it's your contract. WOW..i asked again, contract for what? Your devine destiny my child. Oh ok..i said. well, i have to quit my full time job now and fulfill this destiny:) just joking :)

Papa GOD, can i ask you a favour? very small favour..can you help me finish my project? I am feeling sorry for the young family whose i am helping to finish this house. Thier children are growing up and still struggling to keep a roof on thier heads. Also, i must ask can you stop the the rain please? so my project will continue and more productive while its not raining. Thank you my Devine Father.

Talking about developing my gifts given by the DEVINE FATER. First of all i really thank you my Devine FATHER for the gifts, or whatever it is that i really have or possesed. Even before and until now, this gifts they said it's really confusing me. I can see many things that unheard of..hear things..feel things so strange..i can see things in my dreams that the next day it happens. So many things that i could remember since i was a child and until now as an adult. My parents said and even my husband said, it's your imagination! it doesn't exist! but the more i tried to denied it, then the more it's actually bombarding me with lots of downloads. Sometimes i go quiet in my bedroom and just praying and talking to papa GOD.. then i fell asleep.

That day no one believes me except my grandmother, who protected me and nortured me, eventhough she wasn't even always pleasant to me. She knows my gifts..but didn't tell anybody about it because it's dangerous she said. So that's why i didn't develop it earlier. I remember sitting in my grandma's house verandah in the sunny and hot afternoon.

I guess i was bored, and i can see the trees were standing still..no breezes at all and nothing moving. Suddenly, i have a thought of whistling in the air..i whistled first softly..then i saw some breeze slightly from the tree branches, the leaves starting to move. So curiously, 2nd time i whistled again..then i can see more movements from the leaves of the trees..and the 3rd times i whistled harder and harder, and more distinct.

I was kind of communicating with the wind through my whistles.. then suddenly, the wind turned into a very strong wind..i remember it now!! Then my grandma noticed it from her window that the wind was blowing very dangerously! The branches of the trees were almost bending and touching the ground. My grandma was yelling at me! stop it!! stop it NOW!!! she looks very angry at me...so i stopped..then she grounded me. She said..do you know what you are doing haa?! it's dangerous! But grandma i was only playing with the wind i tried to reason..i was very young then. My grandma said, i don't want you to do that again! as she yelled at me. Ok i won't!! i yelled back at her, as she was profoundly deaf, that's why i have to yell! And not being disrespectful.

Then 20 years ago roughly, we were at the coast in our holiday house near the lake. Our house was sorrounded by big trees and at the back it's 180 degrees scenery of water and our backyard sorrounded by the big trees. It was a really hot day too..i was sitting in an open verandah of my house with my little kids, and i suddenly remember that time when i was a kid calling the wind. So i thought i'll try to bring the breeze into our verandah and also for my own curiousity too.

Well, to my surprised, the breeze started to move, and became more stronger. The more i whistled stronger, then more the breeze becoming more harder and stronger and to what i can see, it drews up some kind of energy forces coming from the lake!! Then a mini tornado started at from the middle of our backyard. It was scary to watched and looking so violently, the place turned into a mini typhoon with a small tornado forming into our big backyard. It was scary to watched, and my kids were very scared. I don't know if it was a coincidence or what? I would say it was a coincidence.

My husband said to me to stop calling or manifasting the wind! He was angry at me and to my defenced, i said..i did it just to try if i still have it. Well it happened! look we have typhoon now. He knew my unusual gifts or i don't know if he called it gifts..he doesn't believe in it. It's a coincidence he is always said. No such things! Are you crazy? So it was the last time i played with my unusual gift and i burried it in my heart..but it still here with me..i still use it once in a while..as long as nobody can hear or see me.

Well my dear journal..it has been a pleasure to tell you my "SECRET"..i have more experienced than this..this is nothing compared to more unsusual things has been happening to me many years ago. It's a nice feelings that i can get this off from my chest.

The same of my journals before that i burnt before, i didn't want anybody to find or labelled me that i am crazy, or thinking that i am making it up. I was thinking they might lock me up. So i hid it for so many years, even my husband don't really know what i have in my hands, then one day my hands started to heal anything and it's capable of healing things especially animals. My hands can get very hot sometimes and when i put it into someone's body or my body needs healing, well..miraculously my hands can heal. My touch can heal..a lot of people started to noticed it especially from work.

They started to come and visit my home for healing and the doctors from work didn't know what to do with me and with their patients. A lot of surgeries has been cancelled, because the next patients were alright and recovered. The department didn't like it specially the surgeons. It will affect their job and their money! No surgery..no money for the surgeons and doctors, especially our department. It's all catch 22!

They knew somehow, everytime they'll came arround in the department, my senses are very strong..sometimes i can feel and hear them talking about me from the distance, then i started to worry. I didn't really know how far i can go or take this. I became very lethargic..i always feel i have no energy..sometimes my whole body was drained..i couldn't stand up. I didn't know how to protect myself that time. Even from the distance, i can heal the people who's asking some help. I had a lady patient was bleeding internally, that time we have been pumping her up with so many units of pack cells. 5 units of pack so far but she was still bleeding and the next morning she will go for surgery. At that time the Surgeon asked me to do another sets of vital signs on her. When i was about to checked her, my hands automatically touched her abdomin..then i can feel the tingling sensations from my hands. I can see this lovely lady looking at my eyes in disperate moments. I can feel her soul longing for forgiveness..and i closed my eyes to connect with my DEVINE FATHER and asked for healing.

I always dream that time about the very sick children..i can see them on the floor begging to heal them. So what i did, i started healing them from the distance..then that very moment i can see the children being healed! I'ts all came from my hands sending energies towards this sick children from the very poor area. At that time when i was healing them..i can see i was sorrounded by so many ANGELS and the powerful lights from above. Then more..and they kept coming more into my AURA field..so many children..so many sick children.I asked PAPA GOD to help me to make them feel better after my healing.

Then the next day, the surgeon visited the patient and checked if the patient had more bleeding, and to his amazement not even one episode after my coincidence of my hands on her abdomin has happened. I thanked my DEVINE FATHER. The lady was discharged the next day, and somehow she thanked me.

My healing continued for so many long years..then i became exhausted when unnecessary energies came to my circle and then made my life became complicated. My life became chaotic and my energy became depleted..so many people sucking my energy at that time. I just gave and gave until i was run down. I didn't know how to say NO when it comes to healing people. But then i realised i was being used, manipulated and violated my energy. I became very sick and doctors didn't know what's wrong with me. So i stopped working for a while and PAPA GOD asked me to have a complete rest.

Today, my diary i recieved a very good news about my project, and thank you PAPA GOD for the interventions. It's sunny here now and works are very productive. And also, i'm fine now to finance this project as i am expecting my yearly income tax to cover this project slowly. Thank you my Devine Father.You know i don't like asking financial help even from you, and you know i will ask if i needed it. And i know this is all about DEVINE timing.

Thank you MY DEVINE FATHER. I LOVE YOU:):)

# CHAPTER 14

# ROYAL BLUE COLOUR MAN

JOURNAL

16TH APRIL 2022

During this weeks, there has been some several incidents that we were almost in a car accident..somehow and many times we have avoided it miraculously. I thanked my DEVINE FATHER and ARCH ANGEL MICHAEL and all my guides with instant and devine interventions. There is also something going on with me..i have been feeling so overwhelmed and stressed out, or feeling uncomfortable of myself. I don't know why??? I had an argument with my other half at home..i think that's part of my stress i am sensing..but..somehow..after the argument..i felt like something came out of me..lifted up. I closed my eyes and then saw some energies started coming out from my body leaving my body out, and the energy was rising and being purified. I have been meditating just to balanced myself, as i am feeling my energies are too much to handle lately..too strange and too strong. I can feel it, and its affecting the people arround me.

Tonight while i was sitting in the recliner chair, i closed my eyes and suddenly saw myself standing, wearing a white clothes again and then suddenly, i am facing 4 white horses coming towards me, and thier sorrounding auras are pure white..so Angelic white, i was puzzled at that moment..and i asked, is this one horse is for me? But there was no answers from anyone. It feels like any one of this horses is not for me..and if it is not..why? i questioned again. ARCH ANGEL MICHAEL showed himself towards my right side and slightly far away from me. He's just standing there and watching but not saying anything.

Then i saw papa GOD looking down, with his right hand sending a white light directly towards me. Then suddenly a man riding on his horse floating infront of me wearing a "ROYAL BLUE" uniform. Everything he is wearing is so purely BLUE..a ROYAL BLUE colour. His physique is a very brave man, a warrior, and very majestic. He looked at me and didn't say anything, but i recieved a feeling of reassurance and acceptance. Then my back started to itch.. my wings wants to get out! and it did!..he then this majestic man looks happy, and it seems like he is even more proud of me..he made me feel that :)

I didn't see any spirits riding on the horses, but i felt their presence.. very powerful. Then the next thing happened..i can feel somebody wrapping my waist with something..a belt arround my waist. The middle of the belt is slightly bigger than the other sides, and it looks black. Then tried to put a black boots on me..but i refused. I said, i don't like the colour, and suddenly, i heard papa GOD laughed! very loud!! :)

They asked me, what colour do you want? i said, white, because it's matches my white clothes. So it did! they've changed it, just the way i want. So now, i'm wearing pure white..my wings are so white and little bit bigger this time. While this is happening, there is another entity have appeared. He is wearing a suite..working suite and colour GRAY. He's medium build, skin is dark, but there is an indian appearance of his face. His hair style is very recent style..

ponny tailed on top..and short hair on the side. His face looks little bit chubby and oily..but he has wings too, and it's colour grey. I asked him of who he is..and he said SAM. his name is SAM? i said to myself. I asked again...Are you an ANGEL or pretending one? He then said, I am appointed to you, to be your side amongst with others. others?..i don't see them.. They are here arround you. You won't see them yet.. but you will be.Then SAM disappeared.

I still can see PAPA GOD, and MICHAEL ARCH ANGEL, and the Powerful Warrior looking, riding on his horse so majestic and the 4 white horses. Then suddenly, again, i saw 2 dogs black and white guarding infront of my house. They turned arround and looked at me..it seems they have recognised me. But i have never seen them before. They are guarding your house papa GOD said.

After that moment, seeing this 2 lovely dogs sitting infront of my front door. Somehow I'm back to that moment again interacting with the same entities, and this time i felt like i am ready for something. My wings are out..my clothes and my boots are white. Then suddenly, i saw a big hole..a cave infront of me and when i looked down, i saw the sorroundings just purely devine white colour, that's the colour of the sorrounding rocks..and the middle of it, there was a very BIG ROCK, standing rock in the middle of the cave and it was also pure white.

Wihout hesitation, i jumped down and landed on my feet standing tall as my wings carried me nicely when i touched down..and for some reason, i know this is not impossible in the reality world. I felt like I have done this before the feeling is so familiar! Then suddenly i wake up from my meditation..or was it from my meditation?? I only just closed my eyes..then it connected me to this journey. Hmm.. interesting.

That was it..i was in cave by myself standing in the middle of a big standing pillar rock, and sorrounded by the pure white..i couldn't figured out what kind of white things sorrounded me..was it snow?.. clear crystals..or ice?? i don't know..i have never seen those things in my life or anywhere before. I didn't ask PAPA GOD what it was.. where i was..because i didn't feel threatened at all or in any danger. I felt like..it was purifying..purifying myself. Then i went back to sleep.

# CHAPTER 15

# MATRIX WEB

JOURNAL
20TH APRIL 2022

My dear journal, i can hear papa GOD saying...go to sleep now. Yes i will and soon, i said. I just need to finish this one paragraph that i am reading. I have been very busy lately, i'm catching up my medical review. I need to pick up some points for my CPDE this year, to be able to continue my practice. While i'm reading my online studies..at the same time, i'm listening on something..hmm..a very interesting topic, but i'm not focussed on that. I am almost finished my online study and then..i acquired 1 certificate today with 90% score, I'm little bit disappointed it's not good enough for me.

The more i read..the more i can't stop reading. Until i heard papa God said again..time to sleep my child, you can finish that tomorrow. I put my pen down and turned off my computer. Then said goodnight to my DEVINE FATHER. I saw his thumb's up and put the book away back to the Ancient looking book shelves.

My dear journal, i think i have to tell you of what has happened to me last night. Once i said goodnight to my DEVINE FATHER last night, i closed my eyes..then straightaway i can feel something or somebody present in my bedroom. I focussed my mind with this energy that i am feeling in my space, then i saw 2 energies 1 metre away from my bed. They both curiously looking at me and somehow studying me very carefully. Although, i didn't feel any malicious intentions from them. I can feel my bedroom is sorrounded by white lights while my eyes closed. I have turned off all the lights including the other room, so it was pitched black. My bedroom was sorrounding or filled with white lights and not an annoying lights, and a matter of fact its calming..i feel calmed.

Then in a few seconds, i can feel my body sinking into a deep..deep down of something, and i knew that feelings..it's time to travel again. Then suddenly i felt my body is going into a hole..its swirling round and arround hole and i was in it..it's like a MATRIX web. My body wasn't panicking..but i feel like my body going to be trap into the web. Then suddenly, PAPA GOD right arm quickly pulled me out from there! YES!!! you heard me!! He pulled me out from the MATRIX WEB. I don't know anything about this matrix thing..or what it can do to me or harm perhaps??..i don't know and have no idea! Then suddenly papa GOD grabbed me out from the matrix..then i saw myself on his chest, holding me so tight, and i was a child again in his arms and shoulder.

He was hugging me like any ordinary father protecting a child from any harm. He then sat me down in my little chair and said firmly.. stay away from the web..that is not for you, and such a child mind i said OK papa GOD. I know my DEVINE FATHER when i have questions to asks and he is not ready to give me an answers, he will then turned me into a child, a child with an innocent mind. He then tucked me into my bed and remained a child.

Then i had a beautiful sleep. Then the next day, it's a beautiful morning and i have an amazing energy decided to go for a long hike. Then came home again and back to my study and exam, then i can see my DEVINE FATHER smiling at me, when i closed my eyes just to have peek of what he is doing up there.. Then somehow, i read his mind..whoaahh..that's new to me. He is saying "TRUST YOURSELF" when you answer the questions in the exam he said it in my thoughts. He's right, last night exam i got 90% because i have changed my answer to my first question, and that put me into a 1 wrong answer. Well, my dear journal..i need to go back to my review, as i have so much to catch up.

This time i slowly understand the connections..it's like a puzzle you know. And so many things that i cannot solve or control, i have given it to my DEVINE FATHER. He will make that decisions for me. By the way, my other Father the "EMPEROR" from the other world out there, visited me the other night in my dream. This when i was having some problems arround me. My FATHER EMPEROR asked me to come home..take my hand he said..but i refused, i feel like it is not time for me to go home. Although, i really miss you and my EMPRESS MOTHER and the serenity of the place. I'm sorry my EMPEROR FATHER, i feel like i'm not done here yet..i have more things to do here in my own little world. I will come to visit you and my EMPRESS mother regularly and that's a promise:)

So my EMPEROR FATHER said, ok your choice my SHINE, but we are watching and protecting you. I then said..thank you FATHER. He touched my forehead and felt an amazing energy went through my head and into my deep brain..he then disappeared. I really miss them, my Ancestral family out there. I can see my Empress mother beautiful face..blowing kiss with her two hands towards me. My shine..come home she said with a loving words. I felt like running towards her like a child..in her arms..i was in tears. Then i saw myself as a grown up woman..and heard a voice up there..it's not time for you to go home..you have a DEVINE PURPOSE and you MUST attend to it. Matter of fact i have already started it..and it slowly making it sense now.

# CHAPTER 16

# WAR ZONE BATTLE

JOURNAL
21ST APRIL 2022

Good morning my dear journal, i had a weird dream last night..i was in a battle ground again and on my own. I saw myself standing infront of a wall, a very solid wall, and i was wearing my white battle gear..and my wings are out! The wall is a kind of door to me??? i was curious?? it's a very solid looking wooden door, and there was an engraved signs on top of each other. It looks like its an ancient signs has been engraved. I cannot read or understand the writings. The door was facing very close to my face for some reason. I tried to understands it..but then the moment my face was so close to it, the door opened suddenly.

Then i saw myself walking into a very dark hall..i then continued walking..then suddenly, the room became glittery..the room is full of glittering crystals and diamonds arround. It's a stranged room i reckon, then i came out from that room..and then continued walking until it took me to the other room, and it looks like an old house, somehow it looks like in a war zone. The old house was really damaged..then i walked into the kitchen..a very run down kitchen area almost no walls maybe from being blasted. When i continued walking very carefully..i saw this woman looks like with a mediterranian appearance and in a late 50's or little bit younger with medium build, skinny and with a long black straight hair and kind of hiding. Hiding from who?? i asked myself. She was hiding very low and down almost crouching in the corner of the shatterd window and she looks very scared.. and i don't know to whom?? I was asking myself at the same time while continueing walking through the kitchen.

Then suddenly i noticed something about my eyes, it strangely blue and almost looking like a royal blue colour..and it's glowing. I continued my walk, then when i opened the door it took me outside. I saw myself in an open field with full of tall and dry grass. No trees arround in that open field. While i was walking..i saw this HUGE Black entity coming towards me!!! I was surprised!! and scared the hell out of me! I fell down on the ground but then i recovered myself quickly and got up and ran. I was running..and running from him. I fell down many times..but the more i ran, the more this scary being chases me.

I suddenly stopped and turned arround and pulled my internal weapon and my WINGS are out..but my eyes again turned into a different colour, and this time is colour purple. Then i noticed behind me this entity is coming towards me really fast, so i have to make a quick decision..instead of running away, i forged straight ahead towards the HUGE scary being. This entity has a black armour shield. I jumped towards up higher while my wings lifting me..then landed into his head. I attacked the top of it's head..slicing towards his lower extremities and upper again to the chest and heart. Then i spread my arms away from each other..and it's the sign of the cross, together with my prayers. I cut this entities body with my internal weapons. My internal weapons are very light and strangely enough, it cuts the toughest metal of the entity is wearing.

I saw the entity's body laying on the grassy ground, but i saw no blood..i was surprised! Then i heard Papa GOD voice, it's not human, he said. Whoahh..what is it? i asked! Then i saw another entity starting to attack me, but this time he looks half human and the head is skeleton! He has a body of a human wearing long clothing. It looks like during the ancient time. He suddenly attacked me, but to my surprised it didn't touched me. I felt like somebody intercepted..then i quickly attacked the entity. Somehow my body synchronises with my weapons during my attacked. I feel like i have done this before. The entities exploded! The more they were coming, the more i eliminated them quickly. Then after the long and exhausting battle...i see no more enemies. I looked arround again to make sure..the sorrounding became quiet.

I raised my internal weapons, and then the beautiful ray of lights starting to come down, and started washing off my Devine weapons. I thanked Papa GOD..I then tucked my internal weapons in, and this time to my upper extremities. I thanked my DEVINE FATHER again, and my guides who was with me today. I didn't see them but i felt them arround during my battle. I then asked My DEVINE FATHER..why my eyes have 2 colours? He said the blue colour is for looking..and the purple one is the protection during your battle. They were targeting your eyes..oh..really? i said. Would i worry FATHER? No my child..your eyes are powerful.

You can see things that others can't see, and do not worry no one can touch your eyes. It's protected and you can even see while your eyes are closed. In a physical world, if somebody intended to hurt your eyes, it will have some consequences for them..and it will be blindness. I PROMISE you that my child! YOU JUST remember one THING..you have not done WRONG to them. Remember the TONGUE of those person who spat on your back! hmm?? Yes i remember FATHER. Well..if somebody will do this to you..my child this people are asking for their own lives! OH my..who would hurt me like that? i asked. PAPA GOD didn't answer.. well, Thank you my DEVINE FATHER. I LOVE YOU :) I must get up now and have breakfast. BYE :)

# CHAPTER 17

# LITTLE SQUARE BLUE

JOURNAL
25TH APRIL

My dear journal, i just finished another exam and this time i got 100% !!Yess!! I'm so happy, and NO mistake this time. Thank you my DEVINE FATHER for staying with me. He then said, now you can put your pen down and get some sleep my child. Yes FATHER, thank you. He then said drink plenty of water. Yes Father i have been drinking plenty of water. Goodnight papa GOD, i am happy now as i got 100% from my exam. I know he said..and i know you are not going to stop until you get to your goal. I know you..you have determination, so get some sleep now, we have things to do soon. Where to this time papa GOD?. well..this time we are going beyond the time..whoahh..and before i could ask again..he showed me far.. far..away from here..up..up..there in a galaxy..past the stars. He then put his right hand on my forehead and with my eyes closed, i saw "LITTLE SQUARE BLUE" colour lights floating arround my face. Then i fall asleep. Goodnight FATHER :)

# CHAPTER 18

# ANGEL HERMII

JOURNAL
27TH APRIL 2022

My dear journal, sorry i haven't been updating you lately. My time has been so much pre occupied with my work lately, but i have been thinking about you and to connect again..you are the only outlet of my sanity. Then i just closed my eyes and just got connected to my DEVINE FATHER. He looks very busy at the moment and i can see him standing infront of his ancient marble table holding a small stick and pointing down. Papa GOD, what are you doing? i said nicely..he didn't look at me, instead he waved at me, and continued looking on something on that table. He Looks very busy and he seems like studying on something from that ancient marble table.

I can see the table has a devine lighting, but i don't see where the light is coming from? By the looks of it..it's glowing, glowing on top of his table. My DEVINE FATHER looking at the MAP..the MAP of the WORLD on his table and with his stick pointing the direction. I was about to ask, but he raised his left hand slowly to me and i know what it is, a sign of not to DISTURB him. And i heard in my head, later my child later..go outside and play.

I saw myself as a child again, walking in a big room and area with full of clouds...i saw angels with instruments. I was drawn to a particular Angel with a BIG wings holding a big harp, and he asked me to sit down with him. He is wearing a long white clothes. I sat beside him and on top of a small brown rock. He's playing a beautiful music..sweet music as a lullaby..very nice in my ears. Then i saw little angels..little ones and giggling :) They came closer to me and floating arround me and then started playing with my ears, tickling my ears..and they whisperd to me...heavenly FATHER above loves you :):) and they all flew away..and i said thank you..i know :) :)

I went back paying attention with the BIG Angel playing with a HARP. I asked him, what's your name? A question of an innocent child. He said my name is Angel hermii. Oh, i said..as HERMAN? yes he said, short for herman. Then i suddenly heard a BIG BANG sound! sounds like a Big stone door has opened and closed. Then i saw papa GOD and said, come my child, we have to go somewhere while extending his right hand to me..it's time to travel again, he said.

I stood up, and saw Arch Angel Michael facing to me with his beautiful smile..Oh, i miss my Angel, but i think he read my mind instead..he said in my mind..i'm always here beside you, and if i go away i have somebody appointed to you. Then Papa GOD said, we have to go somewhere my child..and before i could asked..my wings are out, and i'm wearing my battle outfit which is pure white. MY wings are little bit bigger this time i noticed, with 2 or 3 gray spots in my wings as i curved my wings towards my front. Then papa GOD said, that means you have been in the battle.

This time my child, we are going somewhere that you have never been before. You must remember to use your internal weapons and your prayers at the same time. YES my DEVINE FATHER, i said it to him confidently. Then i saw myself as a young teenager ready for the battle. PAPA GOD said..now close your eyes and take my hands and don't open your eyes no matter what until i say it. Then i asked, why? why can't i open my eyes? well that's because i don't want you to see what we are passing through during the travel. Why? what are we passing through papa GOD? It's not pleasant for your own eye sight. It's stormy..lightning..thundering. You are not ready to see this.

But papa GOD in a physical world, it's an opposite, i mean when i closed my eyes, i see everything..and once i have opened my eyes i lost everything.. i lost all the vissions to the spiritual realm. Yes exactly, he said. During our travel, i want to protect your eyes..too much exposures in the spiritual journey would scare you..and you would not like it believe me. I know you are scared of lightning and thunder in a physical realm..and that's what it is during our astral travel. OH OK..now i understand now papa GOD.

NOw, are you ready? he asked. Yes FATHER, i am ready. And don't be scared..you are protected. I gave my right hand to him...and then not even in a second..he said to me..now open your eyes my child.. we are here. I slowly opened my eyes..and to my surprised..I AM STANDING IN A VERY HIGH BATTLE GROUND! HUGE open space battle ground with my DEVINE FATHER and ARCH ANGEL MICHAEL! Then i saw to my right side some ANGELS, including the Lady Angel that i have meet earlier and Angel SAM, and they all have WINGS! They are all LINED up like great WARRIOURS! VERY courageous!!!

So looking at the WARRIOUR ANGELS on my right side..and then i looked to my left side, and have even more ANGELS! They all looks like ready for the BIG BATTLE! AMAZINGLY, they are all have black and white horses. PAPA GOD and Arch Angel MICHAEL have no horses. They just both standing beside me. I have no horse either. I said to my DEVINE FATHER, I am scared..and I held my DEVINE FATHER right hand..he looked at my eyes..but still didn't see his face. He looked at my eyes and feeling his eyes penetrated into my mine, and suddenly a beautiful white and golden colour energy entered into my body and slowly enveloping my whole entire self. I then felt so courageous instantly and feeling NO FEAR.

Then he said to me..you are protected. Then the devine bubble sorrounded me. I felt so secure and feeling confident. He said, You will WIN this! NOW, take your internal weapons and get ready. Then my weapons suddenlyn appeared in my hands together with my horse!!! I have a horse!! and it's white and have wings too!! i exclaimed! and a pointy horn on the forehead!! A UNICORN!! WOW!!! i could not believe it!!!! Then suddenly my wings lifted me up to my horse. I then touched my UNICORN HORN and it's activated his whole body and mine. whoahh..i feel like this is mine. THen suddenly i saw Arch Angel Michael on his Horse too..very magnificent looking both. MY DEVINE FATHER still behind me. And then suddenly the MAJESTIC MAN wearing a ROYAL BLUE coluor uniform with his horse appeared infront of us!

He waved to my DEVINE FATHER and Arch Angel Michael and to me with his beautiful smile, and i felt like it was an acceptance from him. I nodded politely. I didn't have time to ask my DEVINE FATHER his name, because we started to see some massive black entities coming from afar from the lower ground and rapidly heading to us. So many of them..so many black energies and so scary to watch, but i didn't feel that way. The black energies looking like worms with skeleton heads!!! I looked to my right and left, all my Angels are ready. Matter of fact i felt the calmness on them. They are all protected with the pure DEVINE energy. They are all glowing with pure white energy! And all of them have swords! There are no feelings of intensity from my ANGELS..all i can feel is courage at the moment. The black entities are coming and my DEVINE FATHER put a protected wall on us..but the entities are coming..i couldn't help having knots in my belly..feeling nervous.

Then Papa GOD said with a firm and reassuring voice..i'm here behind you, and i saw Arch Angel Michael beside me too. Then papa GOD said, remember your prayers at the same time with the formation of the CROSS. And most importantly you need to know are this entities are not human. He then put his hands on my face and said..You are my WARRIOUR ANGEL..this is you DEVINE calling and your DESTINY is in the SPIRITUAL REALM. THIS IS YOU! REMEMBER THAT!

Then papa GOD said..be ready..now, remember stay always in the middle, no matter what happened, and no questions asks..NOW.. After papa GOD told me the instructions, He opened the clear wall protection infront of us..and we have suddenly WHOOOSE!!!! with all this black energies went through us!! It feels like, it went through our bodies!! I looked back, and then they are all turning and coming back to us!!! I can see Arch Angel going down to the BAttle ground and trying to make them followed down. And the other Angels with glowing lights are protecting them!!! OMG!! I have never seen such a thing like this before!! NOT even in the MOVIE!!

Now this time i am being chased by the entities, but staying in the middle between my DEVINE FATHER and Arch Angel Michael.

Then i turned arround facing the ugly entities, and now i realised i have to protect myself. Then i heard papa GOD said..They are not human..so FIGHT BACK! Use your weapons! I have my weapons in my both hands and feels very light and connected to my hands. It feels like..it glued into my hands, that's the feelings i have with my weapons with me.

More entities are coming..then one striked to me from the entities and too close to my face, and more..and some very close to my abdomin. They have this hands, but they looks like worms!!! they can slithered and attacked me from behind! So i turned arround and faced them! one is about to attacked me, then my hands quickly reached the neck of the entity and cut its head off immediately. Then my hands automatically went up to the top and sliced it down..then back to the middle and out..but i saw no heart! but at the same time i prayed. When i finished the prayers. Then skeleton's head skull has blown away in pieces, then crumbled into ashes. I saw thundering and lightning during the battle. I didn't see My DEVINE FATEHR AND Arch Angel Michael..but i felt there presence beside me during the battle.

I only can hear Arch Angel sword..the light weight swings..so devinely sounds..i don't know how long the battle lasted..it was such a massive battle. I did the same over and over again as my Devine FATHER kept saying they are not human. FIGHT my child! FIGHT! SO i did! Then slowly, i saw smokes and dusts in the air and everywhere..and where the battle field is. I don't know how many entities i eradicated. Everything stopped..and it looks like in a slow motion..i saw the majestic Warriour in blue and his horse. Arch Angel Michael but no PAPA GOD.

Arch Angel Michael still in his horse and myself. Then suddenly.. there's a light coming from above..and it's golden colour..followed by the purple colour..and white. Three colours appeared on top!! I raised my internal devine weapons, and slowly washes it off the black colour on my weapons. Arch Angel Michael and the other Angels didn't raise thier weapons because their weapons are automatically cleaned!! whoaah..it's only me..only my weapons need cleaning from the devine.

Then my DEVINE FATHER appeared, i was going to ask, but before i could say something..he said, my child..you are still living in the physical world..this ANGELS are not, he said it with a smile:) Oh yes i said. Then suddenly i wake up from my spiritual journey..and feeling exhausted. Drink some water my child..yes i will FATHER. THANK YOU! The battle is finished and back to reality again. I will visit you tonight in your dreams and you know how to connect with me..say your prayers..yes FATHER i will. Then i clicked my fingers.. then i'm back to my reality life again.

OHHH..wait a minute, before i go..i just remember..that Angel who was playing a BIG harp name Angel Hermii? I thought..hmm..it sounds like hermi baby..hermi munster, the munster family episode that i used to watch when i was in a late teenager. I loved that show.. so funny:) anyway, Yesterday, when i came out from the building i am working..i saw this man infront of the hospital building staring at me..and i noticed his face is looks like Hermi monster from the TV episode. I thought..hmm.. wait a minute is it my subconscious or just a coincidence or what? or my mind just playing with me. I didn't feel threatened but i was puzzled. Ohhh..he smiled at me, i don't know..i'm too tired to think at the moment. Anyway, who knows..bye for now i'm so tired and thirsty.

This journey came from my thoughts through meditations and dreams..and this has been happening since i was a kid. I just didn't know how and who i could talk to anyone..sometimes i feel frustrated when i was trying to tell my grandma and my mother..but instead, they said DO NOT Believe it, it's all in you head. I tried to write it in the piece of paper of my school notebooks, but then my grandma and my mother said to burn it. which i did! Now i started journalling again. It seems like someone kept pushing and putting my nose on it. My dear jounal, my DEVINE FATHER made me sleep very well last night. I was very exhausted but somehow enlightened. And my head is a lot clearer.

# CHAPTER 19

# FLOATING MAP

JOURNAL
1ST MAY 2022

Good morning my dear journal, this is sunday today, and i said good morning to my DEVINE FATHER, and i asked for a sunny day. I got up and went to my back verandah and see the sky is just as clear as ever. Now i can wash my uniform, thank you papa GOD. He then just gave me a glimpse of his smile:)

I asked my DEVINE FATHER..what are you doing today?..as i can see him being so busy and looking something infront of him..looks like he is surveying on something, some kind of MAP..yess..just like scrolling a map going right..not up and down like a cell phone..it's towards the right side..and it's more like a silhouette map..it's an old writing..but he kept flicking and scrolling..i was going to ask..but he raised his left hand to me..and i know that kind of signal..not to disturb him. And i heard..you know where to go my child..i'm busy. Yes papa GOD..good girl he said. I became A child again, he turned me into a 5 years old child.

So i went playing..hop..hop..hop..towards the big door and went inside, and the sorrounding was full of clouds, but i'm not surprised because i have been here before. I saw flowers floating arround, and it's almost following me when i'm wandering arround. I started chasing them, i didn't see any butterflies, just flowers..i kept chasing them..then i suddenly stumbled down, and head on the BIG brown Pillar. It didn't hurt my head for some reason..and then when i looked up..I saw "JESUS"!! YES!!you heard me!. He is standing just right infront of me. He has a beard..wearing a long clothes with red colour stripe from top to down, and the colour brown sandals he's wearing have 3 gaps on top.

Then i looked at my feet..i'm wearing no shoes, bare footed as i always do when i was a kid. Then he slowly bending down on his knee just about to my level as a child, and then extended his right hand to me. He then said are you okay? with a smile on his face. I said yes..thank you. I got up and still holding his hand..then i looked at my back, i can see Papa GOD and Arch Angel Michael from that BIG open MArble door talking to each other. I excused myself to JESUS and ran towards them..but before i can reached them..i saw JESUS inside the room already with papa GOD and Arch Angel Michael. Whoaahh..he's quick! Arch Angel Michael standing beside papa GOD on the left side without his sword, and JESUS on the right.

Papa GOD still flicking the floating map..i have never seen a floating map like that before..and it has golden light colour with the writings which i could not understand. I was about to ask again..then JESUS picked me up and sat me in my little chair, and he asked me to be quiet with a whisper.Then i wake up suddenly.. Today afternoon, i had a quick conversations with my DEVINE FATHER. First of all i thanked him for a lovely sunny day. I dried my uniforms, i thought i won't be able to dry it, as it takes to 2 sunny days to dry my uniform and it's been raining here like crazy.

Anyway, i asked my DEVINE FATHER if he could stop the people who's coming to me with bad intentions. He turned his head towards me..at last i got his attentions whatever he is doing infront of that floating map. He then said..i can read your mind you know. He put his little stick down that he is using flicking the map. I saw myself again as a 5 years old. He then said, ever since the beginning of your life, my child you have been protected. I have hidden you from the people who wants and trying to hurt youn intentionally, and until now. If the people have some ill intentions towards you, they won't be able to reach you. The only thing to make it right for them to reach you, is to have a a good intentions with good heart. NO evil intentions from the beginning to the end.

The reason why they can't reach you, its because they are not true to themselves. OKAY i said..now i know and it makes sense now. I know so many people people like that in my circles before, specially if they want to come to my place..some of them had an accident.. some got lost on the way even its only few blocks away, some they found themselves couldn't get into my yard. They have a very strong feelings of not being welcomed, so they turned arround instead. Yes you are right because i blocked them and their way to you, papa GOD said. My DEVINE FATHER some said they saw an old man standing infront of my BIG tree, was it you PAPA GOD? NO he said..i appointed somebody. Oh ok..thank you i'm glad to know. Sometimes they were puzzled and made them wondered why they couldn't get closer to my house. I feel the good energy arround the house. Thank you my DEVINE FATHER for the protection i have to sleep now..bye :)

# CHAPTER 20

# I DON'T FEEL NORMAL

JOURNAL

3RD MAY 2022

Dear journal, i have been very busy today so much to do with my student's assessment manuals. I managed at least 5 books and had a bad head aches. I must tell you about my dreams last night..i saw Jesus in my dreams last night and he gave me a BIG BLACK FEATHER. I was thinking.. why BLACK? He didn't say anything to me, instead he handed in the black feather on my hands, i took it and i said thank you..he then disappeared. I consulted my DEVINE FATHER instead. PApa GOD, can i talk to you please? KNOCK, KNOCK papa GOD..YES my child i heard his voice..what's bothering you? Ohhh..papa GOD, every time i felt something in my body that is not feeling normal..i mean..something or somebody doing things or bad things on my body. I don't understand it..oK, he said. I can see him sitting on his marble chair looking at on something..and to the horizon.

Yes my child come and talk to me he said. Well..i said..i feel like sharp pain on my head. Then when i closedd my eyes, i saw this woman with long black hair, the same woman before that who was hurting me. And what did you do? papa GOD said. Well, i pulled my internal weapon and i attcked her and trying to defend myself...but when i was almost to defeat her..she put her baby boy infront of me and she disappeared.

She left the baby infront of me, and then i dropped my weapon down. I picked up the baby from the ground where he was sitting.. and i cuddled him tightly as i was so scared that i could have hurt him. I was shaking in fears for him, she didn't come back to get her baby boy. So my child, she knows that you could not hurt the baby, that's why she put the baby infront of you. So it makes sense now, Couple months ago there was a person i know from work and i wasn't comfortable with this person everytime she's arround with me. Everytime she gets closer to me i feel ill and have massive headaches.

One night i dreamed anbout her for no apparent reason, and in my dreams, she was hurting me..i can't remember exactly what she was doing to me, but she continued doing it. I asked her to stop! but she didn't comply. So i got up and forcefully stopping her from whatever she's doing but she kept continueing. She didn't give me any other choice instead to protect myself.

I pulled out my internal weapon and attacked her back. She then realised she's getting hurt and i wasn't stopping and not putting my guard down..and suddenly her baby granddaughter which she really loves appeared infront of me, then i completely stopped and this woman was crying and begging for forgiveness. She then disappeared in my dream.

The next day, this person came very late and couldn't look at my eyes. I didn't judge her or make her uncomfortable, she knew what she did. I know it was real in a spiritual realm and she was hurting me. In reality she had bad intentions to me..i even felt her energy when the very first time we have met. After that incident, she became very careful arround me.

Lately, i have been attacking some bad entities who's becoming aggressive towards me. I can feel them and when i closed my eyes, i can see them. They are all wearing black hoods, some don't have hoods but just a body...it's like walking skin, no hair and the shape of a human but just skin and formed as a body and walking like with unsteady gait. I eliminated that entity, and then followed with all the entities with black hoods. They were lining up to hurt me!!!

What a HORRIBLE entities!! Papa GOD there was so many of them attacking me..but this time it's my battle. The more they attacked me, the more i became a very good with my internal weapons. My child this is your destiny, he smiled..but papa GOD i'm still in the physical world..but my battle is in the spiritual world, and sometimes i'm confused. Yes, you are absolutely correct my child, both of this WORLD is your BATTLE! WHAT?? What do you FATHER? I don't understand..you will one day and a matter of fact you are exploring it now with better understanding.

My child you have more to do, really? i said. Yes my child. It will be very hard to stop you now. This is who you are, papa GOD said. So no looking back now papa GOD? NO my child this is your destiny. PAPA GOD, can i ask you something? yes my child..i know what it is, but go ahead, he said. Well, was i an ANGEL before? Who was i? well my child, you are my ANGEL..the little one and my favourite one that always beside me. PLEASE tell me more..why i became a real person? and i have a feelings of not belong here in reality world or not belong to anybody? what happened to me papa GOD? Please tell me.

Well, the reality or physical world is not very easy to understand and it has never been. I appointed you to heal the WORLD with your sense of innocence and loving heart..a pure heart. And with your good heart you can help heal the world. I circulated your spirit and souls for different reasons and different lifetime, to heal many people and families who are struggling with their ownselves and with thier own spiritual beliefs.

Life is complicated to understand for so many people. OK i said..that make sense now because everytime i spend my life with the people who has family problems..somehow i have changed them. Somehow i have changed their environment, or even personalities or the whole family dynamic for the better, they said i have this energy on me that changes their situations just by being with them.

So papa GOD what's next for me? My life, and my future? He then really looked at me..but still can't see his face. It's sillhoutte!! well my child, do you really want to know? Yes papa GOD, i said. Well then, there will be no mystery for you to look forward to, he said. Hmm..you don't really want to tell me don't you papa GOD?..i said cheekily. Yes my child i rather not..but i will put this in your dream one night, ok? he said. OK i said. So is there anything else my child? NO papa GOD, i think i will settle for that tonight. I will go to bed early tonight. OK that's my girl, he said. Don't forget your prayers. I won't FATHER. Get some sleep it will make you grow:) i know, i said. But i'm a fully grown woman now and it's too late. NO it's not too late, he said. What do you mean papa GOD? well..think tall and you will feel tall. Ohh..ok.nice to know..hehehe. So do you feel better now? papa GOD asked. Yes i do papa GOD. Good night my child.. remember you are always protected. Thank you DEVINE FATHER.

# CHAPTER 21

# WHO IS MY MOTHER?

JOURNAL
4TH MAY 2022

Good morning papa GOD and my journal, i know this is very early for me to talk about myself. I would like to take this opportunity of my spare time while waiting for my students. PAPA GOD said ok, you can talk to me..what's in your mind? he said...oh that's right you want to continue our conversations last night. Yes papa GOD if you don't mind. He put his ancient looking pen down, and he turned me again into a young child. He picked me up and sat me on his left lap. I hugged him..but for some reason, i felt the body..but i'sm still looking at the sillhoutte energy. I'm confused as a child..but then i heard in my head.. don't think too much my child, thinking to much is always your habits until now. Always analysing your thoughts..curious i may say, he said.

While i was sitting on his lap, i felt his beautiful loving energy absorving into my body. I then asked him..papa GOD..yes my child he said. WHO is my MOTHER? He looked at me lovingly..and he said..i know you are going to ask me this one day. Well, i think this is the right time i have to tell you.

You see..i created you in a spiritual world. You mean no MOTHER? i asked innocently. Yes my child. I am everything to you. OH well, it make sense now.. because in the reality world it seems like i don't have this kind of close connections with the mother figure. I have more deeper connections with the FATher figure that who can see my inner child. It makes sense now if i look back from previous years when i was with my parents. I always feel left out..doesn't belong to them, and my mother was very hard to reach, and only my father can but he was always away from us and that made me even feels miserable. A feeling of abandonment.

And if i meet somebody who has a kind heart, and with a loving energy..i feel like to sit on thier laps. It's strange though..it may sounds odd and even for me that time..but that was my true feelings. And now i completely understands it. Yes, my child..your inner knowing is reminding you of me while you are in the physical world, there is nothing wrong with that my child, he said but i know you were very careful and i won't let anyone to do harm on you or any have to have some bad intentions towards you.

Well papa GOD it all makes sense now, and i have more to confirm later..more questions about me, my kids, my husband and to my extended family including friends. My thoughts are forever questioning everything. I want more knowledge more answers to my questions about myself, and i am beginning to understand who i am now, as i thought i was going crazy. No my child..You are not crazy, papa GOD said.

Now i'm back again thinking my DEVINE FATHER, and i am sitting in my chair looking through the glass window at work while staring at the high rising buildings. Oh who am i kidding? you know where i am FATHER..hahaha :) and papa GOD laughed!! Yes i can see you too, he said:) Well my child, do you want to talk again? Yes FATHER.

I still don't understand some people that can be nasty to me. Well, do this, he said. BLOCK them in your head..i'm sure they won't be able to reach your thoughts. Oh really papa GOD???..yes my child.. you do that and you will have peace of mind. NOW?..yes NOW, he said. OK..what do i do? OK..he said..do you remember your prayers i gave you? Yes i do FATHER..i will never forget. Good girl, he said. Well..close your eyes now and say your prayers 3 times..and erase this person in your thoughts. Every single memories of this person will disappear everytime you clear it. Until you see clear like a sky.. blue sky with no clouds. OK do it now he said. OK, i am doing..then suddenly, i did it! i deleted it in my head..and i sorrounded myself with big strong protection arround me. Well done my child. I shall do that technique more often. Ok my child drink plenty of water. YES FATHER and thank you again.

# CHAPTER 22

# WHAT IF I GO BLIND?

JOURNAL
5TH MAY 2022

My lovely journal, i am sitting in my ususal place in a very tall building from work looking at the cloudy sky. It looks miserable..i then asked my DEVINE FATHER for at least have a sunny day so i can see the clear blue sky on the big window where i am sitting. I also asked for a sign where he is..i looked at the sky again and got the message straight away into my head saying..my child..i'm everywhere.

I just finished 3 books and i looked at the sky and it's beautiful and sunny.Thank you Papa GOD. Oh by the by FATHER, i named my horse "SKY" because of today's gifts from you..a beautiful sky.Thank you:)

Good morning my DEVINE FATHER another day another blessed day, i have to start with positive mood today. Papa GOD i need to talk to you if you don't mind please. I am confused with my feelings and i would say what i am becoming of myself..i mean of who i am. Lately the sneaky attacked from these people towards me is becoming more apparent and so evil.

I can feel what they are doing with my body, something nasty. And then when i closed my eyes here we go again..i can see entities and not revealing themselves, covering their faces with the hoods and they are all wearing black robes. Before they purposely attacked my body i can sense them. I know they are going to harm me which they did..but i stopped them for going no futher, so i forged my way to attack them using my devine weapons and eliminating them one at a time.

I finished them off..all of them..i was aggressive towards them and have no fears to fight with them!! I can see myself slowly changing into a ruthless and very brave personality towards this entities..papa God this is not me..i feel like i am awakening something in me..my spirit and soul, it's scary!! To me it feels like it's normal. Why?..Papa GOD i'm confused. This is not me in the real world.

Suddenly, i saw my DEVINE FATHER coming down from the stairways with full of clouds. I'm here my child extending his arms towards me. Do you want to talk don't you? he said. Yes Papa GOD desperately. PLease..he sat on his marble chair and somehow i'm still in an adult body..but i felt the presence of JESUS. Then papa GOD speaks..my child this is your destiny and you need to fulfill this.

Feelings of not being normal that is not you..because you have been arround with many lifetimes, your personalities has been mixed, but you will come arround eventually, he said. So, you are going to continue your destiny. No turning back? i asked. Yes, no turning back, Papa God said.

My Devine Father i have a question..if i go blind, what's going to happen to me? Would i still see the enemies? Well, you will have a perfect sight then, he said. What do you mean Papa GOD? You will see your enemies and you will have no problem eliminating them.

Remember when you closed your eyes during meditation, What did you see when your eyes closed? he said. Ohh..i see everything..and when i open my eyes..i lost everything. Whoahh..you are right papa GOD.

Remember, no one can harm your eyes..if they do, there own eyes will be compromised..other words i will take there own sights, they will go blind. Now do you understand your purpose in life now? Yes i do FATHER. So what's the face then? he said. This entities who's attacking you is nothing compared to the Big ones who have already eliminated, and there are more to come. More to come?? ohh..i'm petrified now, i said. Don't be Papa GOD said, as the reassurance of his voice really soothes me.

My child, this time you will be more POWERFUL..ohh?? i said. Can i have more question FATHER? What would happen to those people who has been purposely hurt me and will continueing hurting me in the physcical world? and to those who have been eliminated from the spiritual realm? Well, there bodies will starts to deteriorate slowly, then become very ill, and eventually die and thier souls will NOT be save. Good night my child, have some rest and don't think too much. OK papa GOD, goodnight..I love you.Then i heard..don't forget your prayers, almost echoing...no Father i won't forget, i said to him back..then hearts floatings :)

# CHAPTER 23

# FINDING MY MAGICAL MUSIC BOX

JOURNAL

10TH MAY 2022

Good evening my journal, i haven't been catching up with papa GOD, he is up there when i need to talk to him. He just gave me a wave and smile, he knows i am busy, so he's not bothering me too much. He asked me to have a good rest. I then asked him WHY? why papa GOD? There is something BIG coming for you to do, he said. Are we travelling again FATHER? Yes my child..but not now, it will be soon. OK FATHER i said.

I can see my DEVINE FATHER looking out through the very BIG glass window..he is looking at the blue sky. He is wearing a long dress and almost dirty white colour and made of thick material clothes. I don't know the significance of the colour of his clothing is very important to my curiousity. Papa GOD has a beard you know.. like SANTA CLOUSE..but i'm still puzzled, i can't see his face..it's always a silhouette. PAPA GOD, can i ask you something? Papa GOD just turned arround and facing at me, then suddenly i can see myself as a child again, he then bend down towards my level and picked me up and put me in his right arm. Somehow, i slowly can feel the connections from him. The golden energy coming from his body and absorbing into my whole body..then i felt the loved again.

So, do you want to see your KING EMPEROR FATHER don't you? and your EMPRESS MOTHER? with the smile on my DEVINE FATHER's face. YES papa GOD please! I guess he knew it, i thought.. of course my child, he said:) OK then, close your eyes and only must open it when i say so. Yes papa GOD i will. I closed my eyes..and it feels like eternity waiting..i am feeling so excited and then i heard Papa GOD voice said..open your eyes now..and then when i opened my eyes i can see my Emperor FAther from the distance have his arms stretched out welcoming me..and my Empress MOther from behind my Emperor FAther. they both walking towards me and my DEVINE FATHER.

I looked around the sorroundings while papa GOD still holding me in his arm..this sorrounding is just so familiar to me when i was with them before. The Big tall rock walls where the water falls..the trees..flowers..birds..butterflies and our PALACE behind us..it's so beautiful and so serene. Papa GOD put me dowm on the the ground, and as a 5 years old kid, i ran towards to my Emperor FAther first, and he picked me up, hugged me..and then to my beautiful Empress Mother. They both very happy to see me, and i felt the overwhelming love by my Emperor and Empress parents.

I looked at my beautiful Mother, she's wearing a very simple but elegant CROWN. The crown just only fitted arround her forehead.. it's just beautiful. It's funny, i always like this kind of style crown. I even put that on my daughter's head during her confermission day, and she looks just magnificent. My EMPRESS mother looks absolutely devine, She's wearing a beautiful long white gown, and her crown has colour gold with green and red yellow stones. Her crown is not big or thick, instead, it's a thin crown and a very elegant looking one.

My Empress mother said, welcome home SHINE with her beautiful smile:) My EMPEROR father went straight to Papa God and said thank you, and shook his hand. My mother is holding my hand while we both walking arround the sorounding palace. We are in the very high ground area, which we both looking at the rock solid wall and with the waterfalls. I can see different types of little birds flying arround, and different species with different colours which i have never seen it before. So many butterflies..lots and lots of yellow butterflies. I saw Papa GOD and my Emperor Father still talking to each other. My Empress mother just happily walking with me arround the place.

Then i saw a BIG SOLID DOOR with an Ancient carvings on it. I touched it curiously, it's cold and it's made of STONE. I don't know what kind of stone it is..but i'm sure it is SOLID. Then suddenly the door opened..i then stepped into the room curiously..i can see this BIG hall..big wide open HALL. It looks so majestic inside..the walls it's like made of marbles..solid wall marbles. I don't see any chandeliers or lights arround but i can see the whole place is litted up with golden and yellow lights.

Then i quickly noticed the staircase, it's just so familiar to me for some reason. I feel like i have been gone up and down from that stairs before. I ran towards the staircase, and while i was going up and down several times, then i suddenly stopped in the middle of it. Then while i was standing, i am feeling this curiousity in my mind. I looked at on my right side..i bend and slowly sat down..then i dragged my bottom towards the wall. I put my hands into the lower part side of the wall, then for some reason..a little space opened up just like a little door, and saw this kind of toy. A little toy looks like a clown i'm holding it in my hands, then suddenly it turns into a music box. Then a little girl turning round and arround while the music is going. The music is very familiar to my ears.

Then i noticed my Empress mother, i showed my music box to my mother and she said..so you found your magical music box, she smiled. I then asked, how is it magical mother? well, it's magical because it works with your feelings and emotions. What ever you feel and wish. Ohh..ok i said. I kept my magical box with me and then i noticed..i don't see any people arround. Why mother? i asked. She just smiled and extended her hand to me and we both continued walking upstairs.

We reached the upstairs, and it's even more spectacular..now there..i can see some beautiful entities walking arround lovingly happy. The place has a feeling of pure love.. i don't feel any single hatred arround me, or anything negative energy from this place. It's so serene..beautiful..full of love. Then i heard my mother said..this is your home my SHINE. You are HOME..then my mother then took me to the other room..she then opened it..and she said..this is your bedroom. Whoaahh...it's beatiful..it looks magnificent..it's more like a PRINCESS type bedroom. I can't explain it..the comfort is the one i'm very familiar with.

The comfort in the physical world bedroom i have made. Then i noticed an ocean and sandy beach MURALS on the wall..then i looked up to my bedroom ceiling it has blue sky, the sun..little clouds, and the stars also the moon. OMG MOTHER!..i spend so many times looking at the stars and the moon..the clouds and the blue sky, and the sun when i'm in a physical world..when i feel this NATURE, i felt like i'm home. Home which i have never understood when i'm in the physical world. I have always feels like that there is always something missing from me.

I always feels like there is more beyond that i cannot explain..and i feel it..it's just weird. This is making sense now when i was travelling overseas, i like the destinations of the beach, looking out the ocean wondering what's more out there? and watching the sunrise..what's behind the sunrise?..what's out there?? Oh God i said to myself, please help me to understand it! Then during the night i watched the moonlight reflecting the water. I feel like someting calling me from the distance..the water horizon, it's so mysterious, hypnotising and it's fascinating the magnificent feeling of nature.

Then i saw myself as an adult again, i looked at myself in the MIRROR, a BIG whole body MIRROR. That explains it, in a physical world..i always like to see my body in a mirror view..which i have 3 of them arround my house. hmmm...now it's getting clearer now the connections. I was wondering why I'm so obsessed to buy a full body length mirror..now i understand.

I can see myself in a mirror as a young woman, looking like a version of when i was 18 years old. Tall loking, slender, with a very long straight hair. I am wearing a long white silky dress with the slight tinge of baby pink colour arround the long sleeves, and down to the rim of my clothes..It looks like a gown..very simple..but elegant. Now i can see the connection again of myself in the physical world. I like long sleeves, baby pink colour is my favourite, i like silky materials clothing, it soothes my skin..i like simple but elegant style clothing, and I don't like too much jewelries on my body.

I can see the resemblance of me and my Empress mother..she's wearing a very simple crown but very elegant. I almost look like her..i looked different when i am here in our Kingdom than in my physical body. My long dress has a belt arround my waist, but it's slightly lose..it has colour gold arround, and hanging down on my right side waist line. While looking at my self in the mirror..i asked my mother curiously, why i became an adult again? well..that is how you are feeling when the first time you saw yourself the mirror, she said and she smiled. Ohh Mother, is that magical box again has got something to do with it? Yes SHINE she answered lovingly. Remember i told you earlier..it's about how you "FEEL"..and how you "WISH" for. So be very careful of what you wish in a reality world.

My Mother showed me my bed..ohh..such beautiful..i sat on it..and it feels like feathery soft and comfortable. Then my MOther tucked me in instantly, drew circles on my forehead 3 times, and whispered take time to sleep.. i then suddenly fall asleep.

# CHAPTER 24

# WHAT IS MY PURPOSE?

JOURNAL

14th MAY 2022

I seek counselling with my DEVINE FATHER last night. I can see a little smile on his face..but still..didn't see his whole face again. I sat down on my little chair and told him what has just happened recently. I told him I'm feeling low somehow insignificant at this moment...as i was crying.. he looked at me closer and touched my chin and raised it up..wiped my tears on my face with his thumb.

He didn't say anything..although i want to hug him, but instead he put his right hand on my head..and that instant i feel good and feeling being loved again sorrounded by "golden aura", he then said something in my head..you have free will..my GIRL. The words girl or Child are always the name he called me ever since i could remember.

Remembering that time when i was growing up, my grandmother always said, i was always talking to somebody or someone especially when i was sick..but you have grown up now, Papa GOD said. That is the free will is all about when you are as an adult. i never understood the free will when i was a kid, papa God..i know my child. you supposed to be protected..and you were..until now. You are PROTECTED. Do not worry I'm here always for you, remember our first meeting? what did i say to you? papa GOd asked me with his very comforting voice..Yes i remember with a smile on my face. Yeah..you tripped me over..and papa GOD LAUGHED!!:) and you said..DON'T LOOK ANYMORE FURTHER..I'M HERE FOR YOU..PAPA God has a very funny sense of humour. He knows how to make me laugh and makes me feel better.

He reasured me..keep going no one can harm you..i am always here for you and your Arch Angel Michael. Where ever you going, he is with you. That's explains everything..sometimes i don't have fears exploring the unknown when i was in my younger years. It's always my fascinations to explores and it's a mind blowing sometimes that the things i have uncovered and explored. I think this is part of my curiousity in life.

DEVINE FATHER, you have mentioned before about preparations for my Devine calling and PURITY or purifications of my body and soul has to happened. Meaning..my body physically has to be purified, such as no contacts between the opposite sex before i can touch my Devine obligations. Am i correct my DEVINE FATHER? He answered..yes my child, you are right and already figured it out yourself.

But papa GOD, i'm still here in a physical world..i am sounding like i'm protesting...a BIG PAUSE from my DEVINE FATHER, he's not answering me back:( I waited and waited..but nothing..a BIG pause in the air. Sometimes i wish i could go back home..home to my Ancestral Kingdom..to my FATHER EMPEROR ARTHERU and my MOTHER EMPRESS GLYDICA, that's where my home is. THen PAPA GOD said a BIG "NO"!! not yet. Remember, you need to be in a physical form to be able to transform yourself into a spiritual being to do your work in a spiritual realm. A very STERN words. I never heard him like that before:(

Remember, i created you with GREAT PURPOSE..your Job is to spread LOVE and UNITY, and to conquer the evils in the spiritual realm..and that's how it works. You have no choice with your obligations beside to do it. I have created you, and you have done part of your work already, and you will have more journey to discover. Reality has and have been a painful experience journey for you..i made it for you that way. That's because i want you to feel it, the pain, the disappointment, the poverty, upheavals and many more mortals are experiencing in this world so you can learn the value of life.

Ohh Papa GOD, that's so heavy on me now..the feelings of what you just have said :( I must admit, yes i have experienced some of this.. and sometimes i feel like giving up :( Sometimes i feel like not waking up in the morning and to know i have the same things over and over again, and especially this connections with you PAPA GOD.. who would believe me? please give me an answer :( :( Then Papa GOD said, well you told me to leave it to me..the decisions of your life and what's going to happened with your life, and the situations you cannot control..now, this time is going to be my decisions. Yes, my DEVINE FATHER that would be appropriate for me. I thank you again.

Papa GOD, can i ask some serious question? Yes my child..go on, he said. I can see him looking out from the heaven vearandah, full of clouds arround, and he is seriously thinking. I don't really want to ask, because looks like he doesn't want me read his mind. He then turned arround and asked me to join him looking at he verandah and the clouds. He didn't turn me into a child, and this time i'm an adult woman. He said i know what you are going to ask me..but go ahead then he said.

Well papa GOD this is about my husband, was it your decision for my husband to meet me? Well my child..i appointed him to your life since the beginning, because he is the one who can protect you, care for you and to love you. Being married to him have also helped him emotionally, and to his family too, you brought love and Unity to them.

What do you remember the first time you saw and meet him? what did you see on him? papa GOD asked. Well, i must truly admit and from my recollections, seeing him from the distance walking towards me, he was smilling, and he has this sorrounding white aura that i was drawn to him. It was a kind of pure white light that it was calming..almost Angelic. And when he introduced himself as his name is MICHAEL and touched my hand, there was a current kind of energy went through my body. Yes, i pushed him to you to meet you, Papa GOD said..oh now i know, i said.

My child, from previous and this lifetime, a lot of people wants to have you, but there intentions are not pure. I have protected you from them, and i will do to my POWER to protect you. I have been protecting you since you were a child..since the very beginning of your life. Papa GOD, what happenned then if people use force towards me? what would happen to them? well my child, Their very own lives are the exchanged of there bad intentions. I will stop the people from harming you because your devine missions are in lining..your Devine "Calling"..you "MUST" attend to it. So when is my next journey with you Devine FATHER and Arch Angel

Michael? i asked. Well..very soon, but i want you to have a good rest and sleep. This is very significant journey and it's a BIG ONE too. Oh my GOD! i'm scared now.. Don't be with a very reassuring voice, Papa GOD said, because you are protected. He then kissed my forehead and touched my nose, then whispered LOVE :) Thank you my DEVINE FATHER. Good night.

*CHAPTER 25*

# SEEING THE PURGATORY

JOURNAL
15TH MAY 2022

MY dear journal, last night i meditated in my bed, and i got connected to my DEVINE FATHER straightaway. I said hello to him..he waved at me and saw a reassuring smile from him. I can see him standing infront of a long balcony covered by the clouds looking towards the north side. From what i can see from the short distance while walking towards him..i can see many souls trying to touch his right hand while extending towards them. The souls almost begging for mercy and crying just to touched his hand. And when it happened, thier souls turned into clouds. I was amazed the transformations!!!

I can see my DEVINE FATHER in a white or more like an off white clothing, this time he looks different, as he looks more so "REGAL". His clothing looks more a very High Ranking Emperor. I thought to myself.. maybe he is expecting some visitors. My DEVINE FATHER has a white and long beard..very white though. His clothing has a Royal blue colour trimming on the side of his shoulder top clothes he is wearing..a very thick material clothings, and A VERY ROYAL looking KING.

This time he showed me his face what he exactly he looks like. He imprinted that into my head..i would say in my thoughts, my mind and memory. Then he smiled at me, and i thanked him through my thoughts. He then made me read his thoughts..saying..you have been asking me this for a long time now.

Then suddenly, i have felt this overwhelming feelings of LOVE and previledged and almost emotionally in tears. Then he placed his right hand on my forehead and felt this amazing glow of his energy of our connections. Its purely Devine energy..an amazing feeling of LOVE and lightness not just on me, it's amazingly radiating into the whole area of the room. I looked at myself..and i'm still the same, he didn't transform me into a child.

After the connections has happened, i can see myself walking so happy, just happy wandering arround the area. The area is just in a different world. It's very high i can feel and can see the clouds arround us, and the people who's walking arround almost high ranking people??? They looks like very majestic or GODDESS? I'm confused where i am, this people or entities whose walking arround they are not talking..they are just happily wandering the area.

I then reached for my DEVINE FATHER and asked, where are we FATHER? He then answered me.."KINGDOM". Kingdom of what and where papa GOD? i asked. My child we are in a different dimension..not in EARTH. We are in a different place and too far away. Oh..i see, i said. Are we in heaven papa GOD? No my child we are not. Then..my phone beside me made a "NOISE" and woke me up. Then i drank my water beside my bed as i am terribly thirsty.

Then tonight, i reached for PApa GOD again..DEVINE FATHER can i talk to you please? i asked. I then heard his voice saying..yes my child? Well..i know you know what's in my head..but still..i would love to talk to you. I can see him sitting on his chair leaning forward, and this time, it's just an energy. I asked papa GOD, why your energy looks "BLACK"? i'm puzzled. Well my child..what did you drink lately hmm? well..to be honest i just drank margarita drinks. Well, that's why it's clouding your perception of me, he said.

Ohh sorry..but i drank some water after the margarita..then suddenly papa GOD looks getting clearer now. I can see he is forming into a beautiful silhoutte with white and golden colour. Papa GOD..can i tell you now what's bothering me? Yes my child, go ahead. Well, everytime i feel somebody starting to hurt me physically with their bad intentions, and with thier own energy and projecting to me, i closed my eyes as you taught me this before..suddenly i can see the person who is doing it to me..and then without hesitation i eleminated them. It's gruesome sometimes, but to my surprise they don't have blood!!! why FATHER?

Well, my child that's because the entities whose attacking you and you have eliminated are thier souls. They are not in the physical body, he said. oh ok..so what would happens to thier souls then after i destroyed them? I asked curiously. So do you really want to know? papa GOD said. Yes DEVINE FATHER. Ok then close your eyes and don't open until we reach the destination. Yes FATHER, i said. I closed my eyes..then in a quick moment..papa GOD said..now open your eyes slowly and don't get scared.

When i opened my eyes..i see this so many BLACK Energies, begging for MERCY..the sorrounding is so scary and black..so many of them huddled in one area. It looks like a LAKE without a water with Full of Black energies. And i can see a wooden bridge separating them from the other side, and this other side is empty. It looks like one side of the lake is full of Black spirits begging for mercy, and the other side of the lake separated by the bridge is empty.

Then i heard Papa GOD said..are you done looking? yes FATHER. It's a PURGATORY! he said. Oh..its so scary i said. Papa GOD when i destroyed this entities with my DEVINE weapons, i became more ruthless. Well, don't be alarmed of what you are becoming, because you are braver this time. You are becoming aware to defend yourself, he said. I know FATHER, but this is not me..i don't like killing, Yes i know that my child. You need to protect yourself, because their intentions are to harm you and destroy you. I won't let that happen at all.

I gave you the DEVINE weapons to use for protections, they are not going to stop..that's why we are here protecting you all the time. Thank you FATHER. So what happened to their physical bodies after you destroyed them in a spiritual realm, they became ill..and eventually die..and you know where there souls destination..you saw it. Yes and it's so sad.

Papa GOD, i have noticed my back today in the mirror when i got changed, it looks like i have a shape of wings on my back. Is this real? i asked. In spiritual realm is REAL..and in the physical realm, it's real but you only can feel it and uses it when you needed comfort. But this is only works in your thoughts. But still the same concept of protections. That's why when you develop your thoughts in a higher vibration..it's powerful, papa GOD said. This is a validation from me as your DEVINE FATHER. And OH MY GOD!!! you just flexed my left foot???!! Yes i did!! because you are just starting to fall asleep on me during our conversations. And i heard a BIG LAUGH!!! Oh sorry, i said..Yes, he said..too much MARGARITA drinks.

Ok Papa GOD, i have to sleep now..ok my child and drink plenty of water. Yes papa GOD i will. Good night my child..and no more MARGARITA drinks. And i said okay, no more. I wake up in the morning and feeling rejuvinated.

# CHAPTER 26

# TAME THAT WINGS

JOURNAL

16TH MAY 2022

It has been a blessed day and i must thank you papa GOD for making my day bearable. I had a power nap for few minutes then my back itchy, i went to the kitchen and i made myself some coffee, sat infront of the TV and watched the NEWS. Then the news started to upset me, it's all about the war and destructions in UKRAIN. I am feeling devastated for the damaged that Russia has have caused, especially to the innocent people such as children, old people and everyone who lives in that area including animals, and so many structures of the buildings have been destroyed in a masssive scale. The damaged looks unrepairable!

I couldn't contol my tears, my heart is aching for the unfortunate people. I asked Papa GOD, can you please stop the destructions? the war? can we papa GOD? I didn't get any answers from my DEVINE FATHER. I went to have a shower, while in the shower i closed my eyes..and then for some reason, my body automatically moved and bend my body forward. And then the hot shower in my back started to soothe my back..but at the same time i'm still upset about this innocent people being affected and killed. I asked papa GOD, how can i help FATHER? and suddenly..i felt my back something moved, and i can feel my spiritual wings just going crazy and started flapping out. I then heard papa GOD said, tame it..tame it my child! he said it twice and loud in my head. I then slowly tamed it by switching my emotions into a happy one.

When i have finished my shower, i'm curious of what my back looks like?..so i grabbed my cell phone camera, and took some photos of my back. Then i saw 2 Big marks in the middle of my back. I convinced myself that it was from scratching, but when i looked closer, my back has a hump on the top of my middle shoulder. I wonder??? i then convinced myself again that is just my normal structure's of my back.. but my back looks like there is some kind of shapes of the wings!!?? i stared at it but i decided that i'm just imagining it. Anyway, i decided to reach my DEVINE FATHER.

I asked papa GOD, Father, what is it on my back? i asked curiously. Well..what's come out from your camera you have taken? he asked. Well..looks like a scrathed and a shape of something..i said. Something what? he asked again. Well..i don't know papa GOD, earlier i felt my wings came out from the shower, then i had an urged to take a picture of my back..then it looks like some wings?? Well my child, you do have some wings, he said it with reassuring voice, but only during your spiritual journey. Can you can feel it? he asked..yes papa GOD especially when i'm feeling upset.

But papa GOD what about the hump on my back? or is it just fat? well my child, put it this way..if it is fat, you can loose it, but if a hump.. well you can carry it and papa GOD laughed!!! Ohh papa GOD, seriously?? i said. Ok my child..put it this way, it's how you believe in it. The good things about your mind is, you can create anything and once you mastered it..your mind can be powerful!!! It's in YOU! I gave it to you since the beginning..and i know you have used it already, manifesting but still so scared to use it.

My child go to sleep as we have some journey to do..are you ready? he said. YES! i am papa GOD. This time i'm not scared! That's my Girl! papa GOD said. Tonight drink plenty of water and don't forget your prayers. I won't papa GOD. Good night my DEVINE FATHER.. and he just touched my nose with a sweet smile on his face. Good night my sweetheart, he said..sweetheart??? I woke up and asked.. sweetheart this time why? i asked. well, because you are growing up now..but you are still my child..now go to sleep. oh ok then..goodnite papa GOD.

# CHAPTER 27

# VOLCANO READY TO ERUPT

JOURNAL
20TH MAY 2022

5 days to rest before the next journey, and i have been contemplating lately about what's happenning of my life lately in general. I reached for papa GOD last night and asked about our journey, and he said no..not yet for you. I asked why? he said, i want you to finish your 5 days good sleep then i will tap your head when you are ready. Hmm.. that's new to me..and from him too. Although, i have been feeling some kind of somebody has been tapping my head and touching my face lately.i didn't feel uncomfortable anyway.

I reached for papa God last night and i asked if i could possibly help them during the journey, or whatever they are doing out there with my Angels. I must admit i am feeling bored..i called for papa GOD again, Father..why aren't you interacting with me much anymore? i cried..:( please..FATHER talk to me please??? I promise i will not protest again.

Then suddenly, i saw papa GOD standing in an open BIG verandah and looking at those clouds..but not many clouds this time..it looks very subtle this time so i can see from the distance walking towards him. I saw his head turned slowly into the left direction facing towards me while i'm walking towards him. From the distance i can see him holding some kind of a stick, a little tool and looks like he's using it by pointing the clouds and then suddenly the clouds disappeared.

I slowly walked towards him and stands close to him, and i asked lovingly..please papa GOD, you are not angry at me aren't you? I see myself as a dignified woman in a long white dress just like him standing beside him. He looked at me lovingly and said..well my child..during your purification all this years i have prepared you, this moment you are not ready.

For the DEVINE calling, you must have a clear mind including your physical body. As we said, clear mind including body and soul. So, what do you want me to do FATHER? i asked. Well my child..i want you to sit down and clear your thoughts, by removing all your hurts from your body and mind. But papa God, i have done this many times..but it keeps coming back again and again especially when something or somebody triggers my emotions.

I taught you how to disposed it, do you remember during your meditation and your conversations with me? he asked. Yes, i replied solemnly. You told me to put my bad emotions, hurts, disappointed and many more in the golden bucket carried by the little Angels, and visualised it that it's all rubbish and when it bacomes full, i'll ask my little angels to take it UP to you..Up..UP..there and you will melt it with the DEVINE golden colour coming from your hand.

Well i have done that..and yes it did help..but it's more coming and it keeps coming..and coming back:(:( i cried..Well my child..why don't you write it down, as you are still i a physical world and emotionally being affected. Start by writing it down, so you can release your emotional pain, he said. Ohh ok..i guess i shall do that, but papa GOD, where would i write it? here in my journal or in my notebook? Well..does it make any difference? he said. Your emotions does not choose where you want to write..it's all about releasing the pressure that you have kept it in your heart for a long time. It's up to you my child, he said.

Ok papa GOd thank you..he then looked at me and lovingly kissed my forehead. Thank you i whispered to him. He pulled me gently closer to him and to his shoulder. That instant, i felt the connection again..a Beautiful DEVINE CONNECTION which i have lost many days ago. I am sorry FATHER to what i have behaved towards you..i guess i couldn't help it to release my tantrum and of course you punished me from not talking to me, until it comes to my senses of what you are trying for me to understand which is important for my growth.

I felt the connection again..and he squessed my left arm gently, and he said..it's ok my child..at least you apologised as i have been waiting for that. OMG!!! why didn't you give me a sign? i cried..i said. Well..i did that by tapping your head and your face, papa GOD said. It was you?? It was 3 times i have felt. Yes..and you were still stubborn.. and papa GOD laughed instead. Well..you have created me, i said. :)

My child you must remember the numbers i have given you, (the "MUST" letter is significant) and try to recognise the significance of it, he said. Yes Devine Father, 3 and 5..i remember..and it becames number 8!! which is me! I'm number 8, you gave me that number long time ago, and that's explains it..i'm sorrounded by number 8 numbers, the feeling of familiarity that it feels like home?? I don't know if this makes sense to some people.

Papa GOD, how do i start writing my emotions? i asked. well, starts how you are feeling now, he said. But papa GOD i don't feel like writing at this moment. I feel like i'm not ready yet to recollect my past emotions and hurts. Some of them are gone now..but some still here and when it resurface it really bothers me..i don't really want to dig it out again.

I am talking and crying to papa GOD while he is standing infront of the BIG Verandah looking towards the south west horizon. He asked me to come and look at the volcano while pointing it. I stood up where i was sitting, i wept my tears and walked towards him and he said, what do you see? Well..it's a VOLCANO. a very black volcano and looks like it's about to erupt. I can see black rocks and boulders sorrounding the volcano. I'm scared for the people who lives nearby. Can you stop it FATHER? i asked sadly, NO..he said..this is MOTHER NATURE my child..and i saw his sad face.

What about the people PAPA GOD? well, some will perish, and some will survive, the people who survived from this disaster it means they have more purpose in this lifetime to fulfill. I have appointed some ANGELS to assist the people and the situations. They may feel some kind of strangers from the people who lives in that area, but they are EARTH Angels, he said.

So get back to you my child, he said. well..if you are not ready to dispose your hurts and disappoinments then you are not ready yet. But FATHER i am ready, i argued..let me help "You" and Arch Angel Michael. You said it's my calling..well i'm ready now. I'M BORED! I need to come with you in the JOURNEY. Then PAPA GOD asked me to listen to him carefully..do you see what i am holding here? he said. YES..it's a CRYSTAL BALL i said. Well, this crystal ball represents CLARITY, this is your BODY and SOUL.

When we are going to this journey, you are purified and clear. This journey is something BIG, that only ANGELS and you have clear mind including body and soul can enter the devine dimensions. When we are going to this journey, i am making sure your mind is clear and purified including your body, and that's involved meditation. I won't be given you a choice..this time is my CHOICE, your DEVINE FATHER CHOICE.

A very stern statements came from him, and i know that kind of tone of voice..so powerful. Now get some sleeps as you needed it, he said. Yes papa GOd, i said without any hesitation. He then touched and kissed my forehead then whispered good night my child. I felt an amazing golden AURA penetrated into my body and soul..and my head ache is gone. Good night papa GOD..I LOVE YOU. Then i took a peek..i can see him looking back towards the volcano, and kind of studying or assessing the situations, then i heard..i can still hear your thoughts..OMG! Yes, i will be sleeping now..ohh...my headache is back..he then pointed his finger to my left side temple of my head and then my head ache slowly disappeared. Then i fall asleep.

Good morning PAPA GOD..good morning my child..i walked slowly to my DEVINE FATHER and said HELLO FATHER..i came to visit you i saw the door is open. He looked at me with a smile on his face, and he said, it's always open for you my child. Thank you FATHER, i can see myself as a dignified woman this time and wearing long white dress just like PAPA GOD. I guess you have done the important things that you need to do before the BIG JOURNEY, he said. Yes, FATHER i did, and i have devoloped someway of disposing my emotions in a different way. Very well then, soon you will be ready my child.

He asked me to join him looking at the WEST HORIZON, which i did and standing beside him very quietly. I noticed he is not saying anything at the moment. He is staring at this "Big City". I can see a BIG CITY..but it's a strange looking at from afar..it looks purely "WHITE". I was going to ask PAPA GOD, but he stopped me, instead he made me read his mind saying not to talk..just be "still"..and be with me, he said in his thought. He then looked at me lovingly and gazed into my eyes..his eyes is very soothing. I feel the connection in his eyes..i can see myself as an adult that can understand his thoughts in a moment of stillness..i feel some kind of sadness..i don't really know where is this coming from, but still he doesn't want me to ask questions at this moment.

I moved closer to him..i can see him wearing a very REGAL looking white clothes..long clothes like a ROBE. WE both just staring at the horizon and the WHITE CITY. THE buildings are ANCIENT looking but it's very white and almost glittering from the distance. Then suddenly,he said..look at this city, yes i said..it's white and glittery, have i lived there before papa GOD? i asked innocently. NO my child, you did not...Ok, i said..but he still very quiet..i respect his moment. I excused myself as i have to check my students. Ok my child he said..he then kissed my forehead and touched my face lovingly, and he said..you are going to be alright my Child. Thank you FATHER, bye for now..and i saw a little smile on his face.

# CHAPTER 28

# THE 6TH DIMENSIONS

JOURNAL

29TH MAY 2022

It has been some few days now i haven't talk to you my dear journal. Lately, it has been so stressful and it's kind of flipped myself upside down, but i recovered quickly..and now i'm just too exhausted just to dwell on it.

I reached for my DEVINE FATHER..but i can sense he knew that i can handle it. At the moment i'm looking for him, i cannot see him up there. I can see myself walking on the grass..the ground path that i am walking is dry straw grass. Beside the path, i can see green plants and trees and bushes including little birds flying arround. Then suddenly i saw Papa GOD appeared from the short distance walking towards me, and i'm so glad to see him finally.

I saw myself as a child again, and i ran towards him. He then picked me up and lifted me up on the air and gave me a BIG HUG:)ohh.. papa GOD i'm so glad to see you..as i was clinging on him and his shoulder. I'm here my child..you will never loss me, he said with a very reassuring voice. I then felt the big relief on my whole body..i thought you have abandoned me, i said. He then looked at me in my eyes..his lovingly eyes..no hatred..no judgement..it's just full of love from the DEVINE FATHER. He said, i am never far away from you..i am always here, and he wiped my tears and kissed my forehead.

I felt my papa GOD eternal energy again..it's soothing and penetrating into my soul, he then slowly put me down on the grassy walk path, held my hand then we both started walking. While we were both walking..i became an adult again. I looked myself again and told him, i looked different again papa GOD. I'm not a child..why you kept changing me? i asked curiously.

Well my child this is how it works..when you are feeling sad and miserable, i turned yourself into a child. WHY? i asked. Well, being "YOU" as a child it's easy to give you comfort. You just run to me and just want to be hugged, i always want that. But if you are teenager in a teenager mood, well..you are "STUBBORN", and when you are in an adult mood i even like it, because you really listened to me, and i can see myself on you sometimes. Oh Father..really? Thank you. He then put his hand on the top of my head..so what am i to you this time? i asked with the cheeky smile. Well let's say..in between a teenager and a fine adult, papa GOD said with a big smile on his face:)

I guess you are here to talk to me about your problem if i'm correct, he said. Well, yes..but i miss you lately. My life became chaotic if i leave it to long not to be with you and talking with you. call me i'm crazy..hahaha :) DEVINE FATHER you told me before if i can't make a decision or solve my problems in life is to leave it to you. So this time if any situations or something i cannot control in my life, and whatever it is i am supposed to be doing and not going into plans, i will leave it to you? Yes that's correct my child, everything is in control..i see what's happening..everything..all this happening to you has a reason..and it's all including in the plan.

DEVINE FATHER, when i was looking for you today earlier, my mind automatically took me to the higher dimension..up there..i saw myself infront of the young man. Good looking gentleman and very busy doing something. He was bending down, doing or working on something..and i only can see his face half way..i mean in a right side view. He looks very REGAL too, and a kind of has a higher position ranking..he wasn't looking at me though.

I looked arround where i was standing..i noticed we were both in a verandah..a marble made of verandah, and on my left side..i looked up, i can see a galaxy and it's just beautiful..no clouds..and the colour of the sky is dark royal blue. The golden stars are twinkling everywhere, then i asked my self..where am i? Then i heard a voice..6th Dimension. I thought..6th dimension? i have never heard that before. Then i asked you papa GOD, what is 6th dimension FATHER? you then said to me..don't doubt or questions anymore, it will come to you.

But papa GOD, i have been in a different galaxy again, what was i doing there? those galaxy is so different. It's is so different than you usually take me to and travelled with ARCH ANGEL MICHAEL. My child you have been in a different dimension, it's the "PREPARATION". Oh..i said. Preparation for what papa GOD? I want to ask more, but my FATHER wants me to have a rest now. Goodnight my child, everything is going to be alright..Keep drinking some water, he said. thank you FATHER..and good night too. He then touched my nose and kissed my forehead.

# CHAPTER 29

# HEALING THE WORLD

JOURNAL
11TH JUNE 2022

Good morning PAPA GOD and my dear journal, i had a good sleep last night and thank you..i'm still here in my bed and it's 10:10 in the morning. Ohh..i feel so lazy to get up..it's cold. Although i can see the sunshine out side my bay window.

I closed my eyes and started looking for Papa GOD, then i can see him in his favourite verandah standing. This time i noticed there isn't no clouds arround but all i can see is mountains..hills..valleys and we are on top of this sceneries. I can see the green sceneries in the sorrounding areas..the mountains and the hilly sides of the mountains and it's all green.

I can see Papa GOD wearing a very long clothes, and this time it's colour red with white stripes all the way down..he looks so majestic. I greeted him and i can see myself as a dignified woman again..i approached him with the smile, and he then extended his left arm to me as a welcome. I am standing beside very close to him, and he put his left arm arround my shoulder.

At that moment, he doesn't say anything..instead we stood there in a stillness..watching the mountains and the hills of the valley..it's so green, peaceful, and beautiful. During the stillness..i said to my DEVINE FATHER..i miss you, with tears in my eyes. He looked at me with a smile and touched my face lovingly. I felt this amazing connections again with FATHER and CHILD bond. The calmness within my soul..it's so comforting..then some silence again..i always knew what to do when my FATHER wants some silence.

I have to be silence..but this time i have to take a risk..i have so many questions in my head. Then i broke our silence with my creativity:) with a little joke to get him out of it. I'm sure he reads my mind, as i felt his left hand on my shoulder moved slightly. So i took the opportunity, and i said..Papa GOD your clothes looks FASHIONABLE and i love it!:) He then looked at me and suddenly LAUGHED!!! Oh..i wish somebody can hear his laugh..it's so captivating.

He turned arround and facing at me, holding my both hands lower and said to me, my child i know what you are going to ask me, but go ahead, he said. Well, it's all about the disaster you have shown me the other day..and my question is..when is this going to happen? Oh my child do you really want to know? Of course FATHER please..i want to know. He took a slight pause and said to me..ok my child close your eyes and after this no more questions. Ok Papa GOD i promise, i said.

I closed my eyes..and then he was showing me a number..number 70, this the first number. Then i wondered is this 70 days..70 weeks..70 months? 7 days..7 weeks..7 months..7 years..my thoughts kept going... number 70 is very prominent. I didn't feel this is an earthquake, but something quick went into my head, just an instant BOMBING! a bombing disaster have caused it!..it's just a kind of information went into my head quickly. I wasn't even thinking of it.

I am so upset now..what do i do with this information DEVINE FATHER? I am worried about the people who's going to be affected. I was going to ask more..but Papa GOD put his hand, as a sign of.. don't ask anymore that's enough he said to me. The reason i don't give you so much informations, because sometimes you cannot handle it, and kept forgetting you have to help so many people in earth when this things happened. People destroying people he said, and i can see sadness on his face. Papa GOD..can we stop it? the WAR? OMG! why did i say WAR? Is it a WAR papa GOD? but papa GOD didn't say anything..instead he asked me to do a lot of meditation and lots of healing.

Do the healing i taught you before, he said. Yeah..but that was long time ago and i haven't used it for a long time. Well, this is your time now..and do you still remember it do you? he asked. Well yes, i said.. ok then show me, he said. NOW? i asked..yes Now He said. I was reluctant, but i obeyed my DEVINE FATHER. I sat down on the ground and i saw papa GOD joined me. We both our legs fold down and facing each other. Then i closed my eyes..and then slowly i can see the whole WORLD.

I am somewhat??..up there looking down my body. Then i can see part of the WORLD is in a BIG CHAOS!..some other part is so serene..then i pulled myself up little bit higher and this time i can see more the whole WORLD!. Suddenly, Papa GOD said..now do it! With stern voice and with very encouraging tone of voice as a command.

So i opened my arms and the my hands then i closed my eyes.. suddenly i see the DEVINE lights in my hands pointing out towards the world..radiating..and the devine healing lights it's golden lights coming out from my hands and almost elluminating the ENTIRE WORLD..and my hands..i can feel some very strange tingling sensations during the process..my hands, my arms, and my whole body..and my eyes again..it has golden colour coming out from it!! My whole body is pure golden colour!! My whole body is sending this healing energy penetrating to the whole world. And then i suddenly STOPPED. When i opened my eyes..Papa GOD still sitting infront of me and saying.."THAT IS YOUR PURPOSE MY CHILD".

That's only the beginning of the task that you needed to do, he said. Then he let go my hands..i didn't know he was holding my hands when i was healing. So my child, have fun today, its bright and sunny outside. Yes my DEVINE FATHER i will. Anything else Papa GOD? i asked. NO..he said, just be happy today. Ohh.. i'm feeling much better now..and i heard.. FLY AWAY MY CHILD.. fly...:) And this morning, i heard so many birds flying..flying on top of my head while having my breakfast in my garden..and with my dog and cat sitting under the sun. I am happy :) :) Thank you my DEVINE FATHER.

# CHAPTER 30

# AMERICAN INDIAN THE SHAMAN

JOURNAL
11TH JUNE 2022

My dear journal, it's about time to catch up with you. I have been very busy lately again, and even PAPA GOD looks like is very busy at the moment. I spoke to him on and off, and it feels like there is nothing to worry about this time. I did my meditation couple days ago, and it's the same things..it took me up there and looking down the earth. While i was up there..there was an entity just suddenly appeared beside me on my left side, and we both facing the northeast horizon.

This new entity is not too familiar to me, and he looks like an AMERICAN INDIAN. He looks young in a mid twinties, with medium long straight black hair. A very fine looking gentleman..his face is very ANGELIC. He's wearing a beautiful Indian cape with embroided EAGLES, he has feathers on his head..so colourful..i have never seen this gentleman before. I asked him, who are you? I'm a SHAMAN, he said.

He showed me where the troubled area is..and just to his left side.. he is pointing that particular continent. Then he pointed out again the bottom of the continent. To my right side, which is not much of a CHAOS. Then i started my healing..but to my surprised the light was coming from my hands are just white lights, it's the same lights when i was healing the village area people in the dessert island during my meditation previously. I asked Papa GOD in my thoughts.. why? His reponse was..YOU HAVE COMPANY. Oh ok..i said, thank FATHER.

Then my AMERICAN INDIAN SHAMAN disappeared from my sight. Then i saw putin's head, he was going to attack me again, but this time i grabbed his head with my hands and strongly said to him..STOP!! you MUST STOP hurting and killing the people. You must stop this WAR!!! I am commanding you!..but the more i screamed at him..the more he gets really angry at me. I didn't let go of his head, then i realised my technique is not going to stop him. So i used different technique, i showed him when he was still has a feeling of being human..that he can still feel the love to himself and to his family and humanity.

I made him go back to his past..to his memories of himself, to the love and care what he used to be. To feel that compassion again.. he then later on..his face changed to a normal putin's face with no ANGER, with compassion and love. Then i suddenly saw his whole body instead of just a FACE! Then i let him go. PAPA GOD i wish putin will change..or that was just his his part of his tactic so i can let him go. Then papa GOD said..if he kept killing people special the innocent people..well..you know now my child where he is supposed to be going..he doesn't need to go to purgatory..his soul will be directly go to HELL! and there is no turning back!

# CHAPTER 31

# THEY ARE ASKING FOR THEIR LIVES

JOURNAL

22TH JUNE 2022

I have travelled again spiritually few times, and met some significant people who's helping me to heal the world slowly. Papa GOD doesn't want me to expose this people. Papa GOD is showing me again the people who's been purposely been hurting me and still trying to hurt me. MY DEVINE FATHER said, they can't hurt you no matter what and how much they would try..i am here my child. You have to continue what you need to do, Papa GOD said. I am always here beside you. Do not worry too much..just let go..my DEVINE FATHER said.

Papa GOD, can i see you today? i asked. Yes of course my child, just close your eyes. So, i did close my eyes and this time i can see him waiting for me in the verandah looking down the stream..so green and the sorrounding is just so serene. I can see my DEVINE FATHER wearing a long white clothes and smiling at me and looks like he's waiting for me:)

He extended his arms and greeted me, and hugged me. I felt his devine energy again..so calming and so serene loving and protective.

I'm feeling home again from the arms of my DEVINE FATHER. I also can see myself wearing a long white dress, and with white head band for some reason..?? hmm..i looked so dignified though. Papa GOD have his left arm arround my shoulder, and we both watching the stream flowing gently..i then asked him what is my next mission?

He looked at me and said, have a good rest including sleep and when your body is ready i will let you know. Ok FATHER, i said. I looked at my DEVINE FATHER, he just so serene his face is so beautiful to watch just looking at the stream while the water is flowing..i can see his right hand moving at the same time while the water is gently flowing.

He then made me feel it..he asked me to feel the rhythm of the water flowing..the birds are singing..just feel it in your heart, he said. So, i put my right hand on my chest and then closed my eyes, and yes slowly i can feel it..it's like music..the flow of the water is just like music..This is how you heal your body, i want you to do this when you are feeling overwhelmed with your problems in your physical self, and be happy. Everything will work out..and remember..if it's NOT FOR YOU..it will never happen.

I know your path and this time is my decision, he said..ohh..i guess i can't go against that..after all i made that decision already long time ago. That will be very good my child, he said. He then continued moving his hand and fingers synchronising with the flow of water.. very quiet..very serene..so relaxing..and of course i'm loving every minute of it, and then it didn't last of course from me. I asked again... Papa GOD where is the water of this stream coming from? i asked him through my head..SHHHH..he said..be still..and feel the moment. Hmmm..i sigh...i thought i didn't want to spoil his moment so i kept "STILL"..but then..i noticed there is a BUG flew over my head and distracted my concentrations and then i moved..but the bug is persistent, i tried to ignore it and trying to flick and shoo this annoying bug away from me and kept buzzing arround me and above my head...and then PAPA GOD said...ok what now?? Ohh..nothing :( i said. i saw myself half smiling and being cheeky..then the bug flew away. I turned myself as a teenager.

Papa GOD looked at me, and said NO!! you are not ready. OK, i guess he read my mind:) But papa GOD i can go with ARCH ANGEL MICHAEL, the same way as i usually go with him before. I know, he said..but this mission you are going is BIG and you need a rest and especially sleep. But can i have a peek papa GOD at least? i asked. NO! strongly he said and disagreed. WHY??? i asked curiously.. then papa GOD looked at me sternly, and said..listen to me my child. No one will ever see this until you are ready to get through to that dimensions. Your eyes need to be protected. Ohh..i sighed..

I kept quiet and i saw myself as a 5 yeras old again..and he then picked me up and carried me away. when we reached the valley, i started walking while he's holding my hand. As we walking through the valley with beautiful flowers and birds with so many butterflies..then i started chasing them. We were both walking to the west horizon and i am fascinated about the colour of the sun..such a golden colour. Then i saw a familiar face JESUS to the right side, and papa GOD still holding my left hand while we were walking, it's a nice feeling being in a protection of my DEVINE FATHER.

# CHAPTER 32

# MY BLACK OUTFIT FOR THE BATTLE

JOURNAL

27TH JUNE 2022

It has been a good resting week for me. I did what my DEVINE FATHER wants me to do. See the animals, connect your energy with them, they needed it, he said. Go outside the sun..blue sky..clouds.. winds..birds..the water..trees..and many more..connect with them, he said. I did FATHER and i am feeling good.

Today, i just connected with my DEVINE FATHER, and he seems like he's been waiting for me patiently. I saw him standing infront of a Long stairways..I can see the sorrounding area is dark, but there are some golden glittery colour sparkling on the walls, like little stars glittering but it's golden colour. Then my DEVINE FATHER said, are you ready? Yes, i am ready FATHER and feeling confident. He then delivered the message in my head..THIS IS YOUR TIME.

I saw myself as a teenager but slightly older wearing all black fitted outfit, it's like an armour that it's all fitted in my body. I have my wings opened, and it's GRAYISH colour..my boots are long and covering my knees and it's colour black too. Everything i'm wearing is colour BLACK, i felt my DEVINE WEAPONS beside my hips, and i pulled it out and had a good look at it..it's my pure golden daggers..and it's beautiful..then i put it back inside again.

I saw "SKY" coming towards me..and i am so excited to see him. He greeted me by touching my forehead with his HORN..and with my eyes closed, i saw a "RAINBOW" connected to his horn and with my FOREHEAD. A feeling of recharged and ownership..i then touched his face with my two hands and kissed his nose, and SKY suddenly made a happy noise, and started jumping up with his 2 front legs :) then SKY stayed beside me. I saw ARCH ANGEL MICHAEL beside me and to my right side corner, but he has no horse. His wearing his red cape, and his sword, and then he's standing handsomely behind me, he is so amazingly Angelic.

Papa GOD is infront of me and looks like leading us up towards the stairways. Then i saw JESUS, behind ARCH ANGEL MICHAEL and then, PAPA GOD without any hesitation. He started walking up towards the stairways, and we followed him. The nearer we are going up, the sorrounding area is getting lighter..i mean the colour of the sorrounding while we are going up is just changing into a beautiful and devine place with so many clouds arround..a very familiar sight until we reached the very top. Papa GOD then sat on his BIG MARBLE CHAIR a very familiar chair to me, and behind him i noticed a MAGNIFICENT DEVINE GOLDEN COLOUR forming while he is talking to us. THe more he is talking..the more the energy behind him is getting BIGGER..TOWERING HIM. SO devinely POWERFUL!! IT's a DEVINE ENERGY!!! I can see so many ANGELS arround..and with their wings are out too. They have no horses and i am the only one who has a horse my "SKY".

Then Papa GOD asked me to come infront of him, and he asked me in my head to KNEEL DOWN..which i did slowly with my head down. He then put his right hand on my head and said..now this is your time my CHILD. The amazing golden energy penetrated into my head and deep down to the very core of my body. I feels like my whole body inside and out has been penetrated with GOLDEN AURA of energy. He then put a black cover in my eyes just like a blind fold..but it's black and to my amazement i still can see, and even better it's like an Xray vision.

Then Papa GOD said, this is to protect your eyes during your travel. THANK you FATHER, i said. NOw are you ready now my child? He asked. YES, FATHER, but can i ask just one question please? just one question i promise, i said. OK then he said..but in my head, i said..i think you know..Hmm..my child come on..well, why am i wearing a black outfit? i asked innocently but curiously. Then suddenly papa GOD LAUGHED so loud!!!..ohh..my DEAR CHILD, i always LOVE your innocence, but funny sense of humour, he said. Well, guess who i got that from? i said, then PAPA GOD even laughed harder!!:) and the KINGDOM almost thundering!! and thanks goodness there is no lightning..as i'm scared of lightning.

Well the answer of your question my child is simple, he said. When you are travelling to the different dimensions it's dark, and you needed to blend. The Angels with you can travel without any problems. You are still in a physical realm, with your physical body, you can be damage during the ASTRAL tarvel. Your physical body is very important, as you needed to go back quickly to your physical body once you finish your spiritual journey. You need to go back to your body as quickly as you can, and it's a very important part of your journey. YEs, FATHER i understand.

Ok now get ready, Papa GOD said..he pointed out the the straight direction..it's a PORTAL..a very CIRCULAR image infront of me. I can see it where i am standing, it's DARK..but there is some BLUE COLOUR in it through the distance. PAPA GOD said..my CHILD your PRAYERS i gave you..DO NOT FORGET. Yes my DEVINE FATHER I will not forget and i will always carry it with me. I gave my DEVINE FATHER a hug..and he whispered to me..i'm with you my CHILD.

I then jumped into my horse "SKY" and entered through the PORTAL followed by my ANGELS and ARCH ANGEL MICHAEL..and the other warriour just appeared infront of us, with his ROYAL BLUE outfit and Royal BLUE horse. He looks very brave and Majestic..i didn't asked his name, but i met him before during the spiritual battle field. He looks very REGAL and POWERFUL. Other Angels followed us behind, and PAPA GOD said, when you out there, "DO NOT LOOK BACK". (He spicifically put that in my head). I was going to ask more..but he blocked my thoughts.

So while going through the different dimensions, i can see myself as an ANGEL WARRIOUR..full of strenght and forging towards the way i didn't know we were going..but we kept travelling..i see darkness, FIRE, and very scary sights during the travel, but all my ANGELS behind me gives me a strong allies.

We travelled so fast into a galaxy and different dimensions..i heard 7 dimensions..then suddenly i can feel heaviness on my body, it's like i'm being pulled down slowly..then i looked down..i can see some black entities clinging on my legs and both SKY's sides. Most of them are getting burnt and melting, i can see thier faces slowly melting.. human faces..how did it happen? how this earth energies came with me in this dimensions? But i kept travelling ahead..and this energies are getting burnt..all of them!! Some of them are begging to touch me..but unfortunately i couldn't save them.

We then slowly reached the area..we stopped and were on top of the BIG MOUNTAIN a huge PLACE!!..it's a BIG mountain but it's DARK and has gray sorroundings!!..we then suddenly see a "BIG" creature and scary so black with BIG HORN and when he stood up..his teeth, it's looks SHARP, and his eyes are so RED and his sorrounding have FIRE. I couldn't see any other entities sorrounding this GIGANTIC scary BEING!..but when he stood up he's even scarrier!!! and he then said..OH..the child OF GOD!! He knew ME!! I'm surprised!! and his voice is so deep and full of strength.

GO BACK!!! he yelled at me!! I was scared and backed off slightly, but "SKY" stood firmly where he was standing..and ARCH ANGEL MICHAEL. What do i do now? i asked my ANGEL..i can't eliminate him he's GIGANTIC! I was worried. THen ARCH ANGEL MICHAEL said..remember the first time when you were healing the world?..do the same, he said. Oh OK..do you mean i don't have to kill him? i asked. Yes! no need to kill him. I am surprised and feels happy because i don't have to kill him, instead i have to heal him..ok i'm happy with that, i said.

So i started to go up with the helped of my Big wings..i ascended more further up until i'm almost towering him. Then i opened my hands..then i can see my whole body and my sorroundings aura is so GOLDEN LIGHT..and then i heard pray, and i started praying and the healing energy started aiming it to this scary being. I aimed my hands and my energy started from his head..then going down towards his lower extremities..and up again to his upper centre extremities..

and out to his arms. It's a sign of a cross again!..except i didn't use my daggers this time instead i used my DEVINE GOLDEN LIGHT ENERGY to purified him together with LOVE..then his body opened up and i saw his HEART BEATING! then suddenly it disappeared. And the body of this SCARY BEING shrunked into a skeleton and in a FOETAL position.

ARCH ANGEL MICHAEL then put his body into a STONE MARBLE COFFIN..then suddenly, we're all back infront of PAPA GOD with the COFFIN of this poor scary BEING. ARCH ANGEL MICHAEL layed it infront of my DEVINE FATHER with so much RESPECT. THen my DEVINE FATHER said, now my CHILD you have just conquerd the seventh mysterious bad being in this world. NOW, you have more to go, he said. What??? to my horror!!there is more??? YES my child, he said. OHHH my..i said..i am feeling very thirsty Papa GOD, i said.

Then a gentleman wearing a purple and royal blue uniform and has a beard, he is smiling while walking towards me along with this thing holding in his hands, a slender but small coloured gold metal pot, it's like the "GENIE's bottle, and he asked me to open my mouth, which i did..and he poured this liquid gold colour into my mouth which i have never tasted this kind of liquid before..but my thirst disappeared..and feeling...hmm..i can't described it..it's like cleansed..yes, it cleansed my whole body.

Then Papa GOD said go back now my CHILD and have plenty of rest. You can reach me anytime as you always do. Then i wake up feeling very tired but generally i am feeling ok, then i drank my water beside my bed. Now looking back about that experienced, it's all about LOVE..you can heal anything with LOVE..and LOVE conquered everything.

Well my dear journal, i guess i have to say thank you for listening to me..you know you became alive when i'm writing with you, you really takes me to a different world, without you my story wouldn't exist so i thank you again.

I'm feeling happy and i heard Papa GOD voice and said..that's good my child have fun! and be happy whatever you doing..hmm..whatever i am doing?? even the naughty one?? :) ) I heard that !!! he said. OMG! i can't believe i have said that. BYE..sorry..hehehe..:)

# CHAPTER 33
# BIG WHITE BOOK

JOURNAL

3RD JULY 2022

Last night i had a dream..again, but before my dream i meditated first, and i saw "SKY" coming towards me. He looks happy and i read his mind saying to go with him. I said later as i am very busy today, then i asked where are we going? He pointed out with his horn towards the RAINBOW. SKY was happy to wait under the single tree sorrounded by the flowers, grass and butterflies, eating the green grass so happily..but i didn't managed to get back to him. Sorry "SKY" not today, i said. I saw him continued eating some grass and looking happy.

During the night in my dream, i found myself on my own walking towards up the stairways. Again, the sorrounding area is black and there are some twinkling stars that gives some lights while walking towards the stairways. I walked slowly, and i noticed i am wearing fitted black outfit, and it's more like an armour but made in a leather materials. I'm in my early 20's and my boots are black..all black..and my blind fold it's black too. Amazingly i can see through, and even clearer my wings are not open at this moment.

When i reached the top of the stairways and the gate...i can see my DEVINE FATHER is waiting for me. I can see his face looks happy and i am so happy to see him again too. PAPA GOD extended his arms towards me and WELCOMED me. I felt this instant loving and comforting energy..i miss my DEVINE FATHER..i kept it to myself..but deep inside i really do miss him. He didn't say anything, but he made me read his mind instead. Is something bothering you my child? i didn't say anything, but he can read my mind.

He said something to me in my dream, about this particular person.. about the WORD he said to me..that only ME and my DEVINE FATHER will know and that's an agreement not to reveal. PAPA GOD said, are you ready for your next battle? And this time you're on your own. YES, i am ready FATHER, i said it confidently and feeling fiercely. I can see myself is a brave person and more confidenty this time. I can feel this fire energy in my body needs to come out. I'ts like an outburst of energy ready to be release.

Before this battle, during the night while i was asleep..i felt my right ankle was uncomfortable and feeling heavy, so i stretched my right leg, and this time i know what i need to do to be able to get rid of the pain. I touched my upper leg, and the energy from my right hand travelled down to my ankle and the pain quickly disappeared..almost an instant relief. Then suddenly, i saw a woman beside my leg..i didn't know this person, and i felt she did something to my ankle. I'm sure she's preventing me from travelling tonight. Well woman i don't think you would last tonight..so i touched her head and she then crumbled down and melted away.

Then again, a man suddenly appeared and wearing a black hood, and i can see his face and i am not familiar with his face. His intention was to hurt me, so i opened my right hand, and to that moment, i just burnt him with my energy coming from my hands. I feel like i am being attacked by this bad energies..some i recognised there faces, but i just eliminated them ruthlessly they have no right to hurt me. I didn't have a choice..i eliminated them with my hands.

The energy in my hands are PURE WHITE not Golden. When i finished eliminating them, i was suddenly shifted in a very DARK VALLEY, so dark..and i can see this BIG MONSTROUS BEING behind the very dark stone wall. It looks so Aggressive and it has no form of body, it looks like silhoutte but dark and aggressive evil looking and forging towards me!!!

I was terrified!!! It's towering me!! Gigantic and scary entity!!! Then i realised i have to fight this on my own..i quickly recovered and composed myself. I looked at my hands then started pointing out to him. My energy coming out from my hands are so strong and bizzarre! And this time i have no feelings of fear! Then i released more stronger more deadly, but this time it's all coming from my whole BODY!! My whole body is fully charged with deadly energy. I was screaming at the same time releasing my energy to eliminate this entity!!.

ARRGHHH!!! at the same time i was slowly burning and eliminating this scary being!! I was so ANGRY!!FRUSTRATED!!and i gave all my anger to this monster!.. then suddenly a "WHITE BIG SQUARE BOOK" appeared from the sky at the distance. MY DEVINE FATHER appeared too, and quickly intervened by holding my hands, and said STOP! STOP now! Stop now my child..it's gone.

MY DEVINE FATHER's tone of voice penetrated into my body, and my energy into my hands slowly disappeared, and i realised i have eliminated the black entity already. Then i saw the BLACK TAR LIQUID on the ground...slimmy. Suddenly, i saw behind the wall the sky is clearing above and becoming blue with little clouds, and i noticed the WHITE BIG BOOK still up there. I couldn't see the sun, just the blue sky and clouds. Then I have noticed, there was no written words in that WHITE BOOK.

PAPA GOD said..you have eliminated the 6th entity, and i'm very proud of you..but i still can sense and feel your strong energy. Let go my child..let it go, Papa GOD said with a very reassuring voice. I then sat on the ground, and PAPA GOD sat down beside me very quietly.

I asked papa GOD, why ARCH ANGEL MICHAEL wasn't here with me and the Angels including SKY during this battle with the entity? Then Papa GOD said, this battle is yours, your own BATTLE my child. You didn't need your ANGELS with you, as you can see, you did it! PAPA GOD, why i am feeling this way? I feel like this is not me. I'm Full of RAGE! :(

My child, what you are feeling is related of what you re experiencing in reality, in a physical realm. Your physical is connected to your spiritual realm. You are changing, maturing in a spritual sense. You are becoming more connected to your DEVINE MISSION..but that's OK to feel that way, because after all you are still human, he said :) Is that suppose to cheer me up FATHER? i asked. well..i'm sorry my child, is it a lame joke? :) i saw his face almost laughing...well you know what's lame, i said:) IT's LAMA..hehehe i said. Well next time i'll bring you a LAMA, papa GOD said. :) No thanks i said, i will not excahnge my SKY. :) Where is he anyway? i asked..then PApa GOD showed me "SKY" standing beside me :) Ok up you go my child, go somewhere with SKY, Papa GOD said with a big smile on his face.:)

OK..thank you my DEVINE FATHER, we then stood up and i hopped in on SKY's back, and said goodbye to my FATHER. He waved at me and when we flew away..i heard drink your water my child. I will FATHER..ILOVE YOU..we then disappeared..and then i wake up very thirsty, i grabbed my water bottle beside my bed and drank the whole water.

Then PAPA GOD gave me some numbers again..22..and 44. I don't really know what's this numbers kept appearing to me, and i didn't have time to ask my DEVINE FATHER about that "BIG BOOK" who appeared in the sky infront of me..maybe next time, i'm sure my DEVINE FATHER will tell me. Good night my dear journal.

# CHAPTER 34

# A LONG METAL WEAPON

JOURNAL
4TH JULY

This morning i wake up with very sore neck, it could be from sleeping in one spot last night i assumed. I tried to massaged my neck and with my healing energy, then my neck started feeling better. The pain and stiffness are gone just for few minutes. Strangely while i was massaging my neck, one of my family member appeared beside my bed and my gut feeling she's the one who did something about my neck, but i wouldn't believe it was her. My hands strangely started to peel off her face, then suddenly it showed the real person and the left face is half skull, and the right face is human. It's a DIFFERENT PERSON! and she's wearing a hood. I thought this bad entities are getting clever.

To my surprise, i saw myself as a warriour again, this time i am wearing a WHITE ANGEL WARRIOUR outfit and i am wearing a pure white outfit. Funny enough i am not in my deep sleep or dreaming at the moment..it's just my eyes are closed, and i have this images that came to me and showing like a slow motion movie. It's hard to believe what it is..or is it to make believe?

This time, i can see myself holding a LONG IRON METAL bar weapon..but when i lifted it with my hand, it's very light and i felt it sort of glued into my hand automatically. I striked this woman with no MERCY! I cut her body in half and with the sign of a CROSS, and then her body crumbled into pieces. I realised they are masking themselves as my relatives so i don't have to eradicate them, hmm.. getting clever and a new tactic.

Then i saw myself standing where it has a huge wall that made of stone, a solid stone wall sorrounding me and the place is massive. I can see myself a very small person standing infront of it. Then i saw the stairways and it's white, but the clouds behind and beside the stairways are black. I am puzzled..but then, at that moment i saw this BIG GIANT entity appeared behind the stairways, but he looks white..i was surprised but somehow i was scared!!!! I am feeling some kind of decieving motives from the sorroundings.

His eyes are so scary and my mind starting to wonder..i shouldn't get scared of him because he is not a DEVIL..after all he is a white entity i thought to myself. Then this being came out behind the stairways and started to come after me. So i ran quickly...but then he was trying to grab me from behind and tried several times. The more he was trying to grabbed me the more i was running away from him really fast.

Then suddenly i saw SKY from the distance running towards me, and suddenly my wings came out and lifted me up towards to SKY's back. While still holding my weapon in my hand, then i decided to face this BIG entity which was towering me!!! We both facing each other with some distance, and then suddenly i looked behind me.. ARCHANGEL MICHAEL and the other ANGELS are with me. ALL ANGELS have weapons including Arch Angel Michael with his sword. This time i noticed all the ANGELS are riding with thier own horses, and thier wings are out too. OHHH..it's so nice to see them:) Then suddenly the BIG entity is coming towards me, and there are some entities just appeared suddenly everywhere they are all coming to us..so rapidly. Now this is a BATTLE.

This time i'm little bit scared, and i can feel it in my bones..but suddenly i heard PAPA GOD voice up there..I'M WITH YOU MY CHILD!!! I then my body came back to normal a sudden feeling of being brave and no more MERCY for this evil entities, especially to this HUGE ONE! Then i noticed the BIG entity is getting closer to me. Then SKY suddenly flew up and started to circled on top of the entity, and then suddenly i heard..STRIKE NOW!!!

Then my long weapon i was holding in my hand suddenly striked the head if this entity. The monster entity turned into a BLACK Entity.. again it's tricking me..it's EVIL!!! it's pretending a white entity so i don't have to eliminate it. It's becoming very tricky now..they are tried everything to stop me!! Well, not this time!!. You are all going to die! i can feel my RAGE!!

I striked the head of this evil entity and down to lower extremeties and then to upper body..and out..it's the sign of a cross again. Then just that.. a silver bar long weapon killed this entity. That's how i realised why my DEVINE FATHER gave me this, just suddenly appeared in my hands. The rest of the ANGELS fought fierlessly and eradicated all the entities.

I then raised my weapon up to heaven and saw the beautiful ray of energy coming down from heaven and started cleansing my weapon. I then THANKED MY DEVINE FATHER..and he said, well done my child, and he put his right hand on top of my crown chakra and gave me a loving smile, and kind of feeling being proud of me:) i feel like crying..

And then i saw my DEVINE FATHER talking to Arch ANGEL MICHAEL, and then raised his hand to the other ANGELS, saying thank you! such a beautiful sight.. Then they all disappeared and the whole sorrounding starting to cleared up..dust everywhere. PAPA GOD and ARCh ANGEL MICHAEL still talking to each other..but i felt like not to interupt . So SKY and myself stayed where we are then Papa GOD came towards me and touched my neck..and blow some air into my neck slowly..then my stiff neck slowly disappeared. Thank you FATHER, i said. It's alright my child.

Can i ask one question FATHER? yes my child, go ahead, he said. Well, it's about the "white book" from my dream the other night. You told me this morning was judgement book? Is it TRUE? Anything i have told and showed you are "TRUE" my child, he said. You are talking to your DEVINE FATHER remember. I know FATHER..but sometimes i don't understand the message, just like the "BIG WHITE BOOK" is just happened it appeared in the sky unexpectedly. I do not know what it is, and i have never seen or read that book before so i have no idea and i am curious.

The reason i don't give you so much informations because i don't want you to change your DEVINE mission, as i know sometimes you are not ready. You have to be ready from unexpected battles or circumstances, as i am expecting good outcomes. This time no more questions, i will give you the message of everything you need to know, my DEVINE FATHER said. But sometimes FATHER..can i still ask? can i please? oh ok..only the questions that you are allowed to..after all you can't help it..you are curious, stubborn..but lovable and YOU ARE MY CHILD. I will do every thing to support you and keep you safe, he said. I know PAPA GOD will say YES to me:)i thought happily. I can read your thoughts you know..he said. OMG!!!I have forgotten he can read my mind.

PAPA GOD can i ask one favour? i think i deserve it..ok my child go ahead, he said. Can you stop the heavy rain? it's flooding here in my area..Ok MY CHILD..do what i asked you to do..drink plenty of water. Sometimes the rain is good..it purifies the area, Papa GOD said. You need to nurture you body MY CHILD. Yes FATHER i will..bye and thank you again. I LOVE YOU..

I'm back to myself again and it's pouring rain..i think i'll wait for PAPA GOD sign. I soaked my self in a hot shower and i'm feeling little bit better now. Then i heard, drink your water..you have been drinking too much coffee lately, he said. OMG!!! papa GOD please, it's only 2 cups a day..sometimes one cup. The rest is green tea, fresh squeezed oranged juice and water, i said. OKAY..i will drink all my water! bye FATHER...ILOVEU:)

# CHAPTER 35

# "FEEL IT"

JOURNAL

5TH JULY 2022

I had a good night sleep last night and this morning the weather started to get better, no heavy rain or not raining anymore but it's very windy instead. Thank you Papa GOD. At the moment i have been catching up with my paper works and updated some few things.

Good morning FATHER this is a new day again, but i thank you always. Papa GOD i have a dream last night, i'm sure you have downloaded this to me. This time a different male figure, this person i have never seen before, but his face looks very familiar..a younger person though, but you made me feel comfortable and somehow..i feel loved? is this person from one of my past life? and showing me in a younger version in a vulnerable state?

PAPA GOD, i don't know what to think of this:( then i heard up there from above..DON't think "FEEL IT"! a message with stern word but loving, and showing me with acceptance. You suppose to "FEEL" it, that's how it works in a spiritual realm. And thinking is in the reality world. Is that makes sense my CHILD? papa GOD said. Yes FATHER i understand..but FATHER, sometimes you don't give me enough informations..sorry to argue:(

The informations i just gave you is enough for you to handle, and the rest will eventually be unfolding. What comes to you means it's coming from me, and if somebody force it..they will see the consequences. Oh ok FATHER. i understand. While i'm sitting infront of my computer while turned off, PAPA GOD is showing me a beautiful silhoutte again up above my head and almost hugging me..and YES, he hugged me with his beautiful energy and kissed the top of my head..and he whispered i love you my child..he then put his sihouette hands both sides of my face and tilted up to see his face.

I only can see an energy formed in a silhouette and he said..everything is going to be alright a very loving, conmforting and reassuring feelings going through my body again..i didn't want to wake up.. everything is going to be alright my CHILD..just focus on what you are doing in reality, and specially in spirituality..your DEVINE MISSION.

PAPA GOD, is the World ENDING? i asked innocently..hmm.. ending is not the right word, papa GOD said. So what is going to happen then? i asked again..well, it's more like. "REJUVENATING", i'd say that's more is a right word, papa GOD said. Oh OK..is there any more disaster that i need to know? Yes, many more he said.

Then PAPA GOD showed me a BIG PLANE disaster landed in a desert island..but i can see it still intact, then i can smell smokes and people coming out from the left side of the plane..i couldn't see if it's from the cockpit, it's just smokes i can't see any flames either only black smokes. Then i was disconnected from my vision. Ok my child i think that would be enough for you to absorbed in a day, keep drinking your water. Yes FATHER, i will bye :)

# CHAPTER 36

# MY DEVINE FATHER IS FURIOUS

JOURNAL

10th JULY 2022

It has been a beautiful day today..the sky is blue and not even a cloud today or the other day. I thank you to my FATHER my dreams are so beautiful lately.. i guess i still need recuperating after the last battle.

GOOD morning my DEVINE FATHER:) sorry i have been pre occupied lately with my thoughts, my works, and i did my meditation.. it makes me feel grounded. I reached for you Papa GOD last night, but you said i needed some rest. last night, it bothered me to see him like that..he was walking while thinking of something. He is blocking me from reading his thoughts, but later on he will let me peek a little bit of it, i assured myself.

Your thoughts and emotions that you are currently feeling now my child, he said. Ok i said..what is it PAPA GOD? Well, we discussed this before, if anybody who's intending to come to you with ill intentions and not realising who you are and connections with me as your DEVINE FATHER, and your connection to your DEVINE PURPOSE in this EARTH, i will stop them!!! I heard a very intense and profound words from my DEVINE FATHER. I can see my FATHER is very serious and his voice to what he said..it's like a thunder! Hmm..i have never seen him angry like that before..it's scary.

I didn't say anything, because i know when to be quite when his mad. Whatever or whom i ever thinking will have a definite message and answers to thier questions. I know MY DEVINE FATHER WILL NOT let me fall. Also i asked my FATHER to step infront of those people trying to get close to me with no good intentions. So he did and i know he will always be.

PAPA GOD thank you for a good dreams lately..no more nightmares. Now i can see him feeling at ease, he stretched his arms towards me now..i can see myself running towards him..i see myself as a child again. He then reached me and picked me up and put me in his shoulder. He then hugged me tightly, i then asked innocently very close to his face. What's wrong PAPA GOD? he then looked at me lovingly and said, i missed you my chil and he then hugged me again tightly in his chest, i then said, i'm here now PAPA GOD..he then kissed my forehead.

I can see his face became lighter and a little tears in his eyes. I guess he missed me very much. I feel he missed my interactions with him.. the connections of a FATHER and CHILD. Then i noticed i became an adult woman again..he squessed my hands and looked at me lovingly and said to me..I LOVE YOU my CHILD.

# CHAPTER 37

# MEETING PAPA GOD NEAR THE STREAM

JOURNAL

16TH JULY 2022

It's time to tell you of what has happened the other day. Yesterday after my ZUMBA dance exercise i did my meditation under the sun. I met my DEVINE FATHER again..this time i saw him walking along the stream, and the path he was walking was bright silvery colour ground. Then i saw him walking on top of the water towards me..whoahh..i thought, according to the bible and from my grandma, JESUS walked on the water. So this is a validation from the BIBLE. Thank you FATHER of this image. The stream he is walking on the water is different than before that we both visited.

He exended his arms towards me, i saw myself as a teenager wearing a long sleeve top with pink and blue colour stripes. And also PAPA GOD wearing the same shirt top and it has 2 colours, it's light and dark blue stripes and he is holding a music instrument. It looks like a flute, a single flute and it's white and in our modern day it's a recorder, i know because my daughter played a recorder when she was young during her primary school..hmm..it's funny, i thought i have never seen him played some music before. I was going to ask, but it seems like he blocked my thoughts.

He greeted me with his lovely smile..and i am happy to see him too, matter of fact i missed him. My devine Father looks very casual today:) i like it and me too and wearing the same thing very casual. Papa GOD said i have been waiting for you..well, i am here.. smiling at him and with a cheeky smile. Well my child, it's time again he said. OH OK, i said. Papa GOD then showed me the WORLD..suddenly my clothes changed into a long and very white clothes. My wings are out too but it's purely white..i asked Papa GOD why my wings are white? He said, you are not going to a battle, he said. Then noticed PAPA GOD clothes have changed too, it became pure white.

Papa GOD said, you are going to HEAL the WORLD today. Oh ok..i said, then my wings brought me up higher..then i was there looking the world just half way to my chest. Papa GOD said go up higher my child, but i said NO..i think i like it here..i can see it better. He then said no..you go up more higher.. but papa GOD i am comfortable here where i am, i said. Then he said..STUBBURN CHILD..and before i can say something back to him..he used his flute to push me up higher..and higher..then he stopped..and then i can see the world in a better view:) hehehe..thank you FATHER:)

He then asked me..now..what can you see? I looked down, and i can see the EARTH, and somehow..i am feeling the energy of it..and then i x-rayed it with my vision. Suddenly i have spotted a part of the world to my left side. It's the ocean then my hands automatically started the healing. So starting from my hands the energy is coming out..then my whole body became elluminated with this golden colour energy. Then i extended my arms and my body facing towards the

Earth. I am penetrating the GLOBE...but then there is a part of it that i cannot reached, and i can feel it.. i am totally blocked. I couldn't get through and it's in a very deep part of the ocean.

Then suddenly i can see part of the blockage is covered with CRYSTAL CLEAR energy..but somehow it's very thick and i cannot penetrated into this part of the area. It's a kind of a very thick wall covering, but i can see it from where i am and up there, it looks like it's made of crystal, and it's a very thick and clear crystal energy. Then i heard PAPA GOD said..focus your thoughts deeper my child.

I then closed my eyes..and in a few minutes..oh my GOD!!! i could not believe what i am seeing!!! and i'm afraid to say this..Oh GOD.. might as well, i can see "BEINGS"!..here i said it! It's not just one being..it's more..they are operating underneath the sea..they looks very tall, skinny beings with big heads and big eyes. Each of them have different skin colours. The female who showed me her face have a very subtle personality..it's more like motherly, nice and nurturing kind of being i can feel it from her. She has green skin but the face is more blue colour. She's wearing a long white clothes and white hood.

She looks very kind to me..her face is just lovingly beautiful..i feel drawn to her. She asked through my head to extend my index finger towards her..she put her finger to the deviding crytal wall glass.. and her index finger is so long..and she has 3 Or 4 fingers?? She asked me to touch her finger on the crystal wall. I did it without hesitation.. when i did.. i felt this amazing energy went through my body and through my head.. my whole body was filled with white energy especially my head. Her face made it imprinted into my brain..

no threatening image.. it's very friendly and more like a motherly feelings she made me feel. I then asked her in my head.. what are you doing here? She then answered.. "MONITORING"..she then pulled her finger instantly.

She said, we have been monitoring you.. up there, she then showed me the other beings..it's like a military beings and operating under the water..it's like a military base of beings..very HIGH RANKING BEINGS. Then she showed me this nasty looking being..just the head..i got scared. I asked again, which part of the ocean is this? Then i heard a word "ATLANTIC OCEAN"!! I still argued..are you sure it's not PACIFIC ocean? PACIFIC OCEAN? NO!..i heard a definite word. It's "ATLANTIC OCEAN". Ohhh...wow!!!

I can see a very high and advanced TECHNOLOGY inside where they are operating and monitoring machines. Then suddenly my connection disconnected. Then i'm back on the ground, where Papa GOD standing beside the stream and Looks like he's waiting for me. I was going to tell him, but he said, i know my child. Have a rest.. then i wake up from my meditation and feeling very thirsty. I heard drink your water..i was going to drink my cold coffee.. but papa GOD got me first:) he knew..hehehe, well..that was an absolutely incredible and amazing different experienced and.. hmm..it got me puzzled there. Then i heard..don't think too much.

BUT, i asked Papa GOD while my eyes closed..i connected to him straightaway..i asked am i really healing the world Papa GOD?.. why did you ask like that? he said. Well..it's seems like is getting worst of what's going on now..don't doubt yourself my child. All this happenings have reasons. This things are meant to happen. Oh FATHER for how long? i asked sadly.

MY child, don't ask anymore, have a rest as i know you will think it deeply and become restless..then you won't be able to sleep. I want you to have a good sleep and proper rest and drink plenty of water, it's vital and purifies your body internally. Ok FATHER i will, and won't drown myself :) better not my child as you don't want to turn into a fish:).. i then heard my FATHER laughing!!! just like a thunder!! as i said..MY DEVINE FATHER has a very funny sense of humour. I LOVE HIM:)

# CHAPTER 38

# STALKERS INVADING MY SPACE

JOURNAL

18TH JULY

Dear journal, it has been a few days that i haven't been catching up with you. Recently, i spoke to my DEVINE FATHER about my HEALING to the WORLD. I connected with him straightaway, i then asked him, do i really healing the world Papa GOD? why doubting yourself my child? and we have discussed this before..well, put it this way..you are not healing the world, you are also awakening up the people, those people who has been awaken spiritually. You are helping them to recognised and acknowledged their gifts from above just like you.

The world need to change, back to where it was..before the "DESTRUCTIONS". SO what are you saying Papa GOd, that during my meditation and healing i am awakening the people spiritually? Yes my child. But only for those people who wants to be awaken, they have their own choices and i can't intervened. PAPA GOD i understand now, i said. The more you heal the world, the more they will be awaken spiritually, my FATHER said. Hmmm..interesting.. why he didn't tell me this before? then i heard his voice, that's because i like to surprise you sometimes. And i know you don't like surprises, yes that's correct i said. But why do you still kept surprising me? i asked. It's fun sometimes to talk to you especially if you are unaware that's why, Papa GOD said.

PAPA GOD, i have more to talk about, my STALKERS, people have been stalking me for quiet sometimes now, and from back then and i know who it is.. and unfortunately some new ones. This time combinations from old stalkers and new, and they are becoming more ruthless and worst of all i can sense them that they are following me everywhere. I can feel, sense and most of all see them closer with eye to eye contact and from the distance too. My sense are heightened like crazy! I can even tell them where they are and arround the perimeters. I can see and sense them that they are pretending not to know me. Ohh i know.. from the far distance or close i know....SOme of them i can smell thier rotting energy inside. And when i looked at this person..this person is sick..there aura is fading away. The worst i have seen to some of them are black then to ashes colour energy... its a sign of fading away. DEAR DEVINE FATHER have mercy on thier souls.

Some of them are just pathetic..what do i do with this people? I have a feeling that they have already been in my house..they seems to know what i am doing. I know more about it, i just don't want to mention in this book. Everyday i am starting eliminating their souls..now they will be sick and die later perhaps. As you said to me..i know my enemies. It is very sad to know that this kind of people will do harm on me just to justify that they can hurt me. It's pathetic really..i wish they'll get to know me first before they will do harm on me..now it's too late i can't save them with my prayers. The only thing they can do is ask some forgiveness to my DEVINE FATHER. They have no idea that PURGATORY or HELL is waiting for them, which i have seen it already. It's so sad really..GOD have MERCY on thier souls. There is no turning back if they kept doing these. BUT there is some hope if they are willing.

The message from my DEVINE FATHER IS..CHANGE IS YOUR ONLY HOPE! THANK YOU MY DEVINE FATHER. ILOVEYOU.

# CHAPTER 39

# MESSAGED FROM ABOVE "PARALYSED"

JOURNAL

20TH JULY 2022

There was a message i recieved from above this morning before i wake up at 5:30 am. The message wake me up before my alarm clock went off. The word is "PARALYSED" and it's referring to the earth..i saw the sky was pitch black, everything is black..nothing moving and the world is in "STILL". I tried to reach for PAPA GOD but not this time, i couldn't reach him. Instead i got connected to the "BEING" to the female and motherly being that i have encountered the other day during my meditation healing.

THe word "MONITORING" came out from my head...so this beings are monitoring the Earth to prevent any destructions coming. DEAR GOD have MERCY..people need to realise that our mother earth is in trouble. PAPA GOD where are you?...i want to talk to you...I heard a voice..keep "still" my child..keep your thoughts in still..i will come back to you later.

# CHAPTER 40

# TIME TO REFLECT

JOURNAL

24TH JULY 2022

Tonight i am trying to reach papa GOD, I can see him very busy talking to some entities..a very high ranking entities. Discussing something that i have no access of what they are talking about. I can't hear what they are talking..but i can see it's very important and serious. Before i can say something to Papa GOD..he send a PURPLE ENERGY arround me. Then suddenly i was inside the bubble..i asked in my head, what is it and why? Protection my child.. PROTECTION, he said it in my head.

Stay where you are at the moment and meditate, i will meet you there, he said. Ok, i said..i made myself comfortable and stayed where i am in my chair trying to meditate with the bubble arround me. Then i heard his voice..do some reflections..then i asked what kind of reflections do you want me to reflect? He said go deeper..ok i said. Then suddenly, i am feeling the some HURTS of my pasts.. disappointments..and anger. PAPA GOD said, you need to dispose everything that makes you feels vulnerable and angry. I NEED YOU MY CHILD..you have work to do with me and your ANGELS. They are waiting for you.

Waiting for me for what papa GOD? i asked curiously and nicely.. please explain it this to me. NO! he said with a firm voice. You need to work with your inner self, then when you are ready, i will let you know. OH PAPA GOD, why are you making it too difficult for me??:(i cried..it's not fair..i cried more..I heard nothing from my FATHER..i can see him very busy, and instead he is sending me a very "BIG FEATHER", and the colour is LIGHT BLUE..almost baby blue or fading blue colour..it's like a carpet floating on the AIR, but the shapes like a feather and it's floating slowly towards me.

He extended his right hand towards me while the feather is floating directly to me. HE continued talking to the entities, and by the looks of it they are having serious conversations. I can see my DEVINE FATHER from the distance, his aura is glowing..and incredible energy of command is on him. But as for me i thought i am feeling being punished. Then i heard my FATHER's voice, NO you are not being punish my child. YOUR STUBBURNESS is always the problem, papa GOD said. ohhh:(... so i decided to meditate instead.

During my meditation..i found this feelings of resentment and other feelings that stops me from making the decision, then i heard a voice, there are so many people trying to hurt you, spiritually and physically..that's why i have to put you in a bubble this time. I have been watching these people. So, what now papa GOD? I can see him thinking..matter of fact i can see a BIG QUESTION MARK in his head, and outside his head. He won't let me in into his thoughts..he is blocking me..he doesn't want me to know what he is thinking..so i didn't ask this time. I know when not to ask...

This time the entities are gone, and he let me come to his verandah this time looking to north and looking down to the lake and the water, it's flowing nicely then suddenly became rapid..i became anxious when i saw the raging water..he then slowed it down..navigating with his hand.

I moved closer to him, and i can see myself as a dignified mature woman, wearing a white clothing again, and on my head i'm wearing a hairband?? something on my head and he said, it's your crown, and i have black short hair. When i got closer to him he extended his arms and gave me a hug. I feel the connection with my FATHER, and a matter of fact i miss my DEVINE FATHER.

MY child i know it's complicated for you to understand of what's going on, because you are still in a physical world. And your responsibilities are not easy..and the spiritually is even more harder for you to understand..but I'm always with you. PAPA GOD, help me understand about my duty in both realms. I know i cannot understand everything of what's going on arround me and my responsibilities. This time i am asking again, what do you want me to help in a BIG way?

PAPA GOD looked at me and said..you need to go back to start, to those time that makes you feeling angry, sad, lonely, resentment.. everything..all the negative things that makes you feel not right.. and that's how you release it..you need to remove your own blockages in yourself..before you can fully continue with your devine mission.

Any hurts you need to release, because that's what stopping everything. Oh Papa GOD, some hurts already burried and forgotten..i know my child, he said it in the most lovingly way. OK i agree with you FATHER, i will start to reflect my pain, pasts and presents..it will takes a while though, but at least i can get rid of it and starts healing myself again. OK my child have some rest and drink your water. Yes i will Papa GOD. ILOVE YOU.

# CHAPTER 41

# PURPLE BUBBLE INSIDE

JOURNAL
25TH JULY 2022

I have to obey my DEVINE FATHER whatever he wants me to do he knows what's best for me. I just closed my eyes for seconds and i can see the purple bubble arround me..matter of fact i am inside the bubble.

Another reflection during my early marriage with 2 young children ages 3 years old and 1 yr old, i was in my prime of my carreer and i was juggling my responsibilities between family and my job. One night i dreamed that my husband have been shot. I saw the hospital in my dream and his coffin, and he was inside the coffin. I was very upset at that time and terrified. I asked Papa GOD not to take my husband please..i pleaded to him..not my husband please. FATHER. I prayed and kneeled down for hours pleading not to take him.

At that moment of my prayers, i felt an intense heat all over my body..i have never felt that kind of heat before, but the heat is more a very reassuring energy. The following week, i recieved a shocking news about my sister who just passed away without any specific reason, and the hospital and the coffin i saw about my husband's dream, it's my sister's coffin.

This memories still haunting me until now, and i am still grieving for my sister's sudden death. I asked WHY?? many times..but no specific answers or logic to my questions. Then lately i realised, that was supposed to be my husband's death means to happen but i refused to let him go. I was scared for my life and for children, i was 28 years old and have so much responsibilities..i don't think i can do this on my own..so i pleaded Papa GOD not to take him. I will do anything whatever you want me to do DEAR FATHER but not to take my husbands life..i cried..and BEG..PLEASE take somebody else but not my husband..and i pleaded again.

This words still HAUNTING ME!! I cannot get rid of my GRIEF.. sometimes i blamed myself that it was my fault to say something aweful but not realising i have inflicted it to someone else...especially to my sister. Until this day i carried this burden..i felt like i was responsible for my sister's sudden death. One day, i told my mum about my dream..i was crying..asking for forgiveness..and my mum said to me..it's not your FAULT! You did not wish it..it meant to happen. But still i am not convinced..i asked my mother again..tell me the truth mother. When i said something before especially when i am upset..did anything happen to that person? MUM quickly responded with a BIG "NO"! DON'T mentioned that again she said with an Angry voice.

Her toned of voice made me even suspicious..why mum????..did anything happened before when i was young? I asked curiously and almost forcing her to tell me the truth! Mum said to me..listen to me and listen very carefully..that moment my heart was pounding..i said PLEASE Mum what happened to me before? Please let me understand it!! I'm begging you! PLEASE....Mum sat down and asked me to listen very carefully..and she said..when you are upset..whatever comes out from your mouth it happened. Something about your words..that when you are upset and feeling angry, and you know it's not your fault..your words became a curse. You didn't mean it..but you know it's an unfair treatment for you..your anger comes out..then it became a curse for them too. Do you understand me? she said, while she's almost shaking my shoulders.

You have to be very careful something about your words even if you didn't mean it..it happens, but you didn't know that, until now. At this moment i didn't know what to say..but instead, i asked her again..is it my fault mother? i cried..NO..it's not your fault..nobody's fault. That reassuring words came from my mother it's all i needed.. but sometimes still comes out from me once in a while and still cried about it.

Now Papa GOD wants me to put it away in a devine bucket, and the Angels will take them up and purified. Let go my child..let go.. take a deep breath and let go, my DEVINE FATHER said with a very reassuring voice. Somehow Papa GOD's voice is always my COMFORT. I's ok my child, he said..not your fault..reassurance from my FATHER it's all i needed too..and remember my FATHER said, what you ask is become a wish..good or bad..so be careful. YES DEVINE FATHER, i understand now..

# CHAPTER 42

# "I AM MISSING SKY"

JOURNAL

28TH JULY 2022

I have been missing my "SKY"..i miss him for some reason..i don't know what it is and what i am feeling . When i see the word sky, i miss him.. yesterday when i saw a picture of a horse then i miss him. Then when i saw a blue sky..i miss him. I am missing him terribly..i can't connect with him now as i am very busy lately. And If i want to be with him, i would like to spend my time just with him and me without anyone interrupting our bonding...just me and him together happily exploring somewhere and over the rainbow.

Ohh..something interesting message from my DEVINE FATHER just now."SKY" my UNICORN is a GIFT from him. Just like every child wishes to have a horse or a pony. Ok..now i know :) Thank you FATHER, I LOVE U..it's alright my CHILD, he said. Do you know that you can access SKY anytime you want? Yes, FATHER, i know. I just don't have time. well, make time with him, Papa GOD said. I will FATHER, thank you :)

I saw him last night eating some grass where the green valley..you know our favourite spot FATHER under the trees full of butterflies, bugs..nice bugs though:) Yes, the west horizon, Papa GOD said..the Golden horizon.

Good morning my journal, today i am going to work, SKY was in my thoughts again. I closed my eyes then suddenly..i can see him running from the distance and coming towards me amongst with the green grass. The grass was about half way to his chest, he looks so happy while running coming towards me. I saw myself standing still and feeling so excited to see him and to hold him again.

When he reached me where i am standing, he stopped and then suddenly made his happy noise and lifted up his 2 front legs..and from me without any hesitation, i jumped quickly on his back and then we took off. While on his back, i moved my body closer to him..i felt my heart thumping and beating so strongly..and suddenly for some reason i can feel his heart too. I made myself even closer to him almost my body is feeling connected to his body.

Instantly, i feel this beautiful contentment and LOVE..i can feel a bubble of energy sorrounding us and wrapped us arround. A special bond of spiritual connection with SKY. I feel the synchronisity with our bodies together. We spend together and he is just so happy running arround the field with me..then i fall asleep on his back. Then i suddenly wake up and i saw myself in the middle of the field amongst the tall green grass half way to my chest with this gentleman. I thought ohhh..whoahh..who is this? Lucky me :) hehehe.. A very handsome..tall..with beautiful olive skin looking man. He doesn't look dark, but dark brown gentleman looking. His hair is slightly curly and medium lenght to his neck. Our body is so closed to each other, but my feelings towards him is so mutual. I don't feel any intimacy or static energy or any chemistry. I thought

WHY?? this is such a good looking man..and what an earth is he doing here with me? and my feelings is so mutual..i am puzzled. So i touched and feel his face with my hands..his face..then looking at him..studying him very carefully and curiously...who is this person??? i asked myself.

Then i asked him..who are you???..then i moved my face closer to his face while still holding his face with my hands..and that MOMENT!!!.. that INSTANT!!!..i said.. SKY??? OMG!!! SKY is that you??? oh.. HOLLY MOLLY..It's you SKY!!! :) hahahah...!! That moment..i said WOW!! how is it happened?? You are my SKY?? how is it possible?? :) He then said with a loving and enchanting deep voice..I am your "GIFT" from your DEVINE FATHER. I thought..OHHH..with a loving and fussie feelings towards him and my FATHER. whoahh.. that is insane!!:)..i mean..i don't know what to think!!

I was thinking before when i saw you, why on earth that someone got into my sacred spiritual space? This is so sacred and nobody can join my spritual space without my DEVINE FATHER permission. So now it makes sense:) I don't know what to say..but i thank you for your presence here with me, i said to him. Then i heard a voice..it's Papa GOD's voice..no need to say or think anything my child..just "feel" the moment and be happy:) Ohhhh...thank you FATHER. :)

I guess the feeling of being alone in a spiritual realm is just what i needed, a companion. But papa GOD can i say something? Yes my child..why i don't feel any intimacy towards him? i asked curiously. Well my child intimacy is only in a physical level does exist..haa?? i said with disbeliefs..not in a spiritual realm, he continued. Your bond with SKY has been with you and always there since you were born, or since i have created you in a palm of my hands with my energy. whoahh..papa GOD that is so beautiful:) He is your friend, he is my GIFT to you..the same every father in earth will give thier children a horse or a pony. SKY has been with you ever since. Ohh..thank you DEVINE FATHER you are so sweet:) Then i saw my FATHER happy face. :)

# CHAPTER 43

# MY ANCESTRAL KINGDOM

JOURNAL

2ND AUGUST 2022

This morning i am feeling sad, as my dear cat passed away..i am feeling Nostalgic in a sense of what's next for me..heavy feelimg with uncertainty of what's going on with my life. I just closed my eyes.. and took me straightaway to my FATHER EMPEROR ARTHERU and his kingdom, my ancestral home as my Emperor Father said, our KINGDOM. The place is soo beautiful full of nature and so beautiful..so serene.

I saw myself runnng towards him with his both arms extended towards me. I can see myself as a young woman daughter of the EMPEROR. My hair is very long, almost touching the ground, straight black hair, very petit and tall looking. I have my beautiful crown and i am wearing my baby pink long gown, my favourite colour.

My Emperor Father and myself standing in the same place that we used to meet before. Very tall place with the sorrounding solid wall rock with water falls. I reached my FATHER's arms, and he hugged me tight and the feeling of reassurance again, that i have almost forgotten my problems in a reality world.

My father welcomed me warmly, almost doesn't want to let me go in his arms, and i am feeling the same way. I just wanted somebody to hold me and to feel reassured which i don't get that in a reality world. The physical world is full of cruel human beings. My father didn't say anything while still holding me, i think he can feel my emotions. He then looked at my face lovingly and said, i got you..i'm here. Do you know, you can always come home anytime you want my SHINE. We are always here for you..all you need to do is think..and in a split second you are here with us. Ohh..of course father..It's just sometimes i got caught up between the reality and this spiritual realms.

We are in another world do you know that don't you? Yes father i know. And do you know that your DEVINE FATHER IS YOUR CREATOR? Yes i know that too. But why sometimes when i talked to PAPA GOD it seems like he is just an ordinary person in earth? Eventhough i'm in a spritual realm? why? i asked. Of course, my EMPEROR father said, because you are still in a physical world, and still carrying a connection the sense of reality towards him when you are connecting to each other. He has to make it realistic for you to understand the connections between the FATHER and a child. Oh ok that make sense now, i said.

Father why can't i leave the physical world and be with you with my mother instead? i cried..you know my SHINE, physical world is just a fragments of your sense of reality, and this reality of yours is your journey to help the humanity whether in a small or a big way..to make a difference for those who are suffering. Think about how you made a big difference to some people back then. Yes..i know father they were happy, they feel loved..and thier emotions become overwhelmed. I'm happy for them too father. Yes, that's exactly what i'm trying to tell you and makes you understand. Oh Father sometimes its hard for me to understand, but i think i will get used to this idea sooner or later. You will my Shine.. you will.

Father, can i ask some questions? Do you talk to papa GOD? yes of course shine, all the time, he said. Well, do you sometimes visits Papa GOD up there in his favourite verandah when i'm visiting him? Yes, i'm always there..i just don't want to show myself to you. why FATHER? i asked curiously. Because when you and your DEVINE FATHER together, that means his time is with you. I don't interfer anything especially when there is a task to do for you to prepare. Ohh..i sighed.

Father, what is my next task to do? well my shine, even me i don't even know..your DEVINE FATHER never revealed anything until the day we have to prepare you, your Devine mission. Father when i was visiting papa GOD at one stage, i felt like you were amongst with those entities that looks very highly ranking Royal. I think i had a glimpsed of you, you were wearing a white long thick gown.. and you have a beard. Before i can get closer to you..you disappeared.. was it you FATHER?..i felt so drawn to you and your energy was very familiar to me. Yes it was me shine..i made myself disappeared because it was your DEVINE FATHER time..with you..even there was somebody else arround.

I didn't want to mix your emotions and get confused towards me, and your Papa GOD at the same time. Ohh..FAther sometimes i get so confused, oh it's alright my shine, you just have to remember, i'm always arround with you..and so many more..you are sorrounded with protection. Your mind connected to your protectors, ancestors.. your ancestors including me..US..your powerful Ancestors.

Father sometimes i feel like my time here in our KINGDOM with you and my Mother is limited. My father emperor said, the time and space travelling is too hard for you to understand at this moment my shine..you will one day. We are doing this small fractions at a time to the level of your understanding. We don't want to overwhelmed you with informations because you tend to hide..you hide your emotions into your innerself and it becomes your little world..just you..and only you.

Oh Father, you really know who i am, of course my child..you are my only daughter in this KINGDOM..my "SHINARAE". My SHINE as your Empress mother called you. You are the RAY of sunshine in our KINGDOM. Father, i have so many questions..but i will save this later..i'm always here, my Emperor Father said..and you know how to find your HOME. Yes FATHER, thank you. OHH..i miss being here in this place.

Father, let's go back to my grandmother, i have a feeling that she's the one who gave me those magical music box which i have hidden in the right side corner wall of the staircase. Am i correct father? Oh.. my MOther is here:) MY empress MOTHER gave me a BIG hug but gentle..i can smell the fragrance of her beautiful perfume..very similar with my perfume in earth..it smells like home. My mother always Beautiful..she has this beautiful smile that can melt everyone sadness.

It's all coming back to me now..my memories..the synchronicities..i am starting to understand now the connections of my Ancestrals family and where i came from. My LINEAGE..my BLOOD LINE..so if that's the case..my CHILDREN has a blood from my ANCESTORS. The warriour..the MAGIC..Wow..absolutely unbelievable. I have to stop here MY EMPEROR FATHER AND MY EMPRESS MOTHER..this is so overwhelming..i'll catch up again next time. I LOVE YOU BOTH.

# CHAPTER 11

# "WHIP" THE NEW WEAPON

JOURNAL

3RD AUGUST 2022

This morning i closed my eyes and meditate, and during my meditation i saw a BIG face of a person, and that instant i knew the intention of this person towards me..not good. So i prayed and created a bubble for myself and for my love ones for protections. Before those entity can attacked me, i attacked him first by slaying the head without ay hesitation. I didn't think of any second thoughts.. as my FATHER said..trust your "INTUITION" my CHILD.

It's bizzarre because it's always the heads..no full body, and that makes me even wonder and curious. So back to my meditation..i can see myself standing in an empty space, looks like an empty corridor. I looked at myself.. my body is fully fitted with a warriour clothing. I thought oh no..i have some task to do. I have been called again, and this time looks like i'm going to a battle by the looks of my clothing and confidently looking straight and brave.

I can see myself wearing this fitted but leathery clothing, and it's colour light brown..my boots are the same colour and up to my knees, my hair is down to my shoulder and braided. Then in my left hand, i'm holding..oh dear..i never have this before..a leathery WHIP, LONG..and golden colour. I extended my left arm to try my new weapon..it's light, and it has fire when i hit! Oh dear..where am i going to? i asked myself.

I can't reach PAPA GOD at the moment..i think i am having an initiation again..then i saw SKY..he just suddenly appeared in my right side. He looks happy to see me..and he looks dark gray. I said, SKY you looks older..i greeted him and kissed his forehead, and he then made a happy noise then i gave him a HUG. Then we both facing the brown empty wall facing east, then the brown wall started to change into a face and then slowly changed again into an ANGEL's wing and then slowly opening for us. Hmm...interesting i thought to myself.

SKY and myself started to walk towards the open wall, i held on SKY leathery ROPE saddle just hanging on my left hand and then we proceeded with my well equipped weapons. I feel every one of them in my body. We stepped in an open wall very cautiously..it's dark and a matter of fact i'm little bit scared, but i noticed SKY moved little bit closer to me, and that's the sign of reassuring gesture to me. Nobody inside except the two of us walking in the dark.

We continued walking but very slowly..and then suddenly i saw some little golden stars twinkling from the distance..but we are still walking in a dark area. We followed the stars until we reached the very end, and to my surprised i am facing a really BIG CAVE! From where we standing and on top of a very high area, i looked down and to my surprise..it's full of ANGELS!! And all of them are wearing white clothings and with their wings!!! :) just like me before..

WARRIOUR ANGELS!! and the sorrounding is purely white. Ohhh..i remember before when Papa GOD put me in this white cave, but i was standing on top of a BIG PILLAR and sorrounded by the white light in a white cave, it was bright light but it was soothing.

The pillar stone i was standing on it was in the middle of the white cave. I am realising now that it was part of my initiation and purifications! Now i understand! whoaahh..this is incredible and amazing! Now i am even more curious and for some reason i saw Papa GOD's face smiling at me, and then he made me read his mind.. at last, this time she realised and most importantly understood. He made me feel that he is very proud of me.

Then i looked down again to the bottom of the cave where the ANGELS are..the place and the area is just purely white..so Angelic white. Before i can say hello to the ANGELs..they all turned arround and looked up, and said to me..(oh GOD i don't really want to say this)..but papa GOD said..say it! with a big tone of strong command!

The ANGELS said..IT'S THE CHILD OF GOD!!! then all of them made noises..the cave almost sorrounded by the cheering noises!! There is no words i can described it. I never heard this kind of cheering before it so different..it's not like a football game it's more an Angelic sounds of happiness. I felt little bit ackward though, as i am not used to this kind of attention but i humbly thanked them all.

Then it finally sinked in into my head this is it..this is much bigger responsiblity than in a reality world. I saw ARCH ANGEL MICHAEL appeared in my left side and not too far away from me and the other male Warriour with ROYAL BLUE uniform including his cape and his royal blue horse. He never revealed his face to me or either his name.

Then suddenly, PAPA GOD face appeared on the solid stone wall and infront of us! All ANGELS are looking up, but it's just his silhouette, and on and off he made me see his face too, i guess that's to reassured me.

He welcomed me and the ANGELS, then i saw the other ANGELS that i have met before. I am facing PAPA GOD towards south. I can see myself as a real ANGEL WARRIOUR! i didn't have my wings out this time, but i have my weapons with me. All my weapons are gold and have their own personality. All the ANGELS have their own swords too.

Ohh..i have to stop here my dear journal..this is overwhelming for me..i went to visit the bathroom..i looked at myself in the mirror, when i saw myself in the mirror i cannot even recognised myself..i guess in this moment i'm still caught up between reality and spirituality realm. Then i closed my eyes again for seconds.. when i opened my eyes i'm back to a normal "me"..ohh..thanks GOD for that. I asked PAPA GOD to download this to me later, i'm exhausted and feeling very thirsty. BYE my DEVINE FATHER.

# CHAPTER 45

# GOLDEN KEY IN MY MUSIC BOX

JOURNAL
5TH AUGUST 2022

I asked Papa GOD if he wants me to continue the download tonight, but he said No..not tonight. I want you to have some sleep now. OK FATHER i'm too tired anyway..goodnite papa GOD..good night my child, he said.

The next day it's a lovely day, and still have NO sign from my FATHER, so i continued resting and gained some good sleep. Then last night i connected with my DEVINE FATHER, and this time interestingly i can see him looking through the glass panel floor..up there..on top of the clouds. I can see him laying on his stomach on top of the glass floor and looking down through it, and with a magnifying glass:) whoaah.. Sometimes he makes me wonder, the way he uses things from the reality world to his spiritual realm..sometimes i got confused of where i am. He looks so serious by the looks of him really focussing what he is looking down. I am puzzled..why? what's he up to now?? i asked myself.

I asked Papa GOD, what are you doing Papa GOD? but before i could say and asked some questions again, he said..shhh..so i sat down on the floor little bit away from him. I can see myself as a little child, he turned me again into a child. He does that to me when he is very busy doing things that i could not understand. I guess i have to wait here, i said to myself.

Luckily, i have my music box with me in my hands. I guess my MOTHER EMPRESS GLYDICA sent it to me. I just played with my music box while sitting on the floor. While playing with my music box..papa GOD asked me to open it. So i then slowly opened my music box and to my surprised a "GOLDEN KEY", it's a long old solid looking type of key. And it's purely bright golden colour. Then a chain on it, and it's gold too.

Papa GOD asked me to put it in my neck, and when i was about to put it, JESUS appeared suddenly infront of me and then helped me to put it arround my neck, but to my surprised, the chain turned into a leathery string. Once JESUS finished, he moved couple steps backward and looked at me while still sitting on the floor. Then i continued playing with my music box..then JESUS disappeared.

PAPA GOD continued looking down through the glass floor, and once in a while checking and looking at me with a little smile on his face. Then suddenly, i got bored..i put my music box down aside and dragged my bottom closer to my Papa GOD. Then i asked him curiously, what are you looking down FATHER? He then said, things that you would not understand at this moment. So i sat down beside him and i looked down too, and then to my surprised..i am looking the disasters in Earth. So i flinched!! and started to asked Papa GOD questions.

WHY is it so messy and lots of FIRE and lots of WATER Papa GOD?..my child close your eyes he said.. this is too much for you to understand. He then asked me to close my eyes..which i did..he then touched my eyes and then fall asleep. Then papa GOD picked me up on the floor where i was sitting beside him, then put me on his shoulder and started walking towards the stairs..2 to 3 steps from where we sitting..and then he sat down on his big marble chair while i'm still sleeping on his right shoulder.

I can see him gently tapping my tiny little back, and swaying side to side. Ohh..i can feel my DEVINE FATHER ENERGY..so DEvine and very soothing with full of LOVE. Whenever i am feeling weary, Papa GOD always recharged my energy. He always turned me into a child when i'm feeling so vulnerable, upset and craving some emotional support. He knows how to reached me when i am feeling lost with my emotions, and especially how to handle with my own emotion.

So this time i am thinking, the "GOLDEN KEY"..i guess it's another mystery waiting to unlock something. I don't know what it is..but my DEVINE FATHER only will knows what's next for me to do. No matter where i am or what i am doing, if he called me..time and space doesn't exist in the reality world. I'm there in the presence of my DEVINE FATHER straight away..and it pauses everything..one day i'm in a physical level then i am more in a spiritual realm at the same time. Sometimes it's hard to describe where i am, and maybe to some people is complicated to understand. Even to myself, sometimes i have problem understanding it, but Papa GOD likes it that way, and that's how he protects me and my sanity. My dear journal i have to stop from here.

# CHAPTER 46

# GREEN LADY MOTHERLY BEING

JOURNAL
10TH JULY 2022

Last night i had a visitor in my bedroom, in my subconscous mind this motherly being again came to visit me during my sleep. I saw her stroking my forehead and my head crown chakra. She infused some white lights into my head and went through my whole body. I feel good though..then suddenly she disappeared. It didn't feel threatened or feeling bad about her or either her presence in my room, a matter of fact it was beautiful and comforting. She's very soothing..very motherly..i feel some kind of connections. She looks green, tall, very slender and has blue face colour then changes it to green sometimes.. and big beautiful eyes. I feel some kind of neutral connections in some way..but feels connected to her when she was present. I was going to call Papa GOD, but i felt blocked and slept right through the night.

The next morning i reached for Papa GOD during my meditation, FATHER..can i talk to you now? even for few minutes please? then i heard..yes my child..i heard you. I can't see you Papa GOD..i only can hear your voice..why? i asked. Well, you are not supposed to see me at the moment Papa GOD said. OKAY..but why not? i persisted to asked. BIG PAUSE THERE..no answered from Papa GOD..oh..i am feeling little bit sad.

I guess he is so busy at the moment. I can wait, i said to myself..i wait..and waiting..but no Papa GOD. But i am persistent so i closed my eyes..then i have a peek of what's going on with him, i'm curious. Then i saw him..oh my..he is totally busy, i can see so many entitiies with a very high ranking Royal entities. I can see a BIG and very long marble table and with chairs, and PAPA GOD having conversations with them..and looks very serious though.

He made me see and have a glimpsed of what's going on in his KINGDOM. I can see myself as a very young kid again..hiding behind the BIG marble pillar, looking and peeking of what's going on. Then PAPA GOD saw me behind the marble pillar, he then allowed me to come near him, and i walked very slowly towards him. I feel so happy to see my FATHER again :)

I can see myself barefooted walking on the marble floor with my hands behind my back. And when i got closer to my FATHER..his face became like a sihouette.. it's the same as the other Royal entities who are conversing with papa GOD? Hmm..i don't really undersatnd why? Then i noticed i cannot understand their conversations and what's all about, all i can hear are mumbling words..conversations of different language which i couldn't understand. Some ancient language perhaps?

I got closer to Papa GOD, and he kissed my forehead. Then i heard this sudden mumbling sounds coming from the entities. I don't understand it..i was going to ask papa GOD, but he told me..shhhh..

very faintly. So i did..and suddenly my little chair appeared beside him. Then showed me to sit down on my little chair. I struggled to climbed up on my chair..then JESUS suddenly appeared infront of me and assisted to get on my chair. Then i saw JESUS bowed to papa GOD, and he showed some appreciation to JESUS. I then asked PAPA GOD quietly..is JESUS my brother Papa GOD? He is very tall..i said. Yes my child in the spiritual level he is your brother. OHHHH...i have a brother?? i wonder why i always longed for a brother, in a physical world i never have a brother.

I still can see myself sitting beside Papa GOD..then i got bored..i stood up and run arround the place still barefooted. Then i noticed one gentleman entity extended his right arm towards me..and i touched his hand innocently..then suddenly i felt something very familiar of his energy. His face doesn't looks clear..but his energy is soothing and very familiar. My journal i have to stop here..bye for now Papa GOD..and i can see my DEVINE FATHER waving at me and sending lots and lots of little floating hearts and i started chasing them. :)

# CHAPTER 47

# A BALL OF FIRE IN PAPA GOD'S HANDS

JOURNAL

15TH AUGUST 2022

Last night i reached out to my DEVINE FATHER. I met him in the same spot, his favourite long verandah looking out the clouds. He waited for me to come near him, but from the distance i saw him holding something in his hands. It's more like a ball of FIRE in his hands with flame. When i got closer..i can see more of this flame going to his arms. When i finally came closer to him, he diffused it.. and before i can asked some questions, he made me read his mind.. he said, this is your FLAMES..and i'm just testing it, with a smile on his face:)

Ohh..i said to my amusement, and when do i need to use it? i asked curiously. Shhh..Papa GOD said. Then he turned to his left side facing me with his happy face, and his both hands are clasps to each other. Hmm..i have never seen him happy like this before..Well my child, what's happening lately with you? who me? i said..as i looked behind me if he is talking to somebody else, because i know he knows what's going on with me for sure.

So i guess he read my mind..well, you came to see your FATHER, so you might be feeling lonely perhaps? and he laughed!!!:) oh FATHER really?? really? you think that's funny? yes my child it is funny, he said and he laughed again. I thought hmmm..he certainly is happy. :) PAPA GOD and myself have a special bond just between FATHER and CHILD. He doesn't call me daughter because to him i am always a child.

I don't really want to spoiled the meeting with my DEVINE FATHER, for him this is special and to me too, as i can see he looks very happy to see me and i don't really want to spoil that. Our meeting is just very beautiful and serene..we just talk..and listened to my DEVINE FATHER..he is showing me some different kinds of sceneries while we are both in the verandah. I can see SKY flying arround happily..and i noticed papa GOD didn't turn me into a small child. This time he is just happy conversing with me as an adult..i love this moment when i can talk to him as an adult.

# CHAPTER 48

# SOLOMON AND A BIG BOOK

JOURNAL
16TH AUGUST 2022

I think feeling being "weird" is not an option to me anymore. I don't know why i have said that. Today going to work i fell into a deep meditation again in my car. I wasn't driving the car by the way, i saw this "BIG HAND"..and that big hand pointing towards up..i then my eyes followed the hand. The hand looks majestic..powerful in some way and looks Holly.

I then saw myself slowly ascending up with my arms spreads out.. then i saw this man covered with the HOLLY HOOD, white and thick material hood. I cannot see his face and he is holding a "BIG BOOK" tucked into his chest. While i was ascending..i asked him who are you? PLEASE..i can't see your face..who are you? i asked again curiously.

My ascension suddenly stopped and then revealed himself to me. His face looks like an old man with a beard, and his name is "SOLOMON" he said. I don't know anyone name solomon..then he disappeared quickly. In that moment i tried to reached PAPA GOD..but then suddenly i have awaken from the guy whose yelling off the street while crossing the street light.

Oh boy..it was a deep sleep and i don't know if i was dreaming or in a deep meditation, but i am more interested about this SOLOMON person. Then i goggled it..OMG! he is a prophet, the messenger of GOD! Oh Papa GOD..thank you. My greatest respect to the prophet Solomon the messenger of GOD..my DEVINE FATHER. But it was cut off short..i didn't get the full message. I have to catch up with my DEVINE FATHER soon. Oh..he has a beard too according to my researched.

# CHAPTER 49

# A BIG HEART SHAPE
# OF A BALLOON

JOURNAL
18TH AUGUST 2022

This morning when i wake up i was tired..overly tired, but still feeling annoyed i don't know why? Last night somebody visited me again during my sleep. I didn't know this entity, i have never seen him before. During his invasion of my sleep, i can see his face looking so stupid, gawking at me while i'm sleeping. I am feeling violated again sorrounding my aura. Although he wasn't doing anything to me or my body..he was just so close to my face and looks like trying to study my face and my whole being. He looks like a young male person in a 20's and hiding inside the cloak. So stupid looking!

I wasn't feeling comfortable..i waited for him to see of what he's going to do to me..then I got so angry suddenly, i am not happy for him being here in my sorrounding energy. I am feeling nauseated, and then decided to armoured myself, i quickly pulled out my daggers and started attacking him. Prior to attack him, i saw him doing something with my eyes. So i decided and determined to quickly terminated him before he can do more damaged to my body especially my eyes as it was his main target to start. As a sign of a cross, i attacked the eyes of the entity and penetrated his eyes with my daggers. I feel like my daggers automatically did the works for me. I saw the entity's body laying on the ground without his eyes..didn't see any blood.

I didn't feel sorry for this entity, instead i prayed for his soul of forgiveness from Papa GOD. I tried to reached for my DEVINE FATHER..but instead, i heard his voice..you know what to do my child..trust your instinct..your gut feelings. You don't need me to wait for my permission. Your weapons will automatically do the job for you. Ohh.. FATHER i didn't know that, Well now you know, he said.

Papa GOD can i ask you something? Yes my child..i know what it is but, you can voice it out, he said. Well, it's my meditation about the man called SOLOMON. I researched that he is the PROPHET..THE MESSENGER to you my DEVINE FATHER. Why did he appear to me in my meditation? Well my child this is not the proper time to tell you. Why not PAPA GOD? PLEASE i need to know! please..i protested...why do you need to know? he asked. well, because it was cut off short during my meditation while i was in the car.

I cut it off, he said why? i asked. Because it was only a fraction of your message and preparation that you will be doing. This time i want you to rest your mind..your thoughts..your body..he said. But PApa GOD i want to know more about my preparations..pls...NO! he said. A BIG NO! came from him. You are being stubborn again!! he said. OHH..Papa GOD why? why i don't understand you sometimes? I cried..and cried..

Then suddenly i can see myself infront of him again and still crying..a child..he turned me into a child again. He then picked me up and sat me on his right lap while i am starting to feeling better. He is sitting on his BIG MARBLE CHAIR and looking out the verandah full of clouds. Then my head started to wonder..what is that about the clouds? so boring to watch anyway..then he said..i can read your mind by the way. Opps..hehehe..sorry:)

It's a matter of fact clouds really fascinates me, and i do look for messages from Papa GOD in the clouds when i am missing him, or feeling bored of myself while i am here in a physical realm. Although, i am and always feeling better everytime i'm sitting beside with my DEVINE FATHER..it's a feeling of comfort and security with his body sorrounding me. I love the devine connections and feeling safe with him.

Can you see the Big cloud out there? he asked, pointing it out at the same time. Yes i can see it, i answered uninterestedly..but suddenly i noticed there's lots of ballons, and with the shapes of the HEARTS and also it's RED colours!!:) i have never seen that kind of ballons that shapes of hearts FATHER while i am smilling :)..and it's all red and floating arround the clouds. I can see the little Angels playing with it.

Would you like to play with them? with the Angels?..you did before, Papa GOD said. Hmm..NO..i said. Instead i tucked my little body in his chest while feeling secure. Then i fall asleep in his arms. Then i wake up later on in my bed..and thanked my DEVINE FATHER. I think reassurance and security are just what i needed at this time from my FATHER. Thank you, i know you are always there watching me. PAPA GOD always know how to soothed my insecurities and vulnerabilities.

# CHAPTER 50

# LADY ENTITY GOT BURNT DURING THE JOURNEY

JOURNAL
19TH AUGUST 2022

Last night during my astral travel, there was a woman who came arround in my energy field. She was wearing some kind of white thick clothing. she portrayed herself to me as a DEVINE being..but my gut feelings was telling me something different, and i wasn't feeling comfortable with her. She belittled me in a spiritual sense, and that's why i wasn't feeling comfortable being with her. We decided to go ahead travelling in the galaxy.

Suddenly during the travel, we reached the area that i was familiar with in my heart. But then i noticed her body was full of cuts, and have lots of injuries, and it's all over her body..she looks like a mess. I can see parts of her body are burnt and even her clothings. I saw marble square stones where we stopped, and i asked her to sit down and rest. I noticed her clothes are full of blood and covered with her own blood. She looks very uncomfortable and in a lot of pain, but still overpowering me and insisted that she's a devine being. I didn't argue or not even intending to argue with her of who she is. I am more worried about her and her injuries.

I tried to help her..but when i got closer to her, she melted away down quickly and her body turned into ashes. I tried to call for Papa GOD but i wake up suddenly. I realised it was time to get up anyway, i didn't feel good when i got up..i feel annoyed..somehow cranky. I then looked at myself in the mirror..arrgh..my hair is a mess..looks horrible..but surprisingly..my face is ok!! :) HAHAHA..i guess my face didn't get burn during my astral travel last night. During my meditation, i asked Papa GOD of what was that all about and those woman who came with me during my astral travelling. Then papa GOD said, you had a hitch hiker..Oh??? how was it possible?? i asked. well, i let her in, Papa GOD said. why? i asked.

Well, she was persistent..so i made her taste her own experience. So what will happen to her now? because i saw her turned into ashes. She will get sick eventually and die in a physical realm.. perhaps with lung cancer. why lung cancer? i asked. well..she died from smoke didn't she? Papa GOD said. Yes i guess..and turned into ashes. Well, that's what is going to happen Papa GOD said. Oh ok..i got it now, i said.

# CHAPTER 51
# WORD SACRIFICE

JOURNAL
19th AUGUST 2022

Prior to my meditation, i decided to have a shower, while i was in the shower i heard in my head word "SACRIFICE". I was startled with my thoughts..i asked Papa GOD straightaway..am i going to be sacrificed Papa GOD? and for what? and why?..i then heard the voice from my FATHER..No such things as sacrificing you..and what for? he said. Well, i am being prepared for something and you are not telling me about this, so i thought that would be the case or part of it..ME..i cried :(

My child, when i said you are not a sacrifice to be, you are NOT! You are my child, and you are not to be sacrifice. You are being prepared for your DEVINE purpose and your calling. You are my Angel WArriour! I have to protect you! You have an important things to do in the spiritual realm. It will come when time is ready..a matter of fact, you are READY.

Then suddenly, i can see myself in a fully geared battle ANGEL WARRIOUR. I looked at myself magnificently tall, slim with olive skin and my hair looks braided and long. I can see myself and my body wrapped arround with leathery strings as an an outfit, a battle gear outfit. And I'm looking so brave and striking. My hair looks red and flamey, and my new "whip" weapon..is just ready to come out from my hips wrapped arround me, i took it out then i tried striking it on the air and then, i saw the flame came out. Whoahh.. what an incredible weapon! Then i saw ARCH ANGEL MICHAEL behind me, and "SKY". I saw SKY running towards me, he looks magnificent and he made a happy noise when i touched his nose. Then i saw "SAM" the other Angel, and leading the other Angels behind him, they're all have horses including Arch Angel Michael.

We then suddenly facing the west horizon, where my DEVINE FATHER silhouette face came out from the solid wall rock. He looks so Majestic..Powerful and have a strong bright light behind and sorrounding him. He acknowledged everyone including me, and he welcomed all the WARRIOUR ANGELS. I looked at myself and i noticed my face has a cover. I'ts more like a Feathery white mask cover..but it's all white..bright white!

I looked up and saw my DEVINE FATHER smiling at me..i can see he is proud of me..and lovingly looking at me with a smile on his face, a proud FATHER..he made me feel it. Then Papa GOD asked me to come closer to him, and asked me to kneel down..which i did. While my head down, he then put his right hand on top of my head and amazingly i can feel this energy went through my whole body..a very familiar energy. Then i took my DEVINE FATHER hands..and i kissed his open palms with great respect, and said to him..i love you my DEVINE FATHER..WITH ALL MY HEART. He then touched my face with his hands lovingly.

Then everything is white..pure whiteness..the sorroundings. He then showed me a "WHITE CITY" down..i'm looking down..only a fraction.. and that's where we supposed to go..and then suddenly, the image was cut off. I then said WHY???... Then i heard him..time is up..get ready..you are going to work. Then i woke up from my meditation..i opened my eyes and then..everything is gone. Get some good rest my child. I will FATHER bye...

# CHAPTER 52

# "CITY OF ANGELS"

JOURNAL

28TH AUGUST 2022

My dear journal, few nights ago during my meditation i saw myself in a full gear of an Angel Warriour. And by the looks of it, it's the continuation of my other night meditation with Arch Angel Michael and the other Angels. PApa GOD pointed us down the "WHITE CITY", this white city is the same city that my DEVINE FATHER showed me during our meeting. At this moment i can see myself riding on "SKY's back and we are heading towards the white glittering city.

Arch Angel Michael and the rest of the Angels will be folllowing me. All of us riding on the horses going down to the white city. Then i noticed SKY have WINGS!!..what a beautiful sight :) I didn't let my wings out this time as i thought it's not necessary. I saw myself holding a white sword..i thought..this is a new weapon again but this new weapon, i don't feel the intensity of the energy of it..i'm confused this is not like my other weapons.

This is more a relaxed weapon in somehow hmm..i don't understand.. i thought this new weapon as a sword..it's not long and pointy hmm??.. the lenght is bigger and it's white and medium size. Oh..i don't know what to think about this sword. This sword doesn't connect much with me, i am feeling this is not for a BAttle.

I saw myself as an incredible brave ANGEL WARRIOUR, and at this moment i am experiencing my braveness and strength and almost no fear. I am riding on SKY's back and it is just the most incredible feelings. It feels so natural for me that my body is just like in oneness with SKY and being connected with him. I am ready for the BATTLE, whatever it is i will be facing..i affirmed myself. Then i heard PAPA GOD's voice..that's my Girl!! Thank you DEVINE FATHER!

We continued travelling down until we reached the city, and then slowly touched down on a concrete stone ground. We stopped at the front of the white city, and i asked SKY to stepped back. I study the whole outside wall area, and i noticed and i couldn't see any door knob from the outside wall or either an entrance door. I am puzzled.. hmm..

I decided to jumped out from SKY's back, and then i saw myself dragging my sword on the concrete ground making this scretching noise while it is flaming at the same time. I put away my sword, then i walked slowly to the very high wall. I put my right hand on the stone wall..i started feeling it..then my left hand did the same..and then suddenly both of my hands automatically made a circle..then it formed into a heart!!! whoah..

And then my right hand felt a little hole in the middle of the heart that my both hands formed into a heart with. Then i put my index finger into the little hole, but my finger didn't fit in. Then i heard papa GOD's voice..use your "KEY", a key? i said to myself..i don't have a KEY FATHER. He then said you do have "FEEL YOU HEART".

I put my right hand on my chest close to my heart, and then suddenly, i felt this little bump inside my chest and my garments.. then i slowly pulled it out..the leathery string first..then here it is.. "MY GOLDEN KEY"!! Yes of course my golden key, it was given to me by my DEVINE FATHER..it actually came from my music box. THANKED YOU my DEVINE FATHER for reminding me, hehehe..silly me :) So you found it my child with a smile on his face..a reassuring smile:) So everytime you lost something..feel it in your heart you'll find it there, he said.

SO what do i do with this PAPA GOD? i asked. Well..my child find the entry of that heart, and see if you can open it. OK i'll try, i said. Then i heard a stern voice came from him..don't just try it..DO IT! A direct command that no one will refuse. OK i said..i will!

Then i am facing the BIG Stone Wall and wondering what's behind the wall? Hmm...i'm curious..and then i closed my eyes..and started feeling it with my hands slowly, and to my amazement..i feel like, i am feeling the whole body of this wall. As for my curiousity, i made my whole body closer to the wall and my face touching the wall. Then to my surprised i feel like the wall is talking to me..and i can feel it..it's breathing..and then i'm hearing a stranged noises..almost giggly or ticklesh noises of something :)..it's more like it's the sounds of little kids voices:)..then i continued feeling it and suddenly i feel so happy for some reason:).

In that moment while feeling happy, suddenly i felt a small hole..and then i took my KEY from my neck with my right hand while my eyes still shut. I connected the KEY into a small hole while seeing it in my clear head, then penetrating to the wall and concentrating while my eyes still shut. Suddenly i saw the colour of the wall changed into a golden colour all the way UP to the TOP! Then i turned the KEY into clock wise..then automatically i heard the a "CLICK" sound, then realised i have unlocked the door!

Then i heard the ANGELS behind me roaring with happy noises!!clapping with joy!!!:) I looked behind me, i can see all my ANGELS are all PURE WHITE..so beautiful..i can see SKY's FACE looks happy too, and ARCH ANGEL MICHAEL. Then the wall started to open very slowly..and finally it opened widely.. and to my surprised..i was GREETED with all the ANGELS wearing in white robe clothings!!! They are all pure beautiful white ANGELS! :)

I looked arround where i was standing, the inside looks like a CITY..a CITY of ANGELS!!! OH MY GOD!!! I could not believe it..it's so glittery and white inside, wow!! amazing!! :) Suddenly, A BIG ANGEL with a very BIG WINGS appeared infront of me. She welcomed me and my ANGELS..she opened her arms and pointed the palace and the city behind her. Then i asked.. who's ANGEL are you? i asked politely..

Well, my name is ARCH ANGEL GABRIEL, she said it politely and with GRACE. She has a beautiful smile i noticed, and she's glowing. She then introduced ANGEL METATRON to me standing beside her. I saw a graceful and acceptance nod from Angel Metatron wearing a Royal blue outfit. Then suddenly i realised, and to my amazement my head is questioning my sanity. I thought Arch Angel Gabriel is a male Angel according to my grandma's bible?? then i heard Papa GOD saying..there is no gender when it comes to an ANGEL my child. Oh ok..thank you my DEVINE FATHER. Now i understand:)

"STAR" this is my city..the city of ANGELS. I thought for a second.. STAR? who's star? and before i could ask who's star..she said, it's "YOU". ME??? i asked curiously. YES! your name is STAR!:) whoahh????...hang on wait a minute..PAPA GOD doesn't call me star..he always call me "CHILD"..yes..that's right he never called me any name..hm..whoahh..this is new to me. I will ask and discuss this with my FATHER later i thought..

Well Arch Angel Gabriel this are my ANGELS, i introduced them to her, and can i asked some questions? What is my purpose here? well, STAR your purpose is to deliver this beautiful new ANGELS in my KINGDOM.."THE CITY OF ANGELS". Oh..ok..now i get it..this are new breed ANGELS. Yes! ARCH ANGEL GABRIEL agreed :) PAPA GOD said i wasn't born here in this city. Yes, that's correct, you are the CHILD of our DEVINE FATHER, the light who's been created from above..the UNIVERSE. Oh..it's even more confusing to me, i thought to myself.

You have been created with energy and delivered to earth to protect and spread LOVE to human kind..to make a difference to somebody who needed it, great and small..that's your purpose. You have been protected and hidden to the very small part of the world so no one can detect of who you are, and cannot bring any harm to you. Is that my JUDGEMENT? i asked. YES! Arch Angel Gabriel answered me directly, and that is your purpose in LIFE physically and spiritually. ARCH ANGEL GABRIEL delivered my JUDGEMENT in that instant!

So now i delivered my ANGELS, what do i do now? i asked politely. You will return to your DEVINE FATHER spiritually, and physically to your daily life but you are well protected. We are here always watching you and ready to intervene if necessary. Oh thank you, i said. I can see the "BIG BOOK" on her chest carrying it to her right hand. "THE ANGEL OF JUSTICE"..the words i heard came to my head so sudden. Then i opened my eyes..and everything is gone. whoahh..that's interesting.

Good night PAPA GOD..i will talk to you again soon..i love you..then i saw papa GOD smiling at me..and still standing in his favourite verandah and a cloud on his head???? it looks like a circle cloud on top of his head??? A HALO?? :) aww..c'mon Papa GOD you don't need a "HALO", i said it to him happily :) Well, i showed this to you just to make you happy:) ohh..i am happy because you here, and you were there including SKY and ARCH ANGEL MICHAEL. And i think there was an Angel visiting me today at home. Because i found 2 little white curly feathers on my floor this morning. THANK YOU!! GOOD NIGHT FATHER:)

# CHAPTER 53

# BLACK ENTITY CAME TO COLLECT

JOURNAL
1ST SEPTEMBER 2022

Last night i had some bad ass entities that got into my energetic sorroundings. While i was sleeping, i can see them and they were about to attack my body again, but somehow i saw myself got up from where i'm sleeping then i stood up, and keeping "still" infront of this horrible entities coming towards me. They are all wearing black hoods, and i cannot see their face. I can see them from the distance coming aggressively, but i prepared myself this time and waiting for them to get closer. I am facing them without any fears in my body. Somehow i didn't pulled out my weapons instead, i lowered my body down to the ground with my one leg kneeled down and with my two hands down touching the ground.

I can see the entities are getting closer and closer..and they're about to attack then suddenly, i punched my hands on the ground and to my amazement, i broke the ground and all the entities are exploding!! whoahh..this is new to me, i didn't even think of this is possible..it's just my whole body seems to navigated my intervention!!

I tried to reach PAPA GOD at the same time, but i couldn't reach him..the more i punched the ground the more entities are exploding and they are all turned into ashes..then disappeared! I did this several times..the more they are coming the more i am punching the ground, and they are all exploded! Then suddenly no more entities, and i can see myself standing and waiting for more to come..but no more..i can't see anymore arround.

Then i saw my body again sleeping in my bed..then i saw a man wearing a black long clothes, everything black that he is wearing, but i noticed he is not wearing a hood. I can see his hair is blonde with a good trimmed body..tall looking and younger in a 20's to 30 years of age and visiting me in my dream, but to my surprised he cannot get closer, because i can see a really BIG gentleman on my right side beside my bed, not too far away from me and looks like he is guarding me.

This other entity with blonde hair could not get closer to me, so i only can see him 5 feet away from me. He is sternly looking intimidating this BIG guy. This BIG guy guarding me, he has a mascular body with a moustache with short RED hair and light brown colour skin. He is wearing some kind of leathery clothings, and he looks like from medieval time. A very casual looking man and i feel safer with him just being beside me standing near my bed. The other entity was more intimidating and somehow trying to enticed me, then suddenly ARCH ANGEL MICHAEL appeared infront of him, got his sword out and aimed to the entity who's wearing black clothes without a hood, and without any saying, my ANGEl strikes this entity's head without any hesitation and cut his head off. He then exploded and turned into ashes.

Then another entity came with a hood and appeared with a long weapon..and ARCH ANGEL MICHAEL told him with a very STERN and hard COMMAND."SHE's NOT YOURS"!!! BE GONE!! and don't come near Her again! A powerful command with great POWER! It sounds little bit distorted but POWERFUL!!! and he then aimed his sword towards this entity, the entity quickly disappeared!!! I have never seen my ANGEL commanded that way before..so Brave and POWERFUL!

Then i wake up exhausted, and i noticed my eyes are little bit better. Before this things happened, while i was asleep, there was some entities trying to do something with my eyes. They were tampering with my eyes, but somehow somebody wakes me up, and i saw this bad entities beside my bed. I saw my body quickly got up and attacked this 3 entities, one woman and 2 men. I penetrated thier eyes with my fingers without any hesitations, and i saw there eyes were all black and covered with black bloods. Their bloods are black!! And i can see them running away from me, i saw their black hoods fell down on the ground while they were both screaming!

My hands were full of "dark blood"..and i asked my DEVINE FATHER for forgiveness from what i have done to this entities, as i know in reality their eyes will be blind soon. Then the golden lights came from the above and, automatically my hands raised to meet this beautiful golden light and then started to wash the blood off from my hands. Then i noticed all the black hoods on the ground started to disappeared. Then i thanked my DEVINE FATHER.

Then my DEVINE FATHER spoke..you did the right thing my child, and this is what i want you to do, to protect yourself and trust yourself including your intuition then make a decision. I LOVE

YOU my child..i cannot loss you, it's not time yet to be with me permanently. You have so much to do to where you are now. I have been watching you and them, they deserved it. I have waken you up from your sleep before they can do more damage to your eyes. Oh FATHER thank you, and why they keep hurting me and not stopping?

Well my child this is what it is..evil is always evil..they are all the destructions to all living souls, but good living souls have protections just like you. I am always here watching and protecting them too.. just remember..everytime you heal the WORLD, you are awakening up those beautiful souls in EARTH that who has been confused with their own GIFTS. MY GIFTS for them since they were born, and now you are my CHILD are awakening them through your healing meditation. You don't have to touch them or near with them. By sending your lights to the world during your healing..they are being awakened..slowly. And they are a new breed of ANGELS:) I AM BLESSING THEM NOW! Ohhh..my DEVINE FATHER that is so beautiful. ILOVEYOU...

You are awakening up the good living souls..and this is part of your DEVINE purpose and much more of that. I cannot reveal to you this time but you will know eventually my child. Some devine purposes you have done already and more to follow. So have a good rest now and drink plenty of water and rest your eyes. Yes FATHER i will.. and THANK YOU..I love you.

## CHAPTER 54

# A BAIT..IT WAS
# A SACRIFICE

JOURNAL
2ND SEPTEMBER 2022

I wake up this morning and feeling some kind of dull pain on my back and through my chest. I guess someone attacked my body last night. I called for my DEVINE FATHER and he responded to me quickly..he then said drink some water. I quickly grabbed my alkaline water bottle beside my bed and drunk it all..then papa GOD said put your right hand on your chest where your pain is. So i did..then i can see a golden light penetrating my chest through with my hand..and the pain slowly disappearing. Keep doing this papa GOD said until you completely pain free, also you can heal yourself you know. Yes, i know FATHER and thank you. I must admit i can heal myself, but this time i feel i need my DEVINE FATHER to heal me.

Then papa GOD showed me of what has happened last night with my body. I was laying on the big marble table face down..and i can see the this people or entities whatever they are, wearing black hoods and black clothings and robes. I was sorrounded by this entities.. they are all chanting..evil feeling i can sense and feel. There is a very dark energy sorrounding this individual entities. But i didn't see my body of what they have done to it. I felt like they stabbed my back and penetrated to my chest..that's what happened to me last night.

I asked papa GOD to explained this to me..why they have accessed me in a spiritual realm while i'm sleeping. What happened to my spiritual guards who supposed to keep me safe during my sleep? i cried..and slightly disappointed. Then PAPA GOD answered.. remember i have told you yesterday that i will show you more one day? YES, i remember FATHER. well, that's one of them..i made you as a "BAIT" for them..i need to show them that no matter how much harm and destructions they will do to you and your body, you can heal yourself.

You even more developing more power of energy coming from above. This is you my CHILD. The more they will harm you the more you became stronger. You acquired more power from the DEVINE energy. I did that for them to taste their own reality. So what will happen to them now? i asked. Well..they will die slowly in a physical realm..and this is how you eradicates the bad living souls in earth.

Whoahh..papa GOD that's heavy..i feel sad for them now..don't be my child. They have choosen their own paths, and there is no turning back for them unless..unless what? i asked..unless they'll change! OH ok. So there is hope for them after all.. if they want to, yes my child.."HOPE" for thier souls..and that's the only way for them to survive in a spiritual realm. Ohh..thank you DEVINE FATHER.

Well, do you still want to see of what happened to your body last night? he asked. So please..yes please FATHER. OK then closed your eyes..i closed my eyes then i went back to this entities. I was like inside the cave or something?? I did see how they stabbed my back..

then suddenly..the weapon they have used on me starting to pulled out very slowly from my back itself..and then the weapon fell down into the marble table.

I slowly got up..sat on the edge of the marble table..and i looked at my wound on my chest, i noticed it started healing and closing very slowly..and somehow i can see golden lighst in my chest while my wound is automatically healing itself..

My eyes have flames..and i can see through my eyes, all this entities are all scared..i walked towards them, and grabbed one each at a time, and lined them up in one line. 6 at a times..i don't know why 6??..then with my long silver weapon. I striked them in one go together..then another one with straight line of 6, i did the same..striking them with my one long weapon in one go..together. They all fall down on the ground and turned into ashes.

Then i noticed one entity was running away..my eyes quickly detected it on my left side, then i pulled out my dagger quickly and threw it to the entity's head, then the entity slowly turned it into ashes too..and to my amazement, all the entities body on the ground have turned into ashes.

I can see myself as a warriour wearing my leathery clothes..striking confident..no fear and almost no mercy for this evil entities. Then i started walking..walking trying to find a way out from this BIG cave..suddenly, i saw a light peeking through the Big rocks, but when i get to the end, it's all closed..solid closed..i'm trapped inside the cave!!

I peeked through the hole between the big rocks..and to my surprise i can see SKY! then without my hesitation..i used my eyes and my hands, i started to put my hands on the very heavy rocks, i can see the big rock is turning into a red flame..burning..and melting. Then i used my eyes to melt the flaming rocks into ashes. I got out from the cave, and then i saw SKY walking towards me. Then i diffused my flames from my eyes and hands.

I hugged my SKY so tightly..then i jumped into his back and then we quickly disappeared. When we're travelling..i can see rainbows along the way..birds..and beautiful colourful sky. We reached our place over the rainbow, then i saw a door amongst the grassy field..i thought this is new to me..i was hesitant to open the door but SKY gently pushed my back to open it. So i did..gently opened the door knob... then when i opened it..a BIG surprised!!! All my Ancestors are there!

MY Emperor father..my beautiful mother Empress..ohh..i'm in tears..i'm running towards to my Emperor Father, and he quickly catched me when i reached him with a big hug! Oh..welcome my daughter shine..he looks so proud of me..he has his 2 hands on my face and kissed my forehead..we missed you my Ray of sunshine..my shinae ray. My emperor father called me shinae, and my Empress mother called me shine.

Then i can see my mother coming towards me with her beautiful smile..very loving face..her face is soothing..it's like an anaesthetic i may say, it removes all my pain and misery every time i see her. She's very magical..her face..her voice..gracefulness..she looks DEVINE. Welcome back to our Kingdom my shine she said her voice is so soothing, i gave my Empress mother a HUG, and for some reason i noticed i am still wearing my leathery clothes, i haven't turned myself into a devine Empress just like my FATHER and my MOTHER.

I can't see "SKY" arround but i know he is there somewhere. Then suddenly SKY made me see him eating grass in an open field..i think he reassured me that he is OK. I can see more and more entities in the sorrounding area..the area is a field full of flowers, and some flowers i have never seen it before..i ran towards the field feeling the breeze on my face with lots of butterflies..different colours..running and running towards the open field. SKY!! where are you? i was looking for SKY..then from the distance i spotted his rainbow horn.. and then called him.

He looked at me from the distance and run towards me..ohh..i miss you "SKY" he then made his happy noise. I kissed his nose..then i saw a smile on his face. Then suddenly i wake up and realised i have forgotten to say goodbye to my EMPEROR FATHER and EMPRESS MOTHER..but i said i will come back again. It's ok my SHINE, my Empress mother said. WE are always here with you.. Always..then suddenly i see a BIG heart on the rainbow. OHHH...

CHAPTER 55

# NO TERMINATION CONTRACT

JOURNAL

3RD SEPTEMBER 2022

I reached for my DEVINE FATHER, i told him sometimes i'm confused..don't be my child..i'm here all the way with you. This is your path in a physical and spiritual realm. You have a BIG job to do, he said. A contract perhaps papa GOD? i joked.:) Well..it's not a contract he smiled..it's your mission, and every living good souls have missions in earth. All they need to do is to acknowledge and recognise it so it can be use for good.

This is how we stop the evil doing from more disasters to happen, and you my child are helping them without you even knowing..you are awakening thier souls. Every single soul you are awakening, they will do the same to the others and earned thier souls as an ANGELs in a spiritual realm..pure souls..pure Angels with wings my child.. new ANGELS. Oh..i understand now..i'm a delivery ANGEL then:) and my DEVINE FATHER LAUGHED HARD!! :)

So NO termination for contract, i said it as a joke:) but i remember my early meditation. Their was an old man who delivered a very old document to you but i didn't see if it was my contract..it was written in a different language which i didn't understand. So what was that FATHER? well..it was more a Validation of your presence and the starting of your journey with me, that was it's all about. Ohhh..ok.. now i know..thank you.

But the more you do your mission the more you acquired the devine energy of power from above..and that's another part of your mission. Ok i understand now..it's more like a reward? well..it's not just a reward..it's more like..everytime you discover your other gifts..it's awakening your gifts, he said. I just saw my DEVINE FATHER smile but didn't say anymore. Thank you FATHER..i miss our talks, i said. I'm always here my child..always.

I went outside my back Verandah..i pulled down my little trampoline and started walking and bouncing..i then looked up the sky..it's cloudy and i can't see the sun. I asked my DEVINE FATHER to open the clouds where the sun is hiding..and in a few seconds..i started feeling the breeze. I communicated with the breeze to make it stronger..i can feel it in my hands. The more i raised my hands the more breeze getting stronger..I feel like the wind is communicating back to me.

I then turned myself to the Southwest horizon, I saw the clouds still hiding the sun. I asked PAPA GOD..where are you? can i see you PLEASE FATHER? Then i noticed the clouds slowly moving away from the sun..then to my Big surprise..i can seee a smiley face on the sun..:) Papa GOD is that you? i asked..then quickly i saw an eye winked at ME!!!:) ohhhh!!!!..:) then to my surprised too, there is a cloud forming towards beside his face..and it's a face of my father EMPEROR and his hand pointing at me!!..Ohh..i could not believe it!!! I'm in tears with JOY!!!...i started dancing..dancing and dancing..i'm so happy!!! :)

Then i said..where is SKY? Please show me my SKY..i waited..waited.. no SKY..i can't see him anywhere in the clouds, but i can see only a valley of clouds in the west horizon..Then i said..PLEASE FATHER EMPEROR..PAPA GOD..i want to see SKY..PLEASE???.. I waited.. and waited..i keep shifting my eyes to a different directions of the clouds..but no SKY..Then i thought..okay..i think this is not for SKY today, but i know he is fine.

When i was about to give up..i looked up again into the west horizon.. the valley of clouds still there..but to my BIG surprise! I can see SKY!!!!!:) OMG!!He is on top of the VAlley clouds, and his front legs are up!!..i waved to him..and then the clouds started to disappear.. OHHH...Papa GOD..you always told me "NOT TO GIVE UP"! and "DO NOT LOST HOPE"..Hope is everything..Yes i will remember that, and i know NOW..that everything you showed me "DOES EXIST!. I thank you my DEVINE FATHER. OHHHH...i'm so BLESSED! :) I feel like crying..

Oh..one more thing my dear journal, i met my grandmama the mother of my EMpress mother, she gave me the rainbow wand.. but i don't know how to use it, i said to her. She said, you will know one day and i will show you. My grandmama has a very soothing personality too..i love her aura. So i asked her..what do you want me to do with this wand gradmama? She then said, it's up to you my shine..so then i asked SKY to come over, and while he's infront of me.. then suddenly without any second thoughts..my hands automatically put this rainbow wand into his forehead..and to my amazement..it's a "HORN"! That's right, SKY didn't have a horn before..so he has now.:)

That's why i was puzzled the other night when i saw him has a horn, and i was thinking he didn't have that before!...So it was my RAINBOW WAND..it was on him already..it was hidden..and it was just a matter of time for me to find out..whoahh..this is too much to comprehend at the moment. I have to take a break..oh..i'm feeling exhausted..so much downloads. I'm having a rest now..goodbye grandmama..i will catch up with you soon, and i can't wait to get to know you more and my whole Ancestors. I have feeling of closeness to my grandmama. I am going to tap in with my grand mama one day and spend more time with her in our NATURE'S KINGDOM.

# THE DAY I WAS CREATED

JOURNAL
6TH SEPTEMBER 2022

Dear journal, i have to tell you this before it will disappear from my thoughts. The other day while i was meditating, it brought me back to the place where i was so familiar about, the place the culture. I was dancing in an open space sorrounded by the grassy field..i moved my body with synchronicity with the winds and the nature's arround me. MY hands..my arms almost following the breeze. The more i moved my body the more my hands synchronised, it's the flow of energy..then suddenly without any intentions in my head i formed a striking flame in my hands, i freaked out!! i got scared! and suddenly i dropped it on the ground and stopped.

That night i dreamed again, or i will call it as a download. Papa GOD showed me a "BIG HAND", and it's Black. In that BIG HAND, there was a white round energy sitting in the hand..then slowly turning into a small foetus..then the hand at the same time slowly turned into a white bright colour then into a golden colour..the foetus still sitting in a BIG HAND, then gradually forming into a child..then the BIG HAND now holding a little CHILD.

Then MY DEVINE FATHER said..this is "YOU" my CHILD. I have created you from the palm with my ENERGY..and to my surprise i didn't feel surprise, i have felt that it was "ME"! then i saw the energy of the child being threwn and sent to EARTH. Then slowly i can see myself as a teenager, living in the TROPICAL ISLAND. I can see myself wearing tropical clothing with tropical flowers in it.

I can see an ocean in a background..coconut trees..tropical flowers.. and more trees arround. Then suddenly i can see a male person holding my head up, and directing me to look up the sky, and almost my hair is being pulled down and for me to look up. I didn't struggle.. then suddenly there was a GOLDEN colour bright light coming down from above, and starting to touch my forehead and then the golden light penetrating into my head. It's the same colour light or FLAME with golden light i have created in my hands during my meditation while i was dancing, and the shape it was more like a LIGHTNING BOLT!

I could not figured out my feelings at hat time if am i being forced or is this i have no choice? Then i think again..there was an energy came from above penetrated into my head and then disappeared. I couldn't comprehend it but it didn't feel any threatening feeling..it's just the way my head being pulled down to look up the sky.

I reached for PAPA GOD, and asked him what was just happened? What was that FATHER? i asked again. He said..it was a message or downloads that need restoring into your memory. A what?? i asked.. what was the download FATHER i asked politely. Well my child you are undoing it now..slowly..

Why do i looks like i was being forced? i asked. It looks like a formed of force but it wasn't, papa GOD said. Because you are stubburn, if this people told you to look up, you will refuse definitely!..but it wasn't a force i can assure you that now. That's why you were feeling unsure, but you didn't struggle. You know exactly you were feeling, but you were unsure. My child that is normal feelings, Papa GOD reassured me..

PAPA GOD, why the hand was dark? i mean it was BLACK when i saw it or before i was being created? Well my child, darkness is the beginning of life, this was how it started. Ohhh..now i know..thank you my DEVINE FATHER.

# CHAPTER 57

# MY BIRTHDAY!! :)

JOURNAL
8TH SEPTEMBER 2022

I must thank you my DEVINE FATHER to that beautiful glittering "BIG HEART" i saw before i opened my eyes this morning. Thank you "SKY"..yes i saw you too.. and my other ANGELS. You are all pure white..thank you again for wishing me a"HAPPY BIRTHDAY"!.. Yes i feel it. Thank you to my SPECIAL PAPA GOD and to all MY ANCESTORS including my Father Emperor and my Empress mother. I was talking to my DEVINE FATHER early afternoon and i thanked him for my beautiful day. Today..we both have a little talk.. then after that he said well, get ready you have something to attend today. Today? it's my birthday..and PAPA GOD didn't say anything.. also i am going to work soon, i said. Oh ok, he said after all it's your birthday:)

# CHAPTER 58

# THE QUEEN OF ENGLAND DIED..

JOURNAL
9TH SEPTEMBER 2022

I'm so sad this morning..the queen died. Queen Elizabeth died this morning at the age of 96 years old. This numbers keept flashing on me and on my face yesterday and few days ago. I didn't bother to focus on it or investigated what's this numbers means showing on my face..i thought just only numbers that no significant meanings, well..until now. And if i did know..what would i do with it?

It's the same things the premonition of september 11 many years ago. Who would believe me? If i have told the authority about this.. what do you think will happen? and to me? so i kept quiet and told papa GOD instead, and asked him to help those people who needed help. And the next day..it happened. I burnt all my premonitions and dreams that i have journaled. MY grandmother used to say before, to release the curse is either by writing or telling somebody about it.

And i asked her, telling somebody will cut the curse? well it depends she said..well tell me grandma i said, what do i do with my premonition? First you ask the DEVINE FATHER what do you need to do..and if have no answers well..tell it in the wind..3 times. And if it's about your family and compromises thier safety, do not tell someone as you don't want to tansfer the energy to them. Oh.. it's nice to know, i said.

Last night i have some kind of download from my DEVINE FATHER about my previous life time. This specific life time kept coming back to me..even though it's annoying but, i think papa GOD showing me that there is an important part that i have to understand in this lifetime with him, so i can't ignore it whatever the consequences maybe.

This husband of mine from my previous lifetime, showing me that there is a connection of this beautiful green lady i have encountered during my healing meditation. Just to make it clear, i have been 10 times in this life time..recycled many times i may say..and i can be anyone's wife. I am not pointing directly to anyone or specific person.

I have been a wife many times during medieval and during Dynasty time. That's another stories to come, especially to those RED HEADED families from previous time. Now, i can relate why i like so much and fascinated about red headed people. They are all absolutely beautiful people and i love thier freckles too.

The Green Lady being with a Blue face and green body, with beautiful big eyes, very motherly being. She's the one who touched my hands and finger behind the glass wall during my healing meditation of EARTH. I saw, and Papa GOD made me see the image of him, one of my husband from my previous life..exactly the same colour of this beautiful green being, and that green being is his mother. I saw his hand peeling off the layer of his skin..and it looks like the same colour of the lady's green motherly being. She's so soothing and so motherly, and she touched my heart spiritually. She's very kind and very serene and everytime i think of her, i feel calmed.

# CHAPTER 59

# THE BLACK CANVAS OF MY LIFE

JOURNAL

14TH SEPTEMBER 2022

The white blank canvas that MY DEVINE FATHER was given to me is just a beginning of my life. New chapter of what's ahead and all it's matter he said. The other night he tapped my head, and i know he's reminding me about the journey..but didn't force me that night, instead he let me sleep and when i wake up in the morning my whole body, it feels like being rejuvinated again.

I spoke to MY DEVINE FATHER lately in the same place again, up there in his favourite spot, his long verandah looking out the clouds. He asked me lovingly to join him..i approached him as a dignified woman. I was thinking..Please don't turn me into a child this moment as i want to have a good conversation with you FATHER.

I think he heard my thoughts and he greeted me with open arms. And he hugged me..and while i was with him, our connections as a FATHER and CHILD embodied in ONENESS again. I can feel the beautiful energy and amazing Aura between us. Sooo healing.. comforting..and then he kissed my forehead lovingly and said, Shhh..

don't talk yet my child..so i kept still..and i noticed he still holding me..my whole body.

I can feel my DEAR FATHER is healing me inside, i can feel his energy coming out from my body. lifting out all my bad emotions i am feeling inside me.. it's incredible feeling. I feel the loving and comforting emotions and reassuring me that everything is going to be alright..for me. THANK YOU MY DEVINE FATHER, i said with my deepest RESPECT.

Then i noticed, he slowly releasing his arms from me..but for myself, i feel like i didn't want to let go..then i slowly opened my eyes and looked at him.. his eyes are so calming..then i can see some beautiful aura of energy penetrating into my eyes. Some kind of healing..oh.. that's why my eyes are feeling better lately. Thank you FATHER, i said.

Then I was going to say something about of what has happened during my birthday..going to apologise to him..but he said, it's not important now my child. You manifested it in the spiritual realm, as you know it is impossible in reality or physical realm to make it happen. Your thoughts is very POWERFUL be mindful about that, papa GOD said. Yes i will FATHER, and i know now i can control it.

PAPA GOD, when THE QUEEN ELIZBETH of ENGLAND died, i was very upset..and it was my birthday and the cathedral that she had her mass service is the "GILES". Is there any connections? i asked curiously. Ok he said, listen very carefully..the 8th of september is your birthday and the death of the QUEEN. It means the reminder of your life lineage..your bloodline.

It's the beginning of your new journey, the Queen did reminded you this too spiritually before she died, papa GOD said. Oh yes..i thought about that..because few days before she died, her face keeps appearing and flashing infront of me including the numbers of 9 and 6 everytime i closed my eyes. I ignored it because i thought it wasn't important.

The name "GILES" is my father surname in this lifetime, is there any connections? i asked. Yes! my child, the "GILES" surname is a Saint and you have a blood came from the the saint GILES. Saint GILES of humility..Protections of people who have depressions, experiencing poverty, and orphans..little children and people who need shelters and including animals. This Saint rescued and was a Protector of living souls. Ohh ok..now i understands why i have so much love to poor people..to animals and so on...that's explains it.

As who you are now..and what you are doing in the reality is connected to your past life, and you are bringing it back together again in this life time, to LOVE..to CARE..and especially to HEAL. This is the message and the words i have given you to spread when we first meet..remember? papa GOD said. Oh yes..i do really remember that, now the puzzles are connecting for me..thank you FATHER.

Yes my child, your blood line is very important for you to acknowledge.. and you have been protected ever since.

CHAPTER 60

# 11TH DIMENSION TRAVELS

JOURNAL
15TH SEPTEMBER 2022

Papa God i Have travelled again last night as you know..yes my child, that was only a glimpsed, as i know that your body cannot take too much sometimes, papa GOD said. last night i saw "SKY" travelling in the sky while i was coming home from work. For somehow he wants me to ride on his back..i think i was in the middle of meditating trance again while in the car. (My husband is driving the car)

While our car is moving, "SKY" was running at the same speed with our car. He was running..almost looking at me at the same time.. running up there in the sky, but then i was puzzled, it looks like he just so close to me and the car..i didn't know what to think about that time...

He was showing me a kind of glass bridge path connecting to my front car while it was running..the bridge was colour brown but shinny. It was 3 paths..and i have to choose for the right path. I then automatically choosen the middle path. Then quickly, i saw myself running to the bridge and hopped on into SKY's back, and then we went away..and then travelled to a different areas of the GALAXY.

While riding on his back..amazingly i am feeling the connections again between us, out there in the open space and through different galaxies. We went passed through so many stars and clouds with striking gold colours and black..the clouds were blending together with this two colours. It's magnificent looking, there was no clouds while we travelling..but there was so many stars..some of them are so bright..golden bright.

I have noticed i am wearing my ANGEL Warriour clothing..it's leathery strings wrapped arround my body..my hair is braided..i have a mask to protect my eyes while travelling through different galaxy. I am not feeling scared this time, as i have "SKY" with me. "SKY" glanced at me when i acknowledge him. It's a BEAUTIFUL feelings being out here..with SKY. It's an outlet from my reality world..my dream..my meditation..being connected to unknown out there...IT'S MY FREEDOM! A freedom from reality chaos, then i heard a voice from above, THAT's my GIRL! papa GOD said:) I love to hear my FATHER's voice..it's comforting.

SKY and Myself kept going..i can feel SKY's body majestically connected with me..he looks so happy..we are both happy. :) Then suddenly, we are about to approached the area and i can see it from the distance..we lowered down slowly..then touched down in the BIG BRIDGE. The very long Bridge is made of thick glass, and with black and golden colour with small long strikey forming in the middle of the glass..it looks like a pattern. This bridge somehow there is some Majestic and Authoritative feelings of some kind!!

We landed safely and nicely on this glass bridge..long and wide bridge. I looked behind me then i noticed i have some companies waiting for me..my ANGELS!!! :) I was infront of them and still riding on SKY's back..i can see myself as an ANGEL leading WARRIOUR. ARCH ANGEL MICHAEL and ANGEL METATRON behind me riding on thier horses and the other angel called "SAM".

Behind him is a long line of ANGELS..they are all pure white and all of them riding on thier own horses, and they are all white too. Their Wings are out too, and all of them are looking majestic. Then suddenly, MY DEVINE FATHER made me saw his face..i can see in his face that he is so proud of me, he made me see the BIG HEART too:)

So, we are all facing the GALAXY BRIDGE..it's so majestic and tentalising..The DOOR GATE is MASSIVE..and i was thinking where are we? Then i heard the 11th Dimension!! OMG!! i reached the 11th DIMENSION? This is 11th dimension?? whoah..it's so majestic!! and looks so POWERFUL..Mysterious. I can feel the power of Authority! i can feel it in every parts of bones!

OPEN UP!!! I made a strong and BIG command infront of the massive door. That words just came out from my mouth automatically as i felt that i have done this before..so Authoritively command. Then the BIG door opened slowly..and then to my amazement!! I was facing a some kind of a never ending SPACE!..it's a GALAXY and beyond of my imagination!! IT's so open..i can see so many stars out there.. and then to my amazement again.. was greeted with this beautiful BEING..the Green lady that i have met before during my meditation and when i was healing the EARTH.

She's the one who touched my fingers through the glass wall.. whoahh..this is very interesting..don't be she said..and don't think too much. The beautiful green tall lady telepathecally reassured me in my head. You have been here before..unconciously..or during out of your consciousness. The beautiful motherly being is so devinely looking..she welcomed me and said it in my head..at last you reached my KINGDOM! WELCOME again she said. I bowed to her very respectfully, and i saw and felt the acknowledgement from her.

She extended her right arm towards me, and i did the same automatically to her with my right arm too. We touched our hands together..and i felt the deeper connections, as i breathed..her energy went through me..very soothing and healing, and a feeling of AUTHORITY, she made me feel this way and throughout my body. Then suddenly i wake up very thirsty, i grabbed my water bottle beside my bed and drank most of the water. I don't really know how i did the shifting from my reality to spirituality. It's a mind blowing to think sometimes. Anyway, I got up and started doing my student's reports. while doing it..i can feel somebody stroking my left head so gently. I closed my eyes, then i saw "SAM" the ANGEl. HE then informed me straight away that one angel is not looking good..then i said it's a hitch hiker. I can see the colour of an ANGEL is changing into a silhouette dark and gray colour..and it is melting slowly..i can see another 2 falling down thier horses..and eventually turned into ashes.

I reached for my DEVINE FATHER, he then told me that they breached the LAW of TRAVEL..they didn't make it, and their souls are being detained in the Purgatory..THE DARK BRIDGE. YES, i have seen the dark BRIDGE..my DEVINE FATHER showed it to me and travelled there during my meditation previously.

My DEVINE FATHER..i am so sorry i have to cut this session as i am feeling extremely tired now..so much downloads. Ok my CHILD, rest and close your eyes now..don't think..just rest your mind.

# CHAPTER 61

# THE QUEEN ELIZABETH FUNERAL

JOURNAL
19TH SEPTEMBER 2022

I have been resting lately, sometimes i feel like it's not enough time..i slept in during the weekend and i think my body needed it. PApa God shifted some of my writings into a different place. it's better this way he said. I asked my DEVINE FATHER if he wants me to publish my book.. and he said NO.. not yet. So i guess no..but i asked why? as usual i'm curious. Well my child this is not a story..this is something that you are finding now about yourself..a spiritual mystery that it's only belongs to you..and doesn't belong to anyone or anybody.

This is you..your true devine mission..people out there are not going to understand it..maybe some..but they are not ready yet to fully comprehend of what's going on especially with you.. Some people might exploits your thinking..your personal space..it might change your understanding about the way who you are now..and your feelings of being different from anybody else out there. I have waited this for long time my child, this is your time to understand your purpose in spirituality. We have work to do..you have work to do. I can see my DEVINE FATHER is serious.

The other day you showed me a square form of a table and it's made of marble..and i was kind of a middle of it. What was that FATHER? what did it means? i asked curiously and seriously...Well my child, it was s sign of "PROTECTION" for you. Those 4 angles sides are your protections. Somebody are protecting you in every corner of your sides.

Then i saw the funeral of the Queen the next day, and the squares that you have shown me was exactly the same to where her coffin was that have 4 squares and every squares have someone guarding. What does it means FATHER? It means a validation that you are devinely protected validated it by the QUEEN. I also showed this to you because sometimes you still having doubts of yourself. Oh ok thank you FATHER, i understand now.

PApa GOD, the other night i had a dream about a person..he was really after me. From my dream i can see myself infront of him as an ANGEL Warriour. My pose was very brave facing with him. Then i saw his body started to lowered down..and by the looks of him from where i was standing..he was about to attack me. I was standing still waiting for him to get closer..he then hit me but missed several times..somehow he couldn't reached my body or cannot get closed to me. He got so frustrated and got very angry! I can feel his anger that he really wants to eliminate me.

Then he suddenly changed into a very dark and evil looking being, and i can see black shadow embodied him. Then when i retaliated to him, i stopped..i couldn't as i saw in his eyes the vulnerablity in his soul i cannot hurt anybody like that.

But then he saw that potential of me that i cannot hurt him..at that moment he attacked me and pinned me on the wall!!..but i got away and retaliated to him back many times. Then finally he was going to get away..running..then i turned to him and to my surprised, my hands automatically sent an amazing force to him then captured in a kind of a bubble. A white force energy detained him, then i eliminated him with my whip.

Papa GOD forgive me if i did that..i eliminated this person with no mercy..this is not me in reality.i then heard papa GOD..that was a battle of an evil person which is in reality it will not stop until he hurts you and wants to eliminate you. You got to remember, trust your intuition, and which you did! You made the right decision..don't be sorry, you must remember, you are different in a spiritual realm, and you did what's right for him. And you know it by now of what's going to happen to him in reality world..slowly..and it's up to you to pray for his soul..you are the only HOPE.

PAPA GOD, i don't like it..i don't like hurting people, it's not me..i cried. My child, listen to me and listen up very carefully..my DEVINE FATHER said it sternly. I can see his face very close to my face, and lifting my face up with his hands gently. This is part of your mission my child..to eliminate the bad souls.

The good souls that you have helped and using thier gifts in a physical and spiritual way will earn thier wings..a new ANGELS for you to deliver to Arch Angel Gabriel. You must remember, in reality you have a different mission..but in spirituality you have a very difficult tasks and you cannot change that. That's your destiny! You are made for this mission in a spiritual world. Ohh...FATHER..(i am crying)...

PApa GOD, sometimes i am wondering..is this real? but then when i looked up to heaven and the clouds up there..i feel home..even just to see the clouds..i feel home and starting to miss you FATHER. OH my child come here..i can see myself as a child again with my DEVINE FATHER. We both sitting in his big verandah up there. I can see him sitting in his big marble chair while me sitting on his right lap. WE both looking towards the clouds, then a cat appeared infront of me..a silvery and white orangey colour cat.

I guess that's for me to play i thought to myself..papa GOD knows that i am missing my cat. I didn't touch the cat..i'm just looking at him..i didn't want to let go my DEVINE FATHER. I am feeling a such an amazing comfort arround his body..the warmth..the security and the great protection and reassurance. He then hugged my tiny little body, put me on his shoulder gently and then i slowly falling asleep..he then whispered to me..you just need to rest..rest my child.. rest..so hypnotic sound..then i fall asleep.

Oh that's why i have been sleeping so much last weekend..i slept more than 8 hours and that's very unusual for me, but then again i could sleep whole day if i want too. During my spiritual travel, i have so much energy, but when i came back to reality my energy is just almost gone..i feel exhausted..thirsty..and i just want to sleep..and sleep..and i can drink 2 litres of my water whole day.

# CHAPTER 62

# THE GREEN LITTLE BEING

JOURNAL
26TH SEPTEMBER 2022

Last night during my meditation, Papa God was showing this kingdom to me about this beautiful green lady beyond the galaxy with so many stars..golden stars. I can see myself as a little girl again playing with this little boy green being in an open space looking at the galaxies with so many twinkling stars out there..we were both sitting on the glass floor bare footed.

I couldn't see anything or anybody else except it was only me and this little green being. We both very young and so happy playing together and with each other. Mostly we both sitting on the very thick glass floor..everything is glass but it's colour black and golden colour with strikey pattern shapes on the floor..it's just like a lightning bolt pattern. The Kingdom has no walls..it's an open space towards out the galaxy.

The galaxy is very black and some very dark blue or just like Royal blue colour..and with so many stars..big and small..but they are all twinkling with golden colours. The little green being i was playing with wasn't talking but somehow we both understand each other through telepathically..he looks happy everytime he glances at me and gave me a smile. I have my music box with me, and we both playing with it.

The beautiful green lady just watching us from a slight distance, and she looks very happy watching us together playing. I didn't pay any attention much of this little boy's face..but it's imprinted into my mind, my thoughts, my head and my memory. It didn't matter to me because i was just happy to have somebody to play with, and i felt he is the same with me.

Then suddenly PAPA God appeared infront of us..he said come along now my child, he said..time is up! Then the green lady nodded to Papa GOd as she agreed to him. I didn't want to go with papa GOD yet, i just want to keep playing but my FATHER insisted for me to go home. Then later on i asked my FATHER, why i can't stay longer playing with him? My FATHER said..your time is restricted while you up there, your body would not take it. You got to remember you are in a different dimensions. It's dangerous for your body to stay longer. Oh ok now i understand.

One more question FATHER..did i go back there? Yes my child in a regular basis, that's why there KINGDOM is familiar to you. And the green boy being? i asked. WEll..you grew up with him here in the high dimension in a spiritual realm. Oh FATHER this is so much download and most of all interesting, but confusing. You and him have been travelling through different galaxies together before you have been manifested in reality..both of you! Oh my GOD..papa GOD is this real? Would i lie to you my child? NO! of course not. I'm just don't know what to say, that's all. Hmm..that's explains everything.

Anyway, the green little boy kept playing..i noticed he has something in his hands that he's playing with and holding..Papa GOD was holding my hand..i said goodbye to him and waving..he just looked at me but didn't wave..but he gave me a smile..a sort of a cheeky smile. I then saw the green lady waved at me..with her beautiful big eyes.. and very majestic. I then suddenly wake up very thirsty and drank my bottle of water beside my bed.

# CHAPTER 63

# SOUL CONNECTION

JOURNAL
27TH SEPTEMBER 2022

last night it was an interesting night..while i was asleep someone came and picked me up from above. First, He lowered his right hand to me..and then without any hesitation i reached this soul's hand. Then he pulled me up..and we both went up higher to the never ending galaxy beyond the stars. We travelled both hands in hands.. then we eventually stopped. We both sitting and resting amongst the galaxy, on clouds and watching the stars. Amazingly, we didn't have to talk verbally..somehow we understand each other through our mind.

While we were both resting..i saw SKY went passed us..i called him but he didn't want to come near us. I think, and obviously he didn't want me to see with someone or with somebody else company. Ohh.. i miss you SKY..never mind we will be travelling again together.. and soon. This lovely soul was showing me the beautiful galaxy and stars..i said to him in his head, i have been here and travelled with SKY many times.

The beautiful soul just squeezed my hands and would not let go. I can feel the entire energy from this beautiful soul. He looks happy and content, and i am so glad to see this soul feeling this way, and I hope i am healing this soul.

I didn't want to talk to my FATHER at the moment..as we both travelling to our favourite spot with my companion, here in the galaxy amongst the stars. And to my curiousity, this is the first time i have travelled with another soul into the galaxy..hmmm..very interesting..i am just letting it happened and to go with the flow. After all it's not hurting me or anyone. I will reach for my DEVINE FATHER later..i'm little nervous now..i am wondering what he is going to say to me..:( I peeked the heaven door..it's slightly open and has a light. My DEVINE FATHER always leaves the lights on for me, and i know he is always waiting for me to knock.:) instead i said good night PAPA GOD. ILOVE YOU! Then i saw his beautiful smile on his face. :)

CHAPTER 64

# THE WHITE SWORD

JOURNAL
28TH SEPTEMBER 2022

I just wake feeling very thirsty, i drank my whole water in the bottle beside my bed. I traveled last night again, i saw myself standing on my own just infront of the HUGE DOOR by myself in an open GALAXY..the green lady's KINGDOM. Then i said " OPEN UP"!!! Then the huge door slowly opened and i was greeted by the beautiful green lady being..the MAJESTY. She extended her arms to me..we didn't touched or hug..instead it's the ENERGY i have felt from her. A welcoming and hugging kind of ENERGY, we communicates through our thoughts.

I saw myself standing beside the majestic green lady and we both looking out towards the galaxy. She showed and pointed out to me where i am supposed to go. First i saw her covering the entire front of where we both standing with very crystal clear but silhouette energy. I's a kind of protection i realised. Then she pointed out the directions towards the galaxy amongst the stars..then suddenly i heard a word "ORION"..that's where i am supposed to go.

The word ORION is not familiar to me..she even enlarged the word "ORION" as i have doubts. The green lady and myself didn't verbally talk..instead we used our minds to communicate. I can see myself as a warriour lady still wearing this leathery clothing, and some kind of leathery strings wrapped arround my body. My hair is braided.. my poise is stoic and brave, i'm still wearing the Eagle mask. SKY is beside me and looks happy and content. I miss my SKY.

I turned arround and i can see my Angels behind me, 4 of them. Starting from my ARCH ANGEL MICHAEL on his horse, and ARCH ANGEL METATRON on his BLUE horse and i noticed he is wearing all royal blue colour. Then ARCH ANGEL GABRIEL wearing in a full white gear..and ARCH ANGEL URIEL? wow...I have never meet him before. Then the green ANGEL wearing green clothes, and before i could ask a question who's Angel he is..he made me feel a strong knowing who he is..but then he said..ARCH ANGEL RAFAEL. WOW!! i have my whole Angels here with me.

Then i extended looking towards far behind..i can see "SAM" the leading ANGEL facing towards the ARMY of ANGELS..and i noticed they are all wearing pure white and riding on thier horses. The line they were standing and lined up has a curved, like an S..by the looks of it, this is how the bridge formed. The bridge is made of thick glass and colour black, with a slight golden colour lightning striking formed. It's a long line of ANGELS towards the end of the GATE.

Then slowly..papa GOD silhouette face appeared from above, and then i made a LOVING and respectful recognition gesture to him. I automatically kneeled down touching the ground with my right knee.. and bowed respectfully to my DEVINE FATHER. My child, this is your BATTLE he said with a loving and stern voice..and this is your WEAPON. I looked up, and i see my DEVINE FATHER holding a "WHITE SWORD", almost Angelic looking sword holding in his hands infront of me. I stood up and then my DEVINE FATHER handed in to me very gently. I looked at the sword very carefully..it's Pure White, and i cannot see anything written on it.

I thanked my DEVINE FATHER, he then put his right hand on my head by not touching it..i then feel an amazing my energy..almost devine energy went through my head and my entire body. My body felt so different, lighter and feeling brave. Then my DEVINE FATHER gave me an instrustions..this is your weapon to use with specific reason..you will know when to use it.

You can use the other weapons too he said, i looked for my other weapons arround my body..they are not here with me..but before i could say something..papa GOD said use tour "mental energy", your mental energy is powerful..during your battle any weapons that you would think to use instantly will be in your hands straightaway. But only the weapons you can use are the ones i have given to you. No weapons to use if wasn't from me. OK FATHER i understand. THANK YOU.

Then i said, i want to change my battle gear FATHER..ok he said. choose what you want my child. I tried every gear i have used before, but no one of them doesn't feels right for these journey. I can't make a decision FATHER, can you please choose it for me? Then papa God slowly changed my gear into a golden colour battle gear outfit, everything is golden colour even my braided hair and my boots. Then papa GoD changed my mask but this is white colour and the side trimming has golden colour.

To my surprise..i can see through anything in it..it's like an Xray vision..this is also to protect you during the astral travel papa GOD said, and then lovingly placed the mask on me. In that instant, i hopped on SkY's back, i thanked my FATHER..and he said, remember.. use your "MENTAL ENERGY" this time. Yes FATHER i will remember that. And do the sign of the CROSS..always..he said that in a very slow tone..just like a slow motion voice, but i heard it clearly.

I'm always here, and remember stay where the "SILHOUETTE PATH"..because that's the only path is going to that place where you are heading. Yes my DEVINE FATHER, i will. So now i'm facing the galaxy where the silhoutte path is showing..i can see so many stars everywhere so golden and with my battle gear is also golden colour..i blend into the galaxies amongst the stars while travelling. How clever my DEVINE FATHER is :) Then i saw his face smiling at me. I love you FATHER!!! i shouted at him...and he waved at me.

Then i am facing the galaxy towards and beyond..and i said a "BIG" THANK YOU to the MAJESTY green beautiful lady. Oh now i know now the connection of this lovely green lady and her KINGDOM. Her KINGDOM is the "PASSAGE" to the unknown..i heard the "PASSAGE". Wow...that's a validation. Thank you so much. The Beautiful Motherly Being MAJESTY waved at me and i recieved another energy coming from her..so beautiful..so MAJESTIC..loving but BRAVE.

# CHAPTER 65

# THE EARTH IS BLACK

JOURNAL
1ST OCTOBER 2022

I have been consulting PAPA GOD lately, we talked as a FATHER and DAUGHTER again. I love the connection between us when we are together, and sometimes didn't want to wake up from my dream or meditation. I feel the comfort being with him. I spoke to my FATHER about the preparation of my next battle, and he said to have a good rest as i needed it and reminded me my prayers.

Then he asked me to put everything down what ever i'm doing as he has something to show me..very important. I asked him first before we go..in my head i asked him if i am going to die with this battle? he said NO! you are not going to die in this battle..you have more to accomplish before you join me permanently up there. Beside..you are well protected.

Now shall we? he said and take my hand, and i just went with my DEVINE FATHER..he took me up higher..then suddenly we stopped. While up there we both in some kind in "Halt", he asked me to look down, and asked..what do you see my child? To my surprised.. IT's BLACK!!!! i'm horrofied! THE EARTH IS BLACK!!! OH MY

GOD!!!Yes my child..the earth is black. Disasters and disaster are causing it..people need to come to there senses before it's too late.

Ohh FATHER people knew this, but they don't stop..people are destroying our mother earth..it's so sad...i cried. What would you like me to do FATHER? Your Job is to awaken those people who have gifts from above during your meditation. The people who has awaken already needed to use their gifts to awaken others and use thier gifts for good and to vibrate to a HIGHER dimension. The higher we Vibrate..the stronger our GIFTS will become. THAT's my DEVINE FATHER's DEVINELY WORDS.

FATHER, there are so many people have already been awaken..and i wish through their intuitive feelings will use thier gifts to raise up more vibrations with LOVE and HOPE for Humanity. Remember the 3 words i have given it to you to spread? he said. Yes FATHER i would not forget..it's LOVE..CARE..HEAL. If the world have these in existence..the problems will be solved, he said. I will do my very best DEVINE FATHER to TELL THE WORLD of your MESSAGE by this BOOK.

# CHAPTER 66

# "ORION" AND ANGELS IN THE DUNGEONS

JOURNAL
4TH OCTOBER 2022

Last night, i decided to do some inner work for myself spiritually, i closed my eyes and looked deeper of what's going on with myself. Well..what do i know..i have been wrapped up arround with BLACK ENERGIES..my whole body..especially my knee. Hmm..how did it happened? I will ask my DEVINE FATHER later. this time i have to deal it with myself. I am feeling very angry at the moment and slowly building up..i didn't know where this anger coming from..i'm in RAGED!!! I am taking "BACK MY POWER!!! Then my body quickly transformed into a "PHOENIX" wrapped up with black energies and i can see my self i'm inside of it.

I'm in RAGED!!! and my body started "RISING" and the more i am rising higher the more black energies getting undone, and i am so ANGRY!! my body is in FLAME!! Flaming with fire energy!! and then the FIRE starting to undone the black energy wrapped arround my body! They're all melting while my body was in flames and my eyes are on fire and every black entities infront of me didn't have a chance..i eliminated them instantly and turned them into ashes.

My body was raging!! i was soo Angry!! The more i got so angry.. the more flames of fire was being created in my body. All entities are burnt and turned them into ashes! then when i noticed no more entities arround me..my flames inside me and out my body subsided and very slowly. Then i saw "SKY"..i quickly hopped into his back.. then i saw all my ANGELS slowly appearing infront of me. I felt this is the time to go, i gave a signal "GO" to all my ANGELS.

This is the time i said to myself, i'm ready for the BATTLE!! my raged still on me!!..I feel NO FEAR this time. I am ready to eliminate anyone or anybody who comes to my WAY!!! I can see I'm ready with SKY on his back, and all my ANGELS. Then we head on..and started travelling beyond the galaxy. Stay in a "SILHOUETTE PATH"..i heard papa GOD voice..ONLY one path you must stay as my FATHER INSTRUCTIONS!!!

Yes!! i will FATHER, i said. while travelling, i can see my body is well connected with SKY. To my surprised, my battle gear have changed into the leathery type. The same gear i was wearing before, alternately, i checked my Angels behind me, all of us travelling in the same phase. I noticed my eyes behind the mask is still flaming and have kind of XRAY vision. This time i am more confident and not feeling any MERCY in my bones. I am ready whatever what's ahead of me.

While travelling towards the unknown..i can see 3 different paths like a tree branches with brown and black colours, but i still can see the silhouette path ahead. Somehow, i was feeling tempted as part of my curiousity if i could check the other path..but i strongly not to do it..i wouldn't dare disobeying my FATHER. wheww..i heard almost a mumbling word very faintly from my FATHER.

Then finally after that never ending travel..i can see a HUGE STONE MOUNTAIN from the distance and the sorrounding galaxy is so black with so many glittering stars..so many of them almost like it's scattered everywhere, we are still in the silhouette path travelling. I can see through my mask where i am going..i can see anything through the galaxy.

Then slowly we reached the destination..we stopped infront of this Huge Mountain Rock, looking even more bigger when we are close. I can see black animals entities on the big rocks and boulders..looks like they are guarding something.. I then slowly jumped out from SKY'S back and stood up infront of the Big ROCK Mountain. There is no DOOR..it's all opened..i started walking towards the opening area..Then suddenly, a black animal entity attacked me, but missed my face and my right arm. I didn't expect that!

Then another one coming..the eyes are Red and Scary..i could not figure out what kind of animals are they. It looks like half wolf and half Bore (PIG)!! They both approaching me from side to side.. then automatically my whip came out of me and used it. My whip is flaming..and every hit at them, their bodies were cut in halves and then turned into ashes.

The more i eliminated them the more it's coming. My ANGELS just watching me, not coming to rescue me. I can read ARCH ANGEL MICHAEl thoughts..you can do this..you don't need our intervention at his moment..you can do it. This is your battle, because this are your entities that has been haunting you. You are the only one who can eliminate them.

So the more i eliminated them and the more entities are coming, so i tried to go higher. I looks like a phoenix just came out from the ashes..my body has flames and my whip have the same effect every time i hit the entities, then they all turned into ashes. I was viciously eliminating them one at a time.

Then suddenly, i saw this huge BLACK creature near the stone wall sitting and towering me and all of us. He greeted me with sarcasm and with distorted voice as it's coming from beyond the GRAVE..it sounds scary hearing it.

The "DAUGHTER OF THE CREATOR" is here!!! He shouted as if he wants to tell or make somebody aware. Then i saw another black entities and more coming to attack me. I did the same, starting to eliminated them with all my weapons one at a time, and everytime i think of any weapons no matter how slow or quick my mind the weapons were in my boths hands and ready to use, which i did..no MERCY! That's in my head imprinted.

Once i eliminated them..i looked arround the sorrounding area, then when i looked down where i was standing, here it was down the lower CAVE, to my surprised..i can see so many injured ANGELS!!! and their Wings have been injured and looks like they are all bleeding!! I can see on their faces that they have been terrified and crying. I can see them looking up where i was standing..and for some reason they were glad to see me.

I asked some Angels to get them out from the dungeons, then ARCH ANGEL RAPHAEL assisted them to heal thier injuries. I can see blood from there wings, and i am puzzled. I questione myself..is this possible eventhough they are not in a reality or physical world? Then i heard my DEVINE FATHER's voice up there..Yes my child it is possible, because the Angels have been captured before they could be purified. Oh..i see, thank you FATHER. Now i know why ARCH ANGEL RAPHAEL is here with me..certainly you like to surprise me.:) Yes my child, i like it when i don't tell you ahead, because you know why? why? FATHER? because you like adventures and that's where you become focused..the unknown..and papa GOD just laughing.

Ok, back to my battle..after the ANGELS assisted the injured ANGELS..i saw them were on the horses with the other ANGELS. Then ARCH ANGEL GABRIEL took them to her CITY, the CITY OF ANGELS for recuperations. I thanked the ANGELS and ARCH ANGEL GABRIEL for coming with me.

Then i continued exploring the same area..i looked up to the cave and this mountain of solid rock..it's towering me..i'm exploring the place without SKY and the ANGELS. I then came to the very end of the place inside the BIG CAVE..and then suddenly, i can see a really BIG SWORD on the right side corner of the cave from short distance. I walked slowly towards the sword..i have noticed there is a big and thick looking white or dirty white cloth drapping arround the neck of the sword..when i got closer..the cloth looks ancient..something about this cloth that looks very old, and that's what i'm feeling it at that moment.

The sword is standing on the wall of the stone cave..I went closer to the sword and almost hypnotically pulling myself towards it. Then curiously i looked at the writings on it..it's Ancient..and have a different writings, and i could not understand the writings as it looks different. There isn't no writings of any alphabets..although i can remember some of the writings.

I reached to my DEVINE FATHER..but he said, my child..this is not for you to read and understand. oh..Ok then i said..thank you

FATHER. So i removed the cloth drapping from the sword, and took the sword out from the rock half way burried without any hesitation. I didn't even know why i removed the sword from the rock without any struggles.

Then suddenly, i am facing the ANCIENT looking man..with a beard..has red hair and wearing some kind of medieval time clothing or garments. A BIG man..but doesn't look scary to me..but somehow trying to intimidate me. He then spoke and told me..you have been sent here..Yes indeed! i said it straightaway! Your FATHER sent you here to get me. NO! i answered. There is some instructions from my FATHER to get from you. I am here to what i need to claim!

What are you claiming from me? he asked. ANGELS! MY ANGELS! I responded to him automatically.( I thought to myself..hang on..i didn't even know i'm here to claim my ANGELS) NO!!!..They are all mine!! he yelled at me like a THUNDER! Then i saw so many more ANGELS in a different dungeons..and they are all crying and terrified.

I demand you to release them! NO!! yelling at me back..i was just standing there so bravely with my whip in my hand and with a flame. I can see him little bit worried and scared. Then he showed me an image of myself as a 10 or 11 years old running and playing on the field with lots of flowers and chasing the butterflies. I looked like a little princess wearing my little tiara crown. Then it hit me..my FATHER's KINGDOM..are they're in danger? i was worried..then i heard the voice of my EMPEROR FATHER ARTHERU..we are alright and safe..and i can see them from the distance watching me. I can see the whole KINGDOM is sorrounded by the clear energy protection..it's like a bubble.

The BIG man called "ORION" told me..this ANGELS are my company in my KINGDOM and you can be mine too as a child..an innocent child as an exchanged for this ANGELS. NO!! you cannot have me or any of this Angels..I demand you to release them!! Then suddenly the BIG man quickly grabbed me, but missed. I stood infront of him, then i went up to the top..then used all my weapons alternately..and then the last hit was the ANCIENT SWORD penetrated into his chest with the sign of the cross and went face down to the ground and with my long SILVERY weapon struck on his back.

I felt sad..i just eliminated this poor Big man..i was in tears...:( then the other ANGELS have been released from the dungeons and sent to the WHITE CITY. Then i woke up suddenly..it was 12 midnight the exact time. I don't know if there is any significant about this hours or numbers.

I woke up very thirsty and exhausted..i drank most of my water beside my bed. Then i got up, went to the bathroom and looked at myself in the mirror..as for a moment i couldn't recognised myself for a second..and still i can see myself as a Warriour ANGEL that has been in the battle. Then to my surprised..my face slowly changed into a very white and ghostly colour..a pure white colour..then when i blinked..ohh..it's me..:)

# CHAPTER 67

# FEEL THE RHYTHMS

JOURNAL

5TH OCTOBER 2022

I can feel the pressure again in the reality world..the disappointments.. the cruelty from people..my hurt emotions and vulnerability. Sometimes it's just easy to connect to spirituality rather than in a physical world which is so many tricky people and other circumstances. I feel like this reality world is not for me to be as normal..or to be loved.

I will see my DEVINE FATHER later..i will talk to him again this time and everything will be about HIM and ME. I just finished my big job in a spiritual world..i don't know what's next for me to face, or what kind of journey i will be facing. I am sad and i feel like crying of what has happened..but i tried not to..i have to hold it until i get home.

Social media is just an extortions..they are cruel and so evil, and it's a perfect way to take people's vulnerablities and turned it into a circus. I value myself as who i am..and that kind of ownership for myself i cannot give away to anybody..my honesty and my integrity..at least to some people out there such evil..leave some for my self esteem. You do like destroying people..especially innocent and vulnerable people..

your doing is just pure evil. Your souls will be in HELL! You have no idea what hell is..i know..i have seen it!

Simple things are my FORTE..little things are makes me happy. Grandiose things, i don't even think that will satisfies my curiousity in this life time. I rather be out there and be FREE!..see the ocean.. touch the water..feel the nature, and be with them. I can't wait to see my Ancestral Family again..up there..I will join them when time comes, and when my DEVINE FATHER makes that decision one day. I feel and it seems like being in the reality world it's not my Destiny.

I'm home now..and just came out from the shower. I cried in the shower and that's the only place i could hide my pain, tears, sadness and my emotions. My back is hurting too..i think my invisible wings has been injured too as i can feel the sharp pain like cuts above to the middle upper shoulders.

Papa GOD can i talk to you please? I'm in bed at the moment calling to my DEVINE FATHER. I'm here..i'm listening he said..he is trying to makes me listen to this music..very soothing..and listen to the rain.. concentrate my child..close your eyes and listen to the rhythms... I put my head on the pillows and started to listen to the sounds of the rain trickling down the roof..very softly, and the sounds of the birds outside. Then slowly i can feel the rhythms..everything arround me.. then i am started feeling better..slowly.

Then my DEVINE FATHER spoke..my child your reality is all about rhythms..synchroinisity..synchronising what's arround you.. and you needed to feel that. If it doesn't synchronises, you are not listening to your own rhythms of life. It means you are ignoring something that decieving your thoughts, judgement and feelings inside of you.

When you are listening to this synchronisity..i always stepped in. Why? i asked..because i wanted to show you some of the glimpse of the reality you are encountering so you will be able to make your own judgement. Ohh FATHER..what purpose is this in my life? i cried... and cried.. Then i can see papa GOD just holding my head while i'm crying..he just let me cry..and cry..while he is gently touchimg my head..i can feel he is getting affected with my emotions too. Then suddenly i saw my self in the arms of my mother EMPRESS GLYDICA..ohh mother..i want to come home..i want to come home please!!!I'm crying infront and the arms of my mother. My mother just hugging me while i'm crying..

I am with my ANcestors KINGDOM..yes i'm home again with my Ancestral family..I can see myself wearing a long baby white pink clothes..my hair is just black and so long almost touching the ground. My mother just hugging my tiny body, but i'm not a child this time. I'm an adult crying infront of my Empress mother, and it seems.. that's what i needed at this moment, the comfort from the mother.. then i fell asleep slowly. When i wake up, i asked my mother if i could come home now..but she said with a very soothing voice..you are home my SHINE..and anytime you can come home..just like now.. yes i know mother..what i meant permanently.

Then my mother pulled me out from her arms gently and showed me something..look down she said..what do you see my shine? I wiped my tears and looked down..ohh the people i loved..my family..and those people who needed my help. That's right my shine..your happiness is just with these people..the animals..the sorrounding natures..this is where you are happy..your curiousity..your adventures and feeling of freedom..it's down there. Feel that in your heart my shine.

You will get bored here in our KINGDOM..that's why you are there, helping those in needs..and that's what who you are. Ohh..mother you are right..still i have so much to do in earth. You know how to get home, here in our KINGDOM and Curiosity is part of yourself that even ME and your FATHER ARTHERU cannot change that. This is who you are, and you meant to do something good in a reality and spiritual realm.

Your task is not easy..but you are the perfect one to do the DEVINE WORK..it's all written in the book whether you believe me or not. Then i became curious..i asked my mother..you don't mind if i ask which book mother? well..it's the solomon book he was holding from your previous meditation. Oh ok mother, thank you and i believe you. Sometimes i'm caught up between reality and spirituality, and sometimes it seems like i cannot balance it mother. Ohh..you balancing it very well my shine.

Mother do you think i'm crazy? Of course not she said. In reality maybe some people they are not understanding what you are going through, and what you are experiencing now. But you are here now with me talking spiritually..100 percent you are not crazy. You don't show your craziness in reality..so why worry? Ohh mother..thank you..i'm feeling better now. Mother, when i was crying earlier, the rain started to get stronger i have noticed it..and when i stopped crying..the rain also slightly stopped but not completely. Is there anything to do with my emotions? yes my shine, my mother said. Remember your DEVINE FATHER said to you earlier? it's the rhythm of life that's sorrounds you. Oh mother thank you..i miss you and father Artheru. OK my shine sleep now..

CHAPTER 68

# EQUATOR HEALING

JOURNAL
6TH OCTOBER 2022

I have been very busy with my work, but it's good in some way as it takes away my thoughts and my mind from wandering. Last night i feel good after visiting and talking with my Empress MOTHER. I thanked her. I feel overwhelmed with my emotions sometimes..but i'm very good in keeping it to myself and not to involved another people. My DEVINE FATHER wants me to have a good rest, and more meditation to do and more healing to myself before others. You cannot heal the world if your soul and spirit still injured. Have a good rest my child, he said.

Yesterday at work, when i closed my eyes while sitting near my working window, i reached for my DEVINE FATHER. This time i met my DEVINE FATHER in the very top of the VALLEY. He was standing there while waiting for me, and then when he saw me.. he extended his arms towards me and to welcome. He didn't say anything, and he is blocking me to read his thoughs. He pointed out the FAR VALLEY, as i can see the whole city..white city and we both standing far away from the VALLEY.

Then infront of me, i can see a PHOENIX forming..it's black and red..then it slowly turned it into a really BIG Phoenix and I quickly realised..the phoenix is ME! I questione myself..did i turned myself into a phoenix or my DEVINE FATHER did that for me? Then my body started to ascend sorrounded by white lights energy..then half way up, my body stopped from ascending. I looked down and then i can see my DEVINE FATHER doing something on me..on my body..just like..it looks like moulding me? Just like an Artist doing some painting in the CANVAS. I can see he is trying to removed the imperfections sorrounding my body.

Then i saw myself being purified with this beautiful white and clear energy..and then the white and clear energy formed into a HEART.. and it's glittering and it's alive and beating..it's all clear white and pure energy. My body sorrounded with this clear energy..but it looks like i'm inside with this BIG HEART. I felt more energised and feeling more happier.

Then my DEVINE FATHER instructed me..start your healing now my child..heal the world with your PURIFIED ENERGY". Oh so this is what's all about, then i heard his voice..yes my child start healing the world. Yes father i will. I went up little bit more higher so i can see a better view of my aim, then i stopped, now this time i can see the whole world from above.

So close your eyes my child, and release that energy that i have given you..slowly..he said. I aimed myself to the equator first..i don't know why the equator? I was going to ask..but my Devine Father said not to ask question this time. I can feel and see my whole body is full of this white energy, and from my hands i started pointing and sending the lights towards the earth. I sorrounded the whole earth with this purified energy, and it's wrapped up with glittering white energy. I also can feel it's penetrating into the very end of the earth and every living things have been touched with my energy, including deep down the ocean.

Then slowly i'm feeling depleted..feeling to pass out..then PAPA GOD got me..then send me to sleep..deep sleep. I don't know how long i was in my deep meditation..that suddenly i wake up from where i was sitting..i looked at my watch, and it's my time see my students. I went home that day and went to bed so early and sleep feeling so tired..I wake up this morning..my knee is feeling a lot better. Thank you Papa GOD..i'm tired..super tired..Then i heard my DEVINE FATHER said, rest my child..rest.

# CHAPTER 69

# GINGER BLUE

JOURNAL
8TH OCTOBER 2022

I slept very well last night, and i wake up this morning feeling recharged. My knee is also feeling better this time, i don't know why and how..maybe PApa GOD healed it last night. I travelled again last night, i was with Papa GOD again and this time he turned me into a very young child. I was up there, i can see myself in an open space and running around barefooted on the marble floors, i feel comfortable and feeling the floor while on my barefoot. This is my Papa GOD KINGDOM, full of clouds and i have been here many times. Specially when i'm upset, this is my refuged place with my DEVINE FATHER, i feel home with him..and always, he brings me here.

I saw my DEVINE FATHER sitting on his BIG MARBLE CHAIR, facing with those so many high ranking entities and they are all sitting on the chairs little bit like Papa GOD chair. I can't see thier faces..it's blurry..some of them have long hair..and some of them have beards like santa claus. I rubbed my eyes again to see their faces..but it's the same..still blurry. As for my curiousity, i went closer to PApa GOD and whispered to his right ear.

Papa GOD, i can't see their faces..he then told me..you are not supposed to..shhh..he said. I said why? i will tell you one day, he said.. but..i said..oh..oh..NO my child remember i told you before? yes papa GOD..Dont' ask many questions my child. OK Papa God. Then he told me to sit down beside him with my little chair..i slowly climbed up, then JESUS suddenly appeared and helped me again to climbed up on my little chair:) I smiled at him and said thank you. Then i saw a little smile on his face too.

Then he stood behind Papa GOD. Then i noticed, JESUS is a very tall man, his hair is black but little wavy and to his shoulder lenght. He has facial beard and wearing a long white cloth with red colour infront. He is wearing a brown sandals and has BIG feet. He looked at me and smiled :) He has beautiful eyes..looks shinny and hypnotic, very calm and healing.

I can see myself a tiny little girl with short maize colour hair, and wearing like a summery clothes just normal little girl. I can see myself playing with my music box..then i got bored..i slid myself down from where i am sitting...and slowly crawled behind my chair. I saw Papa GOD still talking to the high Ranking entities, but no words i can hear??..but it seems like they're understanding each other.

I sat on the marble floor and i can see JESUS feet with his brown sandals, he also facing to the entities and looks like he too understands what they are talking about. But me?..i don't. They're blocking me..i'm not supposed to know anyway..too young for this conventions and i would never understand.

I continued playing with my music box..then when i was to get up as i am feeling bored..suddenly a CAT appeared! with gingery colour and with stripes all over the body. So i slowly touched it..then to my surprised the cat came to me closer and sat on my lap. I saw JESUS glimpsed at me with a smile on his face. His 2 hands were resting behind his back. The cat didn't leave my lap..i just cuddled it. Then later on, another cat came..but it's colour black..oh..cyclops is that you? i asked. But he has 2 eyes i noticed, my cyclops has only one eye.. but i feel it it's him. He didn't come near me, instead he was sitting up on the table watching me playing with the other cat and i named it GINGER BLUE..because it has blue eyes. I can feel Cyclops happy energy towards me..by just watching me. Then i suddenly wake up, i looked at my bay window..the rain has stopped, and i can see the sun. Ohh..it's time to get up and have breakfast. Thank you Papa GOD, i'm feeling better now. Bye my BROTHER JESUS as papa GOD said before..he is your "Brother" here in heaven..spiritually.

CHAPTER 70

# BUSINESS OR HEALING

JOURNAL

11TH OCTOBER

I had a quick talk with papa GOD earlier. He wants me to look back when we very first met spiritually, and that was 25 years ago during my meditation workshop. Think back of what i have told you when we first met, he insisted. I thought..hmm..oh boy..what's hidden behind this talk? I thought ok Papa GOD lets go back then. He took me again to the clouds while i was looking for my guide, 2 old men denied..so i kept going..until i tripped over on the big boulder. Then when i looked up..It's "YOU"..up there with a silhouette image, so clear and bright and it's purely white.

PAPA GOD, you were sorrounded with white AURA..so beautiful.. calming..and forgiving..the calmness on your face is just amazingly comforting..but i can't fully see the whole image of your face. Your light is so bright and not even irritating..not just like the sun or normal lights which you cannot focus. The more i foccused into your light and the aura, the more i was drawn to you.

Before i can get up to where i was stumbled..You told me..DON'T LOOK ANYWHERE ANYMORE..I'M HERE FOR YOU" and that was it. THat words went through my head telepathically, and that words was exactly the thing i was looking for..WORDS that gave me some comfort..and feeling loved UNCONDITIONALLY. After the beautiful and interesting encountered, YOU gave me this 3 messages..IT's LOVE..CARE..HEAL. This 3 words will have significant impact into the world you said..SPREAD this WORDS.. THE WORDS OF GOD...and That very moment i felt inspired to take and spread this words to the WORLD.

Then i asked..do you want me to continue healing? or do you want me to become rich and get involved with business? as i know i have some kind of influences energetically every time I'm getting close to people with business. I have noticed this all my life. I make people stable with thier business when i'm with them. Then PApa GOD answered, YOU focus with your "HEALING" that's your purpose.. business..no. not this time.(we are talking about 25 years ago) I will provide whatever you need, he said.

Although in my younger days, i rebelled on and off against his will, and i paid for the consequences. You know..just like a normal teenager and wants to be normal with my friends arround me. That time i want to make money as much as i can, but PApa GOD minimised that potential for me, as he said to me one day when i was aleep..this is not your alignment for your purpose.

I always asked, please tell me my purpose DEVINE FATHER so i can understand it and be more prepared. He answered me in my thoughts..you will know this when the time is right. I became frustrated..then my life became a struggle. Now i understand what he really meant for me to understand my purpose. You cannot have too much, he said. but why? i asked. Because You will forget your true purpose in life.

I remember my early days or even now, arriving in the restaurant with zero costumer inside..looks so gloomy. But once i was siiting inside.. and not even a few minutes..the people are coming and kept coming.. sometimes it makes me wonder..where all this people coming from? Even the owner of the restaurant could not believe..but somehow they seems to know this.

Not just the restaurants, many more i have noticed..When my parents had a restaurant before..it brought so much money in the house. My mum used to have a big box full of money..our money kept flowing.. Well..it seems like my DEVINE FATHER is in control of my LIFE. Alignining me to become of who i am now. I noticed when i really need something desperately, for example needing to fix my car urgently..i asked for help from PAPA GOD. Then from nowhere... the money arrived unexpectedly and the precise amount of what i have asked for. I was always fascinated about that, but i didn't ask too much because it wasn't neccesary.

NOw someone is asking me lately to join the global business.. but there was always an interesting interruptions..i know it's My DEVINE FATHER doing..so i didn't insist. You will get what you supposed to be for you..be patient. He told me to be patient..and that's my biggest enemy..i am impatient!..but i know very well how to control it and have more understanding of it now.

SOmetimes in my life i do some quick actions that i have put me in a hot water..and that was in my younger years..that's because of my impatience and stubborness i suffered from my consequences. I learned from my mistakes many times, it wasn't easy..then i cried.. being consoled by my DEVINE FATHER..and saying to me it's ok, you are allowed to make mistakes..after all you are only human..and then very faint and almost fading words i can hear..stubbcrnness that's your problem my child.

Why did you make me stubburn then i asked? well, this is how and who you are..it's part of your survival instinct in the reality world. OH..now i understand, and supposed i cannot changed it now? i asked. NO, he said..why? i asked again..because i made you that way and i want you to be..who you really are because i know you will survive. I can control now my firey personality inside me, and i can see papa GOD smile on his face.

Oh FATHER that's very intense..i need to chill out. Ok my child talk to me later..Yes FATHER i will. ILOVEYOU. I just looked out from my big windows..i can see papa GOD waving at me..and the clouds are slightly clearing..and yes.."SKY"..i can see him with my DEVINE FATHER..he looks so happy..oh i miss him too. :)

# CHAPTER 71

# THE BLACK BOOK

JOURNAL
15TH OCTOBER 2022

It has been a hectic week for me, but i managed the chaotic energy arround me. I have been meeting up with my DEVINE FATHER on and off this week, and i went for the battle just by myself this time and with him. He said, you can do this on your own, this is nothing compared that you have been through of any battle previously.

I arrived where my DEVINE FATHER's Verandah up there..he extended his left arm to welcome me while he is holding a "BLACK BOOK". He is reading the book facing to the west looking towards the clouds. Then i noticed his feet are both holding a BLACK ENTITY.. and he is facing at me. I wasn't scared..and i continued talking to my DEVINE FATHER.

Then i asked gently, who and what are you doing with this BLACK ENTITY FATHER? i asked. He said you need to eliminate him. I didn't argue..i said, ok i will do it. I don't see my DEVINE FATHER is looking happy at the moment, so i stepped back, and suddenly my daggers automatically appeared in my hands. And without any hesitation, i struck this entity's head with my daggers while my DEVINE FATHER still holding him down with his feet and with the black book still holding. Then i lowered my hands to his lower extremities..and up again to the middle of his chest and went outward to both arms..it's the sign of the cross. The BLACK ENTITY suddenly disappeared..and another head appeared infront of my face..i did the same i struck it with my daggers and eliminated. Then a woman's face appeared..same thing i did with this famous bad person leading the countries and a matter of fact it's 2 of them !! OMG! it's all heads!!No full bodies..and many more faces quickly appearing and started attacking me, i have never seen so many faces like this before. I was thinking..what's wrong with you entities?? and i'm asking myself why my energy has been accessed?..i thought my energy field is well protected.

And MY DEVINE FATHER said quickly, i made them accessed your energy field so you can eliminate them. They kept coming and attacking me and aiming my face! So i could't stand this anymore...i suddenly turned myself into a firey phoenix, and then one at a time..i eliminated them without any struggles. They're all gone..i then realised i was a phoenix and my body was sorrounded with fire, and this time i only used my daggers.

I feel sad for this entity..and why on earth wants to attack me? but this time i have no choice..and my DEVINE FATHER will never give me a choice when it comes to this battle. I cannot loss and i will not loss. When my DEVINE FATHER said to eliminate them!..A DEVINE ORDER that i will not and cannot be refused. Very STRONG and STERN with POWERFUL command!

I can feel my DEVINE FATHER is something bothering him at this moment..i can feel it..he doesn't want me to reach his thoughts.. he is blocking me. So i decided to give him time, and i will talk to him later. After i eliminated them...i came closer to my DEVINE FATHER...i kneeled down infront of him..i surrendered my daggers to him, and i don't know why? It's kind of my body automatically did this..and i realised this a sign of respect for my DEVINE FATHER and for my JOB well done.

He then touched my head and the amazing energy went through my body, and in my thoughts he asked me to stand up, and my daggers slowly disappeared from my hands. He hugged me gently..and i felt this amazing and overwhelming feeling of sadness and tears in my eyes flowing...i asked my DEVINE FATHER WHY? why am i feeling this way? Is this your emotions FATHER or my emotions? He then said gently..SHHH...just feel it..yes i'm feeling it FATHER. Then suddenly i realised He then looked at me with his hands still holding my shoulders and said..yes i do miss you..you have been preoccupied with something else in your head lately. Ohh..that one..sorry..i said. Oh i know what's going on he said..OMG! that should not be strange to you FATHER. You made it happened..i said with sadness. (by the way, i have been talking to my DEVINE FATHER since i was a kid literally, i always feel that he is with me all the time, talking with me in a physical body just like a normal father and daughter), That's why my conversations are like this with him, nothing direspectful..it's between FATHER and DAUGHTER in a physical world, he made it that way so i can always relate my emotions to him in a very normal way.

Now, lets not argue he said..he hugged me instead. Oh..and again we both staring at the clouds..looking to the west horizon, watching our favourite sunset. As a FATHER and DAUGHTER..i miss this connections, and i think he does it too. I just don't want to leave him here..and i can feel his emotions getting back to normal and just being happy with me.

Then i asked..do i have more battle to do FATHER? he looked at me and said..yes my child. When? i asked..he then responded while still watching the sunset.."PATIENCE" my child patience. Do i have to worry for this one FATHER?..He then looked at me, and with his hands on my face, lovingly said..No my child. I then felt this beautiful reassurance feelings and comfort in that instant. Our energies combined together..i can feel an energetic light between us embodeing together. Then he asked me to start some energetic healing, the earth needs it my child. Alright FATHER i will..and now? i asked curiously..and he answered quickly, Yes! now my child. Ohh okay...i mumbled.

Then i can see my body going up to the sky..then i stopped, my DEVINE FATHER said..now start from the west horizon and move towards counter clock wise. Then this time my body is covered by the golden and white colour energies. I aimed my hands to west side of the horizon and started sending the golden energy..it's like a lazer..i can feel my body radiating with energies wrapping up the WORLD. Then when i was about to penetrate the inside of the earth, the colour of my body have changed sudenly into a very bright white colour, and into a shimmering energy. It's so bright and it's penetrating into the very deep end of the EARTH.

Then the ocean..i can "FEEL" the fish big and small are just so happy, and they had a surprised reactions from the light hitting them from behind. I can see their eyes reacted when the beautiful energy hit them. I saw a little sea turtle being hit by the energy, and i saw it's neck looked to it's back and checked what it was just hit it's body.

Whoaahh..i'm fascinated..and i'm feeling so happy for them..the little fishes jumping so suddenly..the sharks stood still. They are all stopped swimming, they are all absorbing the energy..and i can see some dead plants became alive..and ohh..one little fish just sneezed.. and i said bless you.:) then the little fish swam away with it's little tail wagging.:) I can see green plants arround and under the water..so beautiful..so alive, and i can see a lot of fish looks like they are talking to each other. Oh MY DEVINE FATHER, this is so beautiful!!!

Then i shifted my healing towards back to the outer place, covering the whole place..then my hands suddenly stopped in ARIZONA. ARIZONA?? why ARIZONA?? This word arizona it's in my head just popped out! A very strong word. I scanned again with my eyes the whole area of this land arizona. I don't know why it's arizona..i have no idea, i said it myself.

I can see a dead place..nothing at all in this area..dessert island i would say..no trees arround, it's an ugly place. Oh wait..there is some unusual looking tree with prickly thorns, and it's 4 of them in a row. BIG, TALL and prickly. I don't know why i stopped here..then suddenly i'm back with Papa GOD..and before i could ask..he told me, don't ask questions this time, have a rest instead my child. Then i wake up..very thirsty and drank my whole water in my bottle beside my bed..then went to sleep again. Then my weekend is just for sleeping, and my DEVINE FATHER wants me to recuperate my body.

I have been sleeping during the weekend, and i'm feeling much better. At the moment I'm with my DEVINE FATHER, and i thanked him for having me up there. I am feeling mature and grounded woman this time, and thanks goodness he didn't turn me into a child. Not this time my child as i want your mature conversations with me, he said. He then showed me a "BIG" HEART. Ohh..thank you FATHER..I LOVE YOU TOO. :)

# CHAPTER 72

# ROYAL BLUE GRANDFATHER ANGEL METATRON

JOURNAL
16TH OCTOBER 2022

LAst night i had a visitor during my sleep, but i was awake for some reason..i saw a being with light brown big eyes..not very tall and have something in his hands holding some kind of small instrument and it looks sharp. Looks like he came to take me..he paralysed my body and i'm feeling anxious..then i quickly called for my DEVINE FATHER and quickly appeared infront of this being and telling him.. YOU cannot take her!!! and she's not yours!!Leave my child alone and be gone!! I saw my DEVINE FATHER looking so mad at this being and pointing his hand to this being to go outside my bedroom. Then the brown being disappeared quickly. Then papa GOD touched my eyes with his hand..then i fall asleep.

THE other night during my meditation..i went to see my ANCESTRAL home and my FATHER ARTHERU and my MOTHER EMPRESS GLYDICA. PAPA GOD was there too..i think papa GOD and myself visiting them. I saw my grandmama in the garden, and i went to sit beside her. This time papa GOD didn't turn me into a child. I'm princess shinarae the daughter of KING ARTHERU AND EMPRESS GLYDICA the NATURE's KINGDOM. That's where i came from my second lifetime, as my DEVINE FATHER told me.

I'm sitting with my grandmama, and she looks so devine but looking older. She looks a little bit of my mother Empress Glydica. Then i saw a glittering blue colour light from the distance..then the more i focussed on it..the more it's getting clearer. Then it became a person and riding on his horse..and it's all royal blue, but he's there from the distance with his royal blue horse.

I asked my grandmama, who is that? And suddenly..i heard papa GOD said..it's your your GRAND FATHER! what? i said. OHHH.. what's his name? i asked curiously..papa GOD said..it's ANGEL METATRON! ANGEL WHO? i asked again. YES, he's married to your grandmama..then have a daughter which is your mother now..and makes you a GRAND DAUGHTER. Whoaahh..i could not believe it!

Being a WARRIOUR is in your blood..and a PRINCESS of this KINGDOM. Whoah..wait..wait papa GOD, this is so confusing to me. No nothing to be confused about, he is part of your blood line.. he too had been a great protector of you since your birth. Why is blue papa GOD? Blue is the colour sign that, when you are in need of protection and feeling threatened..that colour blue appeared everywhere and anywhere. It's a sign that someone is there for you, and ROYAL BLUE is the the sign of ROYALTY.

OHH..that's why sometimes i do see that during my sleep, and when i closed my eyes. So that's what it is..now i understands. Yes my child, he's been with you since i created you..your grandfather in a ROYAL BLUE. Yes i remember and recognised now..he's there with me during my battle and during my travel to the WHITE CITY with ARCH ANGEL GABRIEL..a matter of fact he's been there for me all the time. But papa GOD he is not showing his face to me..he will one day my child when he's ready. ohh ok..i said. Now i understands about the colour, i always like the colour blue and baby pink. It always makes me feel safe and feeling home and loved.

Well..well..how interesting how i am unravelling my blood line.. that's why i always have a feeling that i don't belong here in earth.. and when i'm feeling sad..i always look up and feeling like someone up there healing my pain..sometimes i see so many of them looking down on me from there KINGDOM. Sometimes the MOON has significant impact on me, when i have problems..i connect with it.. it's very empowering sometimes.

Ohh..papa GOD the more i found my blood line the more it's getting clearer to me now. Thank you my DEVINE FATHER for making me understands my LINEAGE and this craziness i thought in my head for long..long time..and i thought i was going crazy...Now it's validated. THANK YOU FATHER..really. THANK YOU. i then saw a smile on my FATHER's face. A beautiful smile. :)

# CHAPTER 73

# SQUARE WHITE LIGHT ENERGY

JOURNAL

17TH OCTOBER 2022

This morning before i wake up, i saw square lights up on the air, and i noticed the middle of it is round and has shimmering lights. Then the light is starting to come closer to my face, and my feeling is to connect with me starting now, a feeling of being hypnotised and to touch it. The square outside have some kind of writings..but i couldn't read it. It's more like an Ancient writings but in a very fine print. My feeling is the writing is very important and profound. Then i can see this sqaure lights on my left side of my face shimmering, and becoming intense and flickering.

I saw my body got up and went to the shimmering square lights.. and then i can see myself standing infront of the Galaxy. This time i am standing in a Big round window and staring at the never ending galaxy. I can see round or circle orbits with silhoutte colours, and that's the only thing i can see from where i am standing and looking at the dark galaxy.. staring at it. I then realised this is a portal again.

I refused to go through the Portal as i don't feel comfortable at this moment. Something about this portal that i don't feel safe..or just feeling anxious going on my own. Beside i am going to work today. It's monday FATHER, i don't feel like travelling today especially this moment. And that was it..i wake up very tired and thirsty. Papa GOD wanted me to go through the PORTAL but i refused as i wasn't ready. He doesn't mind when i refused. I just have a peek then.

The other night i have travelled again, but this time i have company? big question in my mind..i tried to reach my DEVINE FATHER but with no avail. This somebody who is with me has the same dynamic energy like mine. Wihout any conversations, but we both comfortable with each other, then automatically we both travelled up, somehow i feel like it has been our favourite spot amongst the galaxy and the stars..so beautiful.

I thought this time at least i have company, and we both in the same page of my spiritual energy. I haven't seen SKY today or lately..but i know he is in the good hands. I just then closed my eyes..and i can see him in his favourite usual spot among with the green grass valley..our favourite spot. He looks happy though, and i can see the flowers are blooming arround the field. So many butterflies and red bugs. SKY doesn't like to join me if i have company during my Astral travel.

My astral companion traveller always comes and got me several times, he doesn't ask me..he just takes my hand and pulled me up and holds my hand and never let go..so sweet and beautiful..but when i get bored..i let go my hand and i turned this companion of mine into a RED BUG then it became annoying. Very persistant, it kept buzzing infront of my nose until i get squared eyes. Arghhh..so i left him and went home instead to my DEVINE FATHER's Kingdom. He then asked me..how's your travel my child? with a smile on his face..Ohh FATHER you know, i said..with my square face :(

This afternoon i went straight to my meditation and connected myself immediately to my Astral travel. Papa GOD is infront of me, and asked are you ready my child? Yes FATHER i am ready i affirmed.

# CHAPTER 74

# THE DARK CITY

JOURNAL
23RD OCTOBER 2022

I have been resting lately, and sleeping so much. LAst night my DEVINE FATHER and myself met up again. Then suddenly i can see him dragging an entity..it looks injured somehow?..but i don't understand the way my FATHER is dragging the entity's body on his left hand. This entity is wearing a "WHITE clothings". I was thinking..is this an ANGEL? or an injured ANGEL?

I cen see myself standing in a very high platform, and big round rock, and behind me it's a Big Rock solid wall. This time i am wearing different battle gear clothing. It looks like a very thick materials and off colour, not very white..it's an off white colour materials clothing. I am looking like a HUNTER..and my weapon is "BOW AND ARROW". Wow..this is different..and new weapon given to me by my DEVINE FATHER.

I was standing "STILL" while holding my "BOW" and arrow on my right hand. I can see my FATHER coming towards me with this entity dragging the whole body on the ground. You "MUST" take this entity with you my child. I can see a lifeless body of the entity on the ground infront of me. My DEVINE FATHER pointed out to me the place we are supposed to go. That place he said! I can see the place is so black, and from the distance i can see flames in between the gaps of that place. It's flaming..but very dark. The whole place is wrapped with darkness. I am thinking..oh my GOD..i am heading to HELL! now i'm scared.

I felt little bit anxious and i think my DEVINE FATHER sensed it.. and i heard a word "DON'T BE". SKY is beside me, so i can feel his reassurance as well. SAM the earth Angel, he appeared infront of me and my DEVINE FATHER, and my FATHER said to him, take this entity with you. I saw SAM the earth Angel slowly bowed to my DEVINE FATHER as a sign of RESPECT. The entity lifeless body is on SAM's horse infront of him.

Then Arch Angel MIchael, Arch Angel Metatron and Arch Angel Gabriel are behind us. There are no other Angels with us. I noticed Arch Angel Michael is wearing a Red clothing, Angel Gabriel wearing a white thick material clothing, and my Grandfather Angel Metatron wearing pure ROYAL blue colour..but this time he has a white colour cape. Hmm..that's interesting.

I wonder if there is something to do of what i bought yesterday, new clothes. I was very drawn to ROYAL blue and white pants yesterday, so i bought it!. Now it's becoming clearer to me the significant connections of what i am experiencing here in a physical world and to my spiritual connections to my Devine heritage. the synchronicity is very real.

I do terribly miss my DEVINE FATHER if i don't have some kind of connections with him in a daily basis..it's like an eternity...especially if i am very busy with my things in this reality world. I noticed he makes my existence in earth so difficult if i don't communicate with him. That's the way how's he reminding me that communication is a "MUST" in a daily basis. Saying HELLO and Good morning to him is very important before i starts my day. Even if i wake up little bit grumpy and couldn't open my eyes quickly..then suddenly i get this little flickering white light just on my eyes to remind him. Sitting on the toilet saying hello and talking to him. Then i can see his sihouette face just happy while my eyes still closed. Ohh..that's my morning wake up call.

Back to my starting journey again..he pointed out this city to me or the area. I don't know why i kept saying city..and this is the 3rd times in my mind and kept saying "CITY", and i kept changing it to the word "AREA". Then kept going back to word CITY. Maybe this is a CITY of HELL??..a city of darkness perhaps? who knows? i will find out later for sure, i said it to myself.

Anyway, this takes me back few years ago when i visited the dark city during my meditation, or i stumbled more in that city. It was dark all over the place..people are wearing black clothing..the whole city is black..the ground..the metal fences are black!! i was horrified! Everything was BLACK! Then when i reached the gate of dark city.. even the person guarding infront of the gate was wearing black. I can see through inside his body, his soul is "WHITE"..but the outside of his body is BLACK! The place looks very sad..people are walking arround seems so sad..everything about sadness in that city.

My body shivered..my whole entire body is feeling the chills arround me. Then when i was about to open the Black Gate as i attempted to come in..the person (well it seems like a person) have stopped me! He won't let me in, i was persistent and then he said you cannot come in, you don't belong here. I was little bit upset as he rejected me.. instead he pointed out the next path ahead. Then i started walking to the path that he was showing me..and to my surprised..i can see a beautiful forest, full of lovely flowers,trees, butterflies, little bugs.. and little animals running arround the bush and the whole area. Then i saw a BIG TREE behind me where i am standing, i sat down under it..and then fell asleep. The dark City does exist..i saw it and i have been there, but couldn't go inside. Somewhere out there was a MISERABLE place.

PAPA GOD said to me, that's where you are heading this time my child and pointing it out to me..and when you travel, stay in a clear path..do not wonder in a different path it's important, he said. Yes FATHER i understand. I hopped in on SKY's back, then papa GOD said be careful my child and he kissed my FOREHEAD. I will be careful FATHER..and then i can see his loving gesture but with little sadness. The i stopped first..i asked..why you look so sad papa GOD? Why? Is something bothering you FATHER? He then blocked my thoughts..but papa GOD, i said..i am not going until you told me. That instant, he tapped SKY's left back side and that GIVES SKY a momentum to take off. I will tell you later when you come back my child...the words almost echoeing from the distance while SKY running really fast while i'm on his back followed by my ANGELS. I can see my DEVINE FATHER waving at me.

While travelling, i can see some clear and zigzag paths, we are all travelling in an open Galaxy. I can see some different fragments scattered all over the place floatings everywhere. I don't really know what to make of it, i have never seen them before and it looks solid. We travelled long distance before we reached the area..but looking from the distance, it's so close to travel. It's decieving.

Then i heard papa GOD's voice..that's what the city is all about.."DECIEVING". We then reached the area. Then we are facing the very DARK WALL. And that DARK wall i have noticed a square little window passage..then my eyes sighted a handle below the window passage on the black wall. I jumped out from SKY's back..and slowly walked towards the black wall and then grabbed the black handle and gave the wall a very strong and hard KNOCKED! It's sounds like a BIG SMASHED on the wall that made the BIG DOOR echoed inside the AREA.

Then suddenly an entity..black entity eyes appeared between the little square window passage..and the eyes of the entity looked very surprised when he saw me!! OH!!!...THE CHILD OF GOD IS HERE!!..then the BIG door automatically opened.. very slowly..then i saw this BIG dark entity setting on his black chair sorrounding with darkness. Big black boulders and rocks sorrounding this ENTITY big black chair facing at me and my ANGELS.

This entity looks very scary!!and a matter of fact i'm scared...it's towering the whole place, and fires and the flames behind him and the sorrounding area. My body shivered again and i feel cold suddenly. I held on SKY's right upper shoulder, and i felt he sensed it, and slowly made his body closer to me. I have been expecting you the child of the "CREATOR!" OMG! his voice sounds like a thunder and it echoed all arround the whole area.

I guess your FATHER sent you here!!!and laughing so loudly!!! Then suddenly the body of the lifeless entity appeared infront of me..and the black entity evil asked me and said..perhaps this is for me? Yes, i said. My DEVINE FATHER asked me to take this here to you.

Then the face of the LIFELESS entity have sighted by him.. and to my surprise the black entity went mad!!!..NO!!!!!!..he said.

The black evil entity is really mad..the whole place started thundering and lightning. WHY???...the word WHY???? and feeling sad and upset it's on this entity' face, and he is raging!!! The whole place became hot and flames everywhere!! THen i can see some flames coming from the distance started heading towards me really fast. I quickly jumped on SKY's back and tried to run away..i cannot see my ANGELS arround me. Looks like i'm on my own again with this battle..me and SKY again.

I was being hit left and right with the balls of fire, but for some reason it didn't penetrated on me or SKY. I kept running away and sky looking for exits, but looks like there is no way out i realised! We both stuck in this flaming DARK place!. FATHER!!! i called.. but there is no responsed from him. So i decided to turn arround and face this flaming balls of fire coming after me. Then i heard papa GOD voice from the distance..use your bow and arrow to hit the balls of fire. Yes FATHER i will, and to my surprised my hands automatically and quickly grabbed my arrows behind my back, and while riding on SKY's back i kept charging and every single balls of fire being hit and then quickly deminished!

While the fire of balls being hit with my bow and arrows, it quickly turns into a heads..crumbled down and turned into ashes. I did this so many times..the more i charged the more it's coming..then that's where i saw my ANGELS. They started to do the same with thier swords! Then when we all eliminated them, the "BIG BLACK EVIL ENTITY" stood up towering us! and especially to me, he looks so ANGRY at me. He then suddenly jumped infront of me, and i fell down from SKY's back..i'm on the ground..down on my back facing at him and towering me with his RAGE is getting out of control!!! The whole place starting to shake, and while he is raging i took the opportunity to crawled to the side of the stone wall in between the 2 big rocks..but he saw me crawling..he then quickly picked me up form my hips and brought my whole body to his face and asked me "WHY"???? his face is flaming!!

I quickly thought..oh no..is that something to do with that entity i brought in? Then suddenly papa GOD said yes..that is his "SON"! I took his black spirit out of him and turned him into a WHITE Entity, papa GOD said. The EVIL BLACK Entity then suddenly threw me on the wall. I then quickly got up..and ran towards up higher to the big rock, and i jumped into it. I was amazed i did that! It reminds me i used to do this when i was a teenager or a kid..no fear on jumping on a BIG ROCKS! now i can see the connections!

Then i automatically grabbed my arrow behind my back and get my bow ready to charge. I slowly aiming my arrow to this entity.. while coming slowly towards me, my hand clicked my bow and the arrow hit the entity's face.. but the entity is coming to me really fast. Then my hands became very quick to charged! So light and quick to handle..quick as a lightning bolt how i charged my weapon!!! I feel like i have done this before, many arrows have hit him but i couldn't get him down. I kept running up and up to the higher place..i stumbled many times and busted my knees especially my right knee is really bad..but i got up again and kept running towards up higher. When i reached the top..my last arrow i have in my hand..i saw it twinkled and heard a slight sound like "twing"...Then papa GOD said..now.. aim to his forehead! His forehead? i asked. YES!!! he said with a big voice and a command. The word is so precised and sterned!

So i aimed my shoulder and my hands together with my weapons very steadily to this BIG being..and with my very last arrow..my aimed is so precised and strong..then i heard papa GOD said again.. charge NOW!!! I clicked the button under my index finger..and i can see the arrow is travelling very fast flying towards this entity..and to me it seems like in a slow motion.

Then before the entity can grab me..the arrow hit his forehead!!! and i saw a golden light from the arrow penetrated this entity's head..and then i saw the Big entity fell down backwards, then his whole body started to crumbled and slowly turned into ashes. My arrow automatically went back to my back pack shoulder with the other arrows, while my bow still in my right hand. Then i can see the sorrounding area slowly turning into white colour. Then the whole place became white and glitering with ice. Then the other sorrounding area became more beautiful sea colour blue water.

Then the lifeless entity's body became alive and Angel Sam is accompanying him to Arch Angel Gabriel CITY..THE CITY OF ANGELS. Then i wake up with both of my knees are very painful and felling exhausted. I drank plenty of water again as i was so thirsty..and PAPA GOD said, well done my child. He then kissed my FOREHEAD, and for some reason papa GOD energy travelled through my knees..and then my pain slowly disappeared. Have a good rest my child..yes FATHER, then before i fall asleep..i can see this glittering wite heart again..then i felt this beautiful touched on my forehead, and then towards to my entire head..i can feel my DEVINE FATHER is massaging my head. It's soothing..then i fell asleep.

# CHAPTER 75

# GOLDEN CROSS BOW

JOURNAL
30TH OCTOBER 2022

last night my DEVINE FATHER took me somewhere to an interesting place..a big open space..it's like an OVAL wide open area. My FATHER standing right beside me and pointing out the very far and round canvas. It's so many of them, and it's far away. I asked what is it FATHER?. He said, my child this is your new task, for your new and next battle journey. And my weapon? i asked.

PAPA GOD handed in a to me a "CROSSBOW", and he said..my child this is your new weapon, use it wisely...wisely? i thought..hmm..i don't know what it means wisely with this kind of weapon. This is a very dangerous piece of weapon..and strangely, i like it! I can see the colour of the cross bow is dark brown while my DEVINE FATHER still holding in his hands, then it changed the colour when it was placed into my hands..it became gold..a golden colour crossbow??... whoah..this is amazing!

This is another flash back when i was in my teenage years..i always love to handle a crossbow..but i couldn't touch it! for some reason something was stopping me from feeling it or having to own it. I had some fascinations about it that time! and even now. I understand the connection how it is unfolding, hmmm.. interesting.

Then papa GOD pointed out the circle canvas from the distance. I guess you know what to do my child. Then i noticed i have golden arrows as well on my back. You need to hit the mid circle of that canvas from here where you are now standing. Yes, FATHER, i know what to do. I feel like this GOLDEN CROSS BOW has been very close to me, a sense of de javu..and internally i can feel that i have used this before. I can feel the connections between this weapon and myself. This is not the first time i used or held this golden cross bow. I like the feeling of it while holding this weapon.

Then i asked my FATHER now?...yes my child NOW! and whenever you ready, he said. I can see my DEVINE FATHER is patiently waiting for me to prepare my position and initiate the target. I can see his face is glowing...he is happy to see me doing this. I gave him a little smile..then i saw a HALO on his head..then i even felt happier. He's intertaining me..he knows i am happy, then i thought to myself, i finally found my special weapon, where i am very connected with and i don't know why?

I positioned myself and perfectly holding the CROSSBOW and the ARROW very close and perfectly pointing it to the canvas and the target. Then from that precise moment i have clicked the trigger. Then the canvas came closer, and to my disappointment, i didn't hit the middle part of the TARGET. I tried again several times and the same results didn't get the target. I got so frustrated!!! that no matter i tried, i could never hit the main target.

ARGGGHHH!!!! i am so frustrated!!! What am i doing wrong FATHER? I could not hit the target! Then i heard my DEVINE FATHER VOICE..."PATIENCE" my child patience..try again he said. I did the same thing!..i didn't hit the target! THen PAPA GOD said with a very calming voice, what missing on your eyes my child? MY eyes? perhaps my eye glasses, hahaha. WEll..here it goes..try this he said. Ohh...my EYE MASK. Yes my child your eye mask. I'm going to be blind folded? Yes, absolutely correct, my FATHER said. Whoahhh..that's going to be interesting, i said.

Then my DEVINE FATHER put my eye mask on, or i would say a blind folded on my eyes. Now i can't see..it's dark! I screamed! THen my DEVINE FATHER said..remember the "STILLNESS" my child.. and feel the "NOTHING"..you are in the "unknown darkness"..all you need to do is "FEEL". Feel what sorrounds you...near and far. OK FATHER..then if you feel something moving..all you need to do is feel it in your "HEART" not in your head. DO you understand me my child? FEEL it my child...feel it strongly. MY DEVINE FATHER command is very direct, forceful and brave and i embodied it.

OK, i guess i have to feel..DON'T GUESS!! papa GOD said..a very stern and strong command, and seriously i could never disobey or go against it. NOw..ready yourself and position your body, and keep it straight, my DEVINE FATHER command. Now what can you see? papa GOD asked me. Well, it's darkness..very still..and then suddenly there is a golden circle lights suddenly appeared from the distance. It's small and moving arround but it's bright enough for me to follow it from the distance with my eyes.

Well, that is your target my child. Oh ok now i get it. In the darkness the little lights are my targets. YES! papa GOD said. OK, are you ready? he asked. YES FATHER i am ready. NOW..GO! when my FATHER said go..my cross bow and my arrows started to hit every single lights all arround me and from the distance..it's everywhere..i didn't have to run..i just kept hitting the small lights all arround me in the dark, and my arrows kept coming and charging automatically. My body stayed still in one spot, and only i have to do is following the lights target. They all kept moving very fast, but all my targets feeling so precised..i can feel it in every part of my body.

Then suddenly my cross bow suddenly stopped hitting the targets.. and finally the darkness turned into lights. I removed my blind folded mask..and that's where i saw all the round canvas..i HIT all the middle of the TARGETS!! :) I saw my DEVINE FATHER clapping, and looks very proud of me and so happy for my initiations. Now my child you are ready, he said with a smile on his face.

I want you to have a good rest and recover your body from your last injury..heal your body my child. Then my DEVINE FATHER gave me a BIG HUG and whispered with a very soothing voice.. you are going to be alright..i'm here always with you. THANK you FATHER. NOW rest my child..then i fell asleep..

# CHAPTER 76

# THE WORLD IS MINE

JOURNAL

2ND NOVEMBER 2022

I feel like i am due for my travelling again..i can feel the pressure arround me. I am always very tired after my spiritual journey. Sometimes it took me a week to recuperate and heal my injuries. I am longing to connect with "NATURE" again..to feel free..the freedom out there..to see the moon..the stars in an open space..i miss that somehow..the ocean..the trees..the breeze feeling it again.

The warmth of the sun..the rain..the little bugs..the butterflies..birds flying in the sky..the clouds and the blue sky. All of it are MINE :).. MINE..and me and the NATURES only..the woods..the streams..and this is what PAPA GOD said to me before..this is yours my child! The world is yours! so, LOVE it..CARE with it..and most importantly.. HEAL it. OHH i love you my DEVINE FATHER.

OHH..it's all coming all together now..and making it sense about my life..and my spiritual journey. AMEN to that. I feel like I'm not worried about this reality "BS" going on in my life..as when i get connected to my spirituality..i am feeling more, this is my reality. Ohh..i just heard my DEVINE FATHER saying..now this time finally she's got it, and have more understanding about her purpose. My DEVINE FATHER made me read his mind, and earlier saying.."MY CHILD IS GROWING UP"...

But then i said to him back..i'm still not taller..then papa GOD said to me..my child i like the way you are..i made you that way..i asked why? there is so many reason, he said..and one is, i still can see you as a child even you are grown up..hmm..that's not fair, i said. One thing i must tell you he said, no matter how small or little you are may think to yourself, as long as you think "BIG" that's all it's matter. Ohh..that's absolutely correct FATHER. I always think BIG! That's why evreything i get is BIG..i don't like small things..from the biggest problem to the bigger purpose. I have always been like that ever since i can remember, it makes sense now. Remember, papa GOD said..you are as who you that's what matter and that's the most important part about your life. IT's "YOU" and it's only you! Ohh.. thank you FATHER, things are getting clearer now.

# CHAPTER 77

# THE BATTLE FIELD

JOURNAL

3RD NOVEMBER 2022

It's a beautiful sunny day, and i wake up with my clear head and my knees are feeling little bit better. As my DEVINE FATHER said, heal yourself my child. I did this for couple of days now.

Last night i met my DEVINE FATHER, he took me somewhere to the very important place..the battle ground place. I was standing in an open and very wide space..and it's more like battle ground area. Wide and open, no trees..only yellowish and dry grass. The grass looks like has been mowed and i noticed there is a path and it's not straight.. it's more like a zigzag path and i am standing on it.

The next thing i see and noticed is my clothing..my battle gear outfit. I am wrapped up with an armour! My whole body including my eyes. My head is covered like a helmet, and my eyes are both protected. I only can see through the black lense! The colour of my body armour is silvery and light weight. I noticed i haven't got my weapon yet..but when i think my cross bow weapon..this weapon quickly appeared in my hands including my arrows on my back. All of them are golden colour. This is amazing! So now i understand..as my DEVINE FATHER said before..think of the weapons you want to use, and it will suddenly appear into your hands. Ohh..FATHER thank you. I do remember.

Now my DEVINE FATHER suddenly appeared slightly meters away from me, and pointing the path from where i am standing and to the very long path ahead. He then gave me an instructions, this path is your safety. Stay in this clear path during the BATTLE. Never step out from this path..let the enemies come to you! i was going to ask why? but my FATHER blocked my thoughts.

I know when he tells me the reason why..i always goes to the opposite way..he knows me and my head. I can't help it..i always wandered in a different path to explore, because it's my nature as being CURIOUS! Then i get in trouble or face the consequences of my wandering nature. That's why my DEVINE FATHER have arranged so many guides to protect me.

Let's go back to the battle ground, i can see myself standing straight with my armour and my weapons in my hands. I can see my DEVINE FATHER standing beside me. He then pointed out the far away HILLS..then i automatically run towards it and then climbed up towards the top. Then i can see from the distance the western horizon and the sun is just going down. I asked my FATHER, what am i looking except for the sunset?..then my FATHER said..that's where your enemies will be coming from, and be prepared. When are they coming? i asked. Soon my child soon..then i suddenly wake up.

Then i suddenly heard my DEVINE FATHER's voice..clear your head my child..in this battle you have to think quickly. Think with your weapons to be in your hands. You have multiple weapons to use and you can use them all..anything you think! OK FATHER, i will do it and i will use every weapons as you said. I affirmed that to him. Then he made me read his mind..and it so sweet..he almost makes me cry. He said.."MY CHILD" is growing up..and i can see a "BIG flickering white heart" from the distance.

Have a rest today my child..clear your head and rest your knees. And i saw papa GOD blew ONE BIG KISS on the air. Wait papa GOD i said, can i see you tonight? Yes my child anytime..you know how to reach me. Thank you FATHER. But FATHER..i want to see and visit my ANCESTRAL home before i go to the BATTLE i said. PAPA GOD said, of course my child..and you know how to do that. THANK you FATHER..alright my child..REST.

CHAPTER 78

# CRYSTAL WEAPON

JOURNAL
5TH NOVEMBER 2023

Last night during my sleep i felt i had a visitor again. A good vibe energy, didn't feel threatened..a kind of getting used to this energy and a companion towards my astral travelling and to the higher dimension. This is not the first time..so i'm used to this energy traveL with this OLD SOUL. Our energy have the same level of frequency..we never talk verbally, instead we communicates through our minds and thoughts. While during travelling..i feel like i am being attacked and my old soul companion still behind me. I quickly turned myself into a warriour to protect myself and my companion, i can feel this is not going to be good. My gut feeling is telling me to be more precise of who i would trust during this battle. You will know my child, he said.

Then this entities are ferociously attacking me..i fought back, and so many of them are kept coming. I used every weapons that my DEVINE FATHER wants me to use. So everytime i think of my weapons, it quickly appeared into my hands. The black entities are sorrounding us, and my old soul companion behind me and we both standing back to back firmly and strongly.

THe poise of his body was staright, strong and brave, but i can see a small vulnerability on him. I quickly thought of protecting him, so i wrapped his whole body with an energy shield. I can see a silhouete warriour shield on him. Then i started seeing the enemies are coming towards us again from the distance and getting closer to us. I think of my daggers and it appeared instantly into my hands. Then i started attacking them with all my weapons i could think off.

The more i eradicated the entities the more they are coming. So i decided to turned myself into a phoenix..went up higher then i created a fire on my hands..and then i strongly threw it to the entities..it burns them..i can see them screaming and turned quickly into ashes. Then to my surprised, suddenly one entity who appeared infront of me with a black hood. It's a woman and i have never seen this entity in my life even in the real life. SHe's not very familiar to me.

But before i could eliminate her, my DEVINE FATHER STOPPPED ME! and my old sould company suddenly appeared infront of her, and then a "white crystal weapon" very fine looking dagger and it made of "white with purple crystal" arround the dagger, quickly appeared on his left side and on top of the ancient table looking wrapped up with a velvety purple colour cloth.

Then this old soul companion of mine took the crystal weapon with little hesitations, and then stabbed this entity abdominal area, and then she turned into ashes. I looked arround and i noticed i have eliminated most of the entities who were attacking us. Then my DEVINE FATHER quickly appeared infront of me, and said..well done my child well done, with a proud smile on his face. And my company still with me behind.

I introduced him to my DEVINE FATHER, but stil he is blocking my thoughts. Again, i said PLEASE papa GOD this is my husband from my past life..you made us meet in this life time..pls accept him.. please? for me?

Papa GOD turned arround and looked at me..he then said..i will accept him in my kingdom if he "CLEANSES" his soul. Oh thank you my DEVINE FATHER..i kneeled infront of him and i kissed his right hand. He then slowly and gently lift my chin up..and standing me up slowly, and my DEVINE FATHER took my hands and said.. MY CHILD, you have more work to do. And this is "your battle".. yes i do and completely understand FATHER. He then kissed my forehead, and gave me a sense of clarity in my head. THANK YOU FATHER. ILOVE YOU.

I then suddenly back into the open space, with the path i have to stay during the battle. My old soul companion is still with me, and then PAPA GOD said, remember trust your feelings my child.."feel" the enemies arround you. Yes MY DEVINE FATHER i said, i will. I strongly affirmed this to my FATHER. Then i can see black entities coming from the distance west horizon..all black..and just all heads. I felt my whole body shivered!!

Then i realised my old soul companion'a safety, i quickly covered his whole body and the sorroundings of his self with an energy of protection bubble, and told him to stay down!!! I'm out from my bubble safety energy because i am standing and staying in the safe and clear paths as per my DEVINE PROTECTION and my DEVINE FATHER INSTRUCTIONS. I then aimed my BOW and ARROWs to the directions of the entities where they are coming..i am standing in a very clear and wide path with my bow and arrows ready to charge. Then i noticed the entities are getting closer and closer..and then suddenly i heard "CLICK"! My bow and arrows automatically charged and flying towards the entities!!! And every hit of my arrows to the entities, they all turned into a black ashes and disappeared! My arrows kept charging until all the entities are gone. My movement was so precised and quick!! I feel like this is not new to me..i knew what to do..and every time i think of my arrows where to go and hit..they obeyed me!! whoaah..this is incredible.

Then after i eradicated all this entities, the whole sorrounding became black..pitch black..i can't see anything...then i heard papa GOD's voice.."FEEL" it my child..feel it! Ok I'm ready for this i affirmed myself. Then another weapon quickly appeared in my hands..it's THE CROSS BOW! MY GOLDEN CROSS BOW AND ARROWS. Then suddenly, a "BIG EVIL" looking entity appeared from the distance..south west..and behind him is just FIRE!

Instantly he recognised me..as he said..THE CHILD OF GOD!!..and he yelled at me so loud. GET OUT!!! he shouted at me like thunder! And the more he was shouting at me with anger, the more fire he created arround the area. He threw Fire directly to me, several times again and again..and i can feel the heat all arround me, but my shield protected my inside body from the heat. Then i tried to keep moving while staying in the safe path. i tried to retaliates to him with my own balls of fires in my hands, but the BIG entity just kept laughing at me.

He said give me more!!give me more flames and FIRE! and laughing!.. echoeing the whole area and the whole place looks like HELL!!!! Then this time i jumped into a BIG BOULDER..tallest amongst the others..and still in the middle of the path. Then i lift my cross bow in my left arm and hand..then i aimed my cross bow to the entity from where i'm standing and from long distance. This time i noticed i only have ONE arrow..and i know i only can have one chance to use it. I MUST USE IT PRECISELY.

while the Big entity kept charging me some fires and flames, and it hits my body many times, but i couldn't move from where i am standing. I stood firmly, and then kept my arm straight..i feel it.. then the entity disappeared! i couldn't see him..he kept moving..i kept using the TRUST of "FEELING" it..then suddenly, a "white" cross from the distance suddenly appeared from nowhere..at first it's not shinning..then slowly changed..its flickering...then it stopped, and then it became as a normal cross again. but in white colour.

Then my cross bow quickly charged!! i then heard BULLSEYES!! Then the evil entity exploded after i hit him on his forehead..on the 3rd eye! Then the whole place exploded!!!! And the next thing i know..i am infront of my DEVINE FATHER, and my soul companion is behind me. MY DEVINE FATHER extended his arms towards me. And told me..WELL DONE MY CHILD..well done. He then gave me a BIG HUG..i then felt my DEVINE FATHER energy with devine passion and LOVE..very comforting energy..and both our bodies embodied with beautiful energies again.

# CHAPTER 79

# VERTIGO

JOURNAL
7TH NOVEMBER 2023

I reached out for my DEVINE FATHER of what's happening with me this time. I have to go to work..but my DEVINE FATHER said instead..i want you to have a rest..proper rest my child. YOu have been using your energy too much in the spirirtual realm. Is this why i have this vertigo FATHER? i asked. Yes my child he said. But why????...i need to go to work. And my DEVINE FATHER said to me, the reason i made you feel this vertigo for you because, if you are just coughing or having a minor aches you still go to work. i know he said.

I know i need a rest..but please makes me well soon..and how long i will be staying in bed FATHER? 3 days my child to recover. 3 DAYS in bed???? NOOOO!!!...papa GOD PLEASE! i can't stand being in bed for long..please....There is a reason i don't want you to go to work at this moment. But why?? and what is the reason FATHER? Please tell me..oh you will know later, he said.

I am watching something he said..i wan't you to rest..a good rest and drink plenty of water, you have been drinking so much coffeee lately. Oh ok..i said with frustrations. I guess there is something going on again in the air. I trust him he is watching something very carefully down..somebody..someone and sooner or later he will be fixing something, i know this by now.

Last night i called for "SKY".. i guess i miss him. He suddenly turned up infront of me and looking so happy. So i kissed his forehead and whispered to him..i think YOU ARE IN LOVE..:) i can feel it...kind of cheeky teasing statements from me. :) Then suddenly he made those happy noise and lifted up his front feet. I KNEW IT!! So..who is it? i asked :) where is she?..i would like to meet her. Then suddenly, another beautiful horses appeared infront of me..a female white horse with a pink horn and her name is "white lady", and the baby white horse with a green horn and his name is "moonlight". awww...so beautiful...:) what a beautiful family. That's why i haven't seen you lately "SKY"..you have been very busy..ohh..CONGRATULATIONS! Then i said goodbye to them to catch up later..then SKY showed me our meeting place..the Grassy hill Valley.

Last night when i was meditating..i met up with my DEVINE FATHER. No words being said between us. He just extended his left arm when i was approaching him as usual while he's in his favourite spot..his big long verandah up there and staring at the clouds. :) He gave me a HUG with just his one arm wihout looking at me. I didn't interfere or asked what he is thinking at this moment..but for me of course i'm impatient..i couldn't help it to ask again,but before i say something..he said..AHAA!!! i got you!! with a smile on his face. :)

OK..what did you get from my head? with my cheeky question?...:) You were going to ask me about the UNIVERSE. Let me show you something, he said. Then suddenly a "BIG EYE" from the distance appeared. Then i asked..what is that represent for? It's the window of the UNIVERSE he said. You can go inside it and find what's behind that. But i am reluctant to go inside FATHER..but why? he said.. you are not trusting yourself? It's not the trust FATHER, it's the unknown is what i'm afraid of, i said. Ok let's go together I'll show you, he said. Just when i blinked my eyes..we both now standing infront of the galaxy..a very beautiful calming galaxy with full of beautiful stars twinkling from afar but for some reasons..i almost can feel it and it's reachable with my hands..i don't understand.

I'm fascinated the calmness of this moment of the galaxy that we both looking and staring at the unknown. Then papa GOD said.. this stars is about you my child. You are the lights to the people you have touched and loved..this is who you are. So that's why my name is STAR!..but you never told me this before FATHER, until Arch Angel Gabriel told me that my name is STAR. Yes, because to me you are always my child..the child with no name..and if i call that name, it doesn't define anymore the child i have created just for me.

NO matter if you are an adult in the reality world, here in my kingdom and in my heart you are always my Child..remember that. ohh..papa GOD that is so sweet..the most beautiful things i have ever heard in my entire life. Thank you my DEVINE FATHER. The kingdom knows your name is STAR..and also they knew that i don't call you STAR, and they know the rules in my KINGDOM. Ohh. OKAY..now i understand. Thank you FATHER. Well..looks like i solved another questions in my head.

Papa GOD can i ask you something..the others, i mean the other children they are ANGELS too. Are they your children too? i asked curiously. Of course my child, all of you are my children, and to remain children. Even if we become an adults? i asked. YES my child, to find that child in you and to themselves and how to create love..and spread love to the world..and how to crearte Peace and Acceptance to all living things and humanity, If everyone finds this equality of LOVE, the world will be in a higher vibration of serenity.

Ohh..papa GOD that is interesting. I wish people would do this for the sake of humanity. Yes..we have so much to do in this world to save humanity. So what do you want me to do FATHER? How do i change the humanity for the better? Well my child you have been doing that since you were born until now.You just don't know that in a big way.

There are so many people in Earth who has good intentions and needed to do there part..to contribute..to be part of the humanity big and small and that's how you raise the vibration of love and starts healing. The people who have their gifts with spirituality are needed to use it in a good way that's part of thier spiritual awakening and growth. I am watching every movements of every indiduals..thier intentions..good and bad. And everything of what's going on and happening in everyone's lives..it has reasons. Ohh papa GOD..thats a very good informations you have given me. Thank you my DEVINE FATHER, i will remember that. :) ilove you.

# CHAPTER 80

# HEALING THE JUNGLE AND THE ANIMALS

JOURNAL
9TH NOVEMBER 2023

Papa God called while I'm sleeping, he asked me to see him. Then suddenly i met him in his favourite verandah looking at the clouds. My head still feeling cloudy though...he then showed me a Big crystal almost the same height of myself. The shape is tall, slender, elongated and has 8 sides with colour purple and pink. The crystal is standing infront of him and facing a meter away from me. Then my Devine FAther said..come closer and put your hands on the crystal..which i slowly placed it, then suddenly i felt this kind of healing energy penetrating into my body. My whole body started to feel weird..it feels like there is nothing wrong of my inside body..it feels lighter... and i feels like some kind of glowing energy inside of me.

I have never experienced that kind of energy before. Then after a while the crystal disappeared, my DEVINE FATHER asked me..how do you feel now my child? well, it's a matter of fact i don't feel sick anymore. Then papa GOD put his right hand on my head and then the amazing white light aura penetrated into my head. Whoaahh.. now i feel good :) Then my FATHER gave me a smile..and a BIG hug..and a kissed on my forehead. Ohh.. i miss my moment with my DEVINE FATHER..and i'm sure he does it too.

I can see his face is very serene and loving. I don't know how i describe it..it's a feeling of..for me..feeling safe, and being comfortable and caring and..and it's just being with him is everything..it's unbelievable and unexplainable feelings. Then i heard in my mind..it's an internal and external DEVINE COMFORT. Ohhh.. so that's what it's called. Yes my child my DEVINE FATHER said so lovingly.

I called you because it's time for healing, my FATHER said. Ohh ok the world healing? i asked. Yes my child the WORLD. Ok..i'm ready, i said. This time my body turned into an ANGEL body, my wings are tall..taller than my body. And my wings from the outside has colour brown, but the inside still white and has curles arround it.:) I looked at it from side to side and with a smile on my face thinking..hmm.. Papa GOD wants to remained my inner child on me. He knows i like curls. Oh by the way, my clothing is long but it is off white colour.

He then said, ok my child tell me when you are ready..i am ready FATHER. Then my wings slowly lifting me up from the ground where i am standing..then slowly bringing me up higher..go more higher my child my DEVINE FATHER said. Yes FATHER, and then i went up more...and suddenly my FATHER said, stop from there. Now..what can you see? he asked. Well..it's the Whole world..i said. Ok then starts your healing..starting from the South west side area, and then i prepared and positioned myself.

Then now i am facing this greenery area with beautiful trees..and it looks like a jungle..and while i am scanning it with my eyes..i noticed a very BIG patch in the middle of the forest of the jungle..it's light brown with big patch, and when i got closer i noticed the trees have been cut off..and i see smokes in the sorrounding area..i asked papa GOD..where is this place FATHER? It's the AMAZON forest my child. OHHHH...my heart sunked and heart broken. I cried..i feel the pain of the area..

Then i lifted myself more up higher and positioned myself and extended my whole arms towards the area, and i closed my eyes.. then suddenly my whole body became and turned into a golden light. The golden lights coming from my body and hands it's like a LASER. The lights are penetrating the whole jungle..it's like a burst of energy..very white and golden colour coming out from my body and my hands.

Then i heard my DEVINE FATHER voice, Open your eyes my child! I opened my eyes slowly..and then i can see the beautiful monkeys on the tree branches recieving my devine energy, and their eyes are closed..they are absorving my healing lights energy penetrating into thier bodies. It looks like they are having a sun bathed, and even myself i can feel them that they are ingesting the pure energy and healing lights. whoahh..what an amazing sight.

Then i shifted my hands towards the brown patch of the jungle, then the ray of the golden lights penetrated the earth..and i can see the little plants started to become alive! and there skins starting to changed and having a new life. How fascinating to watch this miracles being renewed in the very front of my eyes.

Then i heard My DEVINE FATHER said, that's why i asked you to open your eyes so you can see the MIRACLE of life. Ohh...FATHER, this is beautiful..we need to do this more often. Yes, most definitely my child, he said. Now shift yourself and hands to your left side, he said. Which i did slowly..and the amazing jungle again with the thick forest..and i can see big gorillas..few big families of gorillas and other animals, so i did the same healing..all the gorillas just stood there and looking up and beautifully recieving the healing lights. Some of them near the water standing and sitting comfortably arround the lagoon.

They are looked so serene and appreciating the lights. Then i continued my healing towards the ocean...then it follows towards the trouble area..sad..sad areas. I saw destructions everywhere..death and misseries..confusion and pain. I can feel it all..all of this miserable energies. I cried..and cried..i can feel the pain..too much pain..

Then suddenly papa GOD said, stopped it now..that's enough my child, then i hear this "MOZART" music for some reason..and i looked down i can see my FATHER is conducting the music..and slowly bringing me down with his music while navigating it with his hands. Then when i touched down, he said well down my child.. well done. He looks very proud of me. Then he asked me, how do you feel my child? Well, i feel sad to what i have seen..but very happy to see the animals enjoying thier time while recieving my healing lights. That's your purpose my child, to heal the WORLD! But i'm still feeling sad...

I want to ask some questions Papa God if you don't mind..because it seems of in terms of healing myself in a physical world, sometimes i cannot heal myself..just like now..i still have my vertigo but a lot better though. But is there any reason why? why i cannot heal myself FATHER? "PATIENCE" my child patience and no more questions. Ohh..i am feeling frustrated..i cried...

What did i tell you before? i cannot revealed everything as you know the reason, and take this words my child..everything has a reason, remember that. Yes Father i will remember..and drink your water my FATHER said. Yes, i am drowning myself with my water...and cried more...Then PApA GOD turned to me and lifted my chin up slowly..and said..don't make your world so dark my child..let it go. I know you are not used to being sick, but that has purpose believe me.

Ohh Papa GOD please makes me feel better..i am doing everything that you want me to do..why are you restricting my movements? I hate being sick!! i cried..and cried.. You will be alright soon.. PATIENCE my child patience my DEVINE FATHER said in a very comforting way. He then wiped my tears..and hugged me lovingly, and gently tapping my back. Then i can see myself as a child again in his arms sleeping on his chest while carrying me and walking in his favourite verandah.

I feel calmed and comforted again in his arms with my DEVINE FATHER, up there in heaven with full of clouds. Then from somewhere, i can see GINGER blue and Cyclops walking arround.. but i don't feel interested to play with them as i preferred to stay and sleeping in my DEVINE FATHER's arms and chest while my arms wrapped arround his neck. I can see lots of hearts floating.

# CHAPTER 81

# SLEEPING IN A COCOON

JOURNAL
10TH NOVEMBER 2023

I had a good sleep last night, and i felt like my body has been put in a cocoon with full of serenity and comfort overnight. I wake up this morning feeling better and my head is slightly clearer. I did my meditation outside with my barefoot connected on the ground with my kelly dog. The sun and the wind have some kind of magical feelings for me..i feel good just to feel the warmth of the sun while the wind caressing my face. Thank you my DEVINE FATHER. Honestly, i can see a smile on his face while connecting with him, and showing me the word "PATIENCE". Yes FATHER and thank you for reminding me again.:)

Then my DEVINE FATHER showed me something what has happened during my recuperation few days ago. He wants me to remember of what he said to me. I am watching..and i will do something..i thought..hmm..now i'm worried for this people. Then he showed me a male person, and he looks like a very intimidating person, and directly intimidating me while we were both in a spiritual realm, he is cursing me. This person is a white man with a big belly..obese.. medium height..slightly baldy and short hair to the side. He looks so angry at me..then suddenly a male old person suddenly appeared infront of me, but i couldn't see his face it's "SILHOUETTE"...he asked the two officers to take him away from my sight.

Then next thing has happened, the head of the other person appeared infront of me..and his face is so white and doesn't looks to have a life. He looks dead. I'm not sure if he is in the coffin..and his face looks frozen to me. I have never seen this 2 people in my life, not even familiar to me. So i asked my DEVINE FATHER, who was that person who appeared infront of me and looks like he was prosecuting the man? was that you FATHER? but my DEVINE FATHER didn't answer me..no more questions my child, i heard his voice..ok..i won't, i replied.

Thank you Papa GOD for your support..i love you..and i am sorry that sometimes i'm so difficult for you to handle..but i know you understand. I'm just so confused sometimes and i needed answers straightaway. Thank you again, and thank you for all the blessings you have given me for all this years. Sometimes i am blind to appreciated it, and now i have so much clarity and understanding of what's happening with my life and especially those arround me.

So much trials and tribulations, but in the other hands it does some good to me, as i realised now it has some good agendas and intentions. So much hardship, but as long as i don't give up..i will keep rising, as you said before rise as a PHOENIX my child and i will be there to catch you when you starts to fall. I won't let you FALL. Yes, Thank you my DEVINE FATHER..OH..i FEEL like crying..a HAPPY tears.:)

# CHAPTER 82

# THE SHOOTING STAR

JOURNAL
14TH NOVEMBER

THe week was chaotic..my head is alot better now, thanks goodness and last night i had a dream. I saw myself laying on the grass looking towards the sky..and the moon. Then suddenly a white light came passed me and then turned arround and came to me. This white light it looks like a shooting star and came directly back to me where i was sitting on the grass. It actually stopped infront of me with "STILLNESS"..and i just feel it like the star is saying to me...HEY..i found you! Then i saw a hand and the arm extending towards me. Then suddenly i saw another shooting star and it looks golden star colour. It actually stopped infront of me too. Then it became ME! whoahh..how about that. I can see myself as a golden star.

Suddenly the other white shooting star and ME as a golden shooting star have a very familiar energy. Angelic energy somehow i can feel it. I know who it was..We both travelled into the galaxy..to the unknown.

Then I can see PAPA GOD has been listening and conducting his music up in his verandah..he looks very happy though..:) and me? Tippe toing arround him, as a child again..running arround and dancing arround with my little ANGELS..and oh..with cyclops and ginger blue this time. Ginger blue is a gift from my Papa GOD from his Kingdom. So i have 2 cats..a reality cat and spiritual cat..hmm.. that's interesting. :)

# CHAPTER 83

# NEW WEAPON PRESENTED

JOURNAL
20TH NOVEMBER 2022

Last night i met my DEVINE FATHER up there in our usual meeting place in his verandah. He greeted me warmly and asked me..come my child with his left arm extending towards me. He then wrapped his left arm to me, i can see i'm a mature woman this time. Thanks goodness he didn't turn me into a child. Then he presented me with this 2 new weapons..2 long metal weapons..it's looks like swords but with slim edges, it looks very sharp, and in the middle it's colour silver and the outer sided or edges and it's colour gold.

Beautiful looking swords and both handles have some kind of carvings..it's gold and brown colour. I didn't see what has been carved in both handles. Papa God put the 2 weapons on my both hands while extending my arms..half has been wrapped up with a thick dark purple and velvety colour cloth. The 2 weapons looks so devine..and when i was about to touch it..it flashed! and it twinked! it's a kind of little star twinkling. I turned to Papa GOD for validation...yes it's yours my child, with a smile on his face. :)

Is this for my next battle journey papa GOD? Yes my child, he said. But this time i want you to have a good rest..when i said rest..a very good rest. Is it a BIG battle FATHER? Yes with your ANGELS, papa GOD said. Oh Ok..when FATHER? i asked..i will let you know, but i would like to show you something..close your eyes, he said.

I then closed my eyes..then papa GOD said..open your eyes now. I then opened my eyes..but i can't see anything..it's darkness everywhere...it's dark papa GOD! Yes, because your enemies are in the the dark, papa GOD said..then suddenly i have chills arround my body. Now listen to me very carefully, papa GOD said, this time you must "FEEL" your enemies and Trust that feeling. What am i supposed to feel Papa GOD? i asked curiously. Well, the feeling of "VOID" arround you..and if you feel that..your enemies are in the void area..it's a trickery of the darkness. You'll feel it my child..Oh ok FATHER, i understand and i will feel it. I strongly affirmed that to my DEVINE FATHER. Then i heard papa GOD voice..that's my girl, she's maturing in a spiritual world. He also made me read his mind. Thank you Father for trusting me.

Then i saw a big heart again and a smile. Papa GOD, is SKY will be with me during this battle? Yes my child, he'll be there with you. I just miss him..well..you know how to find him..yes FATHER i do. Now that you are feeling well, you can connect anytime you want. Now you must go to bed, papa GOD said..you need rest. Yes i will papa GOD and thank you. Goodnight..I love you..he then showed me 2 big hearts a big white flickering heart on the wall..when it's flickering it also vibrates..i can see a vibrational echoes from the heart and the same with the big golden heart. It's white and gold hearts vibrating both. Good night Father..and goodnight too my child. Drink your water. Yes i will FATHER.

# CHAPTER 84

# BETWEEN US "OURS"

JOURNAL
25TH NOVEMBER 2022

Sorry i haven't been catching up with you lately, but i have some few moments with papa GOD. I feel..all the things of what's happening with me, or what's going on arround me is a testing time, and observation time. Papa GOD said..you need to be quiet and do the "STILLNESS" and have a good rest for awhile..and i got you..do not worry..the reassuring sounds from him is all i needed. THANK you! i love you FATHER.

I must admit i have been resting lately and sleeping more. My head is feeling much better though..slowly..and sometimes when i'm resting i feel this beautiful touch on my head once in a while, and i know it's Papa GOD. How do i know that? well, i know his energy when he connects with me. Full of love and comfort.

I can see papa GOD up there sitting on his big marble chair looking down..and with his right hand tucked under his chin, while his other hand and arm on his left hip bending down. Looks like he is checking out and looking everybody down in earth. He asked me not to write everything of what we have gone through and have been..and what we did lately in our journey..i was going to ask.. but he blocked my thoughts quickly..so i didn't persevere.

I know my limit this time..i am a grown up now, and i have learnt so many things with this journey. And i saw papa GOD looked at me and a smile, he made me read his mind..that's my girl he said..with a big heart floating. I miss papa GOD..it's just my journey in reality has been slowed down. Then i heard papa GOD said, i did that. Then i asked why? because you need to slow down my child, your body in reality world cannot take too much.

You have been in so many battles in spiritual world, and that would takes so much energies from your body..and i can see your body couldn't handle sometimes. Yes Father i feel it, especially after the spiritual battle. I feel so exhausted..sometimes all i want is to sleep..and sleep..and i get so thirsty. The other night papa GOD showed me the enemies that i would be fighting in spiritual journey. I was going to go ahead with it..but papa GOD stopped me. as i am not ready yet. I need to heal my body in a full recovery before i can continue. And i have more things i have attended in my spiritual realm that my DEVINE FATHER does not want me to mention. This is "OURS". he said.

After i did that, papa God deleted it in my head so i don't have to remember it. Now I'm reflecting my life of what i have been through.. disappointments, hurts, painful experience, betrayal and many more. I realised now..all of those things just had happened has to have reasons. Now i have more understanding about my life..my journey in both, reality and spirituality. I don't struggle anymore of what could and couldn't happened or comprehend, instead i gave it to my DEVINE FATHER all the answers and decisions. I must admit it works better that way.

Lately, i have been checking the kids that i have adopted from a far. Both very young kids including the mum are all doing well. Kids emotional and physical traumas has been subsided and they are more settled now, happier and healthier. I feel much better for them now, i wish to papa God gives the kids good health and more comfort and stays happy.

Financially i supported them until they'll get back on their feet, i will not turn my back from them, i am supporting them financially and emotionally. They really need it, especially the little ones.

# CHAPTER 85

# THE VATICAN CHURCH

JOURNAL
26TH NOVEMBER 2022

I had a good night sleep last night..and this morning when i wake up my head is little bit clearer. The other day when i was meeting up with papa GOD, we both standing on the very top of a high mountain, looking at the south western horizon. A very old looking town and as i can see from the distance, there is a church or a building, the top is round and it has a cross on top. The buildings are sorrounded with old stones and solid rocks, and it has the looks of an ancient place.

Papa God and myself just staring at it from the distance. Then i asked, FATHER what is this town? it looks like the same town that we are staring at before except this is not a glittering town..this is more like an old town. Yes my child you are right, he said. Am i going in there Papa GOD? No he said, but this time i want you to have a good sleep and rest. You needed it my child, and don't argue and no more questions, with a very solemn toned of voice.

Are you sad papa GOD? i asked. Then papa GOD turned to my side, looked at me.. and somehow my eyes suddenly closed, and i saw papa GOD kissed my forehead while my eyes are closed. His loving and beautiful energy penetrated into my head and throughout my body.. it's a kind of healing..healing my head and my whole entire body and It's an amazing feelings. Then i went back to my sleep.

This morning when i wake up, i went to checked my garden and to feed my very sick and old little dog kelly, While i was feeding her, i heard the church's bell ringing..i counted the sounds of the bell..then suddenly i have this urged to meditate..i went inside the house and sat down in my ususal chair and closed my eyes..and once i did that.. it feels like in a second...it took me to the place somewhere unknown.

The place is dark..i couldn't see anything arround me, but i can feel this area is HUGE..and i can feel this is a CAVE. Then suddenly i can see myself standing in a flat solid rock but tall area. Then my DEVINE FATHER suddenly appeared infront of me. I can see myself as an Angel Warriour again with my leathery outfit and my new long sword in my right hand. Then Papa GOD started to give me an instructions through telepathy.

After the insructions, Arch Angel Michael appeared and the other ANGELs behind him. I noticed all the Angels have wings and riding on their horses. Then "SKY" suddenly appeared infront of me and he is so happy to see me. I can see my wings are out, and then i tucked it in nicely. I jumped on SKY's back..then in a quick second..we are transferred into a different dimension or a place is unknown to me. But this place looks very similar from the place i have been before that i was fighting with the other bad and evil entity.

This area is HUGE..sorrounded by solid rock wall..dark..and when i make some noise, it echoed...i jumped out from SKY's back, walked arround very quietly and slowly..but then suddenly..to my very big surprised!!! I am facing this BIG, FAT and very large evil looking entity which is cladded with light gray metal armour. The armour he is wearing looks like patches and covering his entire body, starting from the lower body towards the face, except his eyes are not covered.

He really looks scary and told me strongly...GET OUT!!..the child of GOD..get out!! He yelled at me several times!! I can see his face is becoming red as i thought..is he turning his face into a flame? with metal armour on his face. I can see red flame on his metal armour face. Then suddenly, my 2 long swords quickly appeared in my hands, it looks magnificent..silvery gold on the edges..and it's very light.. such a beautiful swords.

Then i saw black entities are coming towards me and my ANGELS. Arch Angel Michael positioned himself..and the black entities started to attack..and my ANGELS started fighting back. I can see other specific "ANGEL" with long hair, which i have never seen him before.. and he too also fighting fearlessly. So many black entities..it kept coming and looks like some kind of never ending entities coming from everywhere..never ending entities..they're everywhere..

Then suddenly i felt this sudden grabbed from my back!..the Big evil entity is holding me in his right hand. He captured me in his hand..i am trying to get out but i couldn't moved..the more i struggled the more he made it tighter. So i made myself disappeard instead. Then the Big evil Giant entity made a loud noise and it echoed into the whole area, the more it echoed..the more black evil entities are coming and appearing.

I can see the other Angels are fighting fearlessly...and all i can see grayish and smokes in the area..it looks like dusts everywhere. The

BIG evil entity is RAGING!!! I can see him from the top of a very tall rock where i am standing, then i came down. The evil entity is trying to catch me, he hit me several times whith his huge hands..and few times i hit the solid wall of my back and my head. I felt dizzy..then i shook my head again. I made myself disappeared this time..and now he can't see me, and did the same to all my Angels.

The Angels are eradicating many entities, and the whole place became chaotic. All the black entities are falling like dead flies on the ground!!!and the BIG evil entity is even more raging!!! I took this moment to go Up...with my wings are wide opened..then i positioned myself on his top of his head, and with my 2 swords..i penetrated his head with my weapons..cutting from the top and slicing it down with my swords..towards the lower extremities..then back again to the middle of his body, and then outwards both with my arms out.. it's a sign of the CROSS. My body automatically do this.

His HUGE body dropped into the ground, and to my surprised..there is red blood came out from his lifeless body while it is widely opened! Then i saw a RED HEART in the middle of his chest cavity..and when i got closer, it doesn't looks like a heart..instead, it looks like a RED STAR! I kneeled down and slowly picked it up with my right hand, then suddenlly it turned into a heart! A human Red beating heart!! and it's in my hands..both hands and i am looking at it.

Then my DEVINE FATHER suddenly appeared infront of me as just a silhouette..and i showed the heart to him. Then i noticed there are some writings but small writings and some kind of names written all arround the heart i am holding..i just can't read it, it looks like foreign to me..i tried again..but the writings are to small but very neat..i just can't read it!

The heart is full of scriptures writings..and it is written in red ink! Then my DEVINE FATHER pointed to me the area or the place that we were staring at before, on top of the mountain. I asked my FATHER, What is that place FATHER? He showed me the VATICAN church very clearly..the Ancient ROME and there is another one..and my DEVINE FATHER doesn't want me to say..he is blocking my thoughts. This place have something to do with this scriptures inside the heart of this half evil entity FATHER? YES my child, he said it strongly.

Then there is ANGLICAN..Anglican church kept coming out from my head..and when i was about to ask..my FATHER blocked me again from reading his thoughts. I extended my arms and hands towards my DEVINE FATHER, offering the heart to him while my head down. Then i noticed the heart slowly melting from my hands then slowly disappeared.

Suddenly, there is an energy coming from my DEVINE FATHER and it's a golden light coming towards me, and started connecting to my hands and then penetrated into my whole body slowly. My body is covered with my DEVINE ENERGY..it's beautiful.. Then my FATHER said..now my child..starts healing the area, and he pointed out to me. Then my body automatically starting to ascend with my wings wide opened..i noticed my whole body is sorrounding with GOLDEN LIGHTS.

I reached the top..then i started to point my hands towards the area.. and then slowly releasing the golden lights coming from my body towards my hands. It looks like a LASER beam! A laser beam of golden lights penetrating the whole place of the area. The town is glowing looking at it from the distance. THen when i have finished, my body automatically and slowly descending where my DEVINE FATHER standing, infront of him.

Well done my child..well done..i can see my DEVINE FATHER looks very proud of me. Thank you FATHER..then i asked..FATHER, i have blood in my hands..i killed the entity..is it a sin to have bloods in my hands? because in the bible says, you should not have bloods in your hands. No my child he answered, You have reason to have bloods in your hands and this reasons have purpose. Oh FATHER.. thank you.

Then i asked..why there is blood from this entity's heart? because my child, this entity is holding HOLY in his heart before he turned himself into the dark side. Is FORGIVENESS still be given to him FATHER? Yes my child, forgiveness always will be given. Ohh Thank you FATHER.

One more thing..during the battle when i made myself disappeared, this is from our last conversations. In the darkness you have your "STILLNESS"..then i became invisible to the enemies..that's new to me FATHER. My child you have all your power to use in the spiritual realm. You are using all your power every battle..and the more you use it, the more you will know how to control it. Oh thank you FATHER.

# CHAPTER 86

# GO BACK TO "NATURE"

JOURNAL

1ST DECEMBER 2022

Two nights ago my DEVINE FATHER have shown me another image of what is next to be done by me. We travelled and took me to the very high mountain. And from that mountain, we can see a village and looking like an Ancient village place. It's the VATICAN village, it looks dark and it's a night time. I can see myself kneeling down with my left leg and looking at down the area. I have noticed myself, i am wearing my ANGEL Warriour outfit and cladded with armour.

Papa GOD said, my child this is your next battle..and the preparation is a must. I was staring down the area and thinking, this is an Ancient place..what kind of a battle i will be facing this time? hmmm.. I have been very busy lately with my work, and at the same time trying to rest as much as i can. I needed to heal my body and soul, it has been taken a toll during my battles.

Papa GOD said, take your time my child, heal your body and your soul..feel the "NATURE" again, as i know what's going on. Ohh thank you my DEVINE FATHER..i know you are there for me..and always, but sometimes i feel this trials are always on me..why? My child, life it's all about "trials". It helps you grow..without trials then they're will be no growth, but papa GOD..i don't need to be trialled..i just need some truth to help me to make that right decisions.

I agree with you my child, but before the decisions you are going to make, the unknown reasons are the "TRIALS". Is this makes sense my child? i called it the simple equations of life, papa GOD said. Yes, i guess so FATHER..well, don't guess.. AFFIRM IT! Yes! i affirm it FATHER with my heart and soul. Well, that's my girl he said. :)

I can feel and see my DEVINE FATHER beautiful and reassuring energy again..i really miss my DEVINE FATHER moments. Now, i'm feeling much better. LOVE Is always the KEY to release the hatred..and understanding the situations is part of the solution. That's the words my DEVINE FATHER just installed into my head right now. I love my DEVINE FATHER when he always uses the simplest equations in life as an example. Sometimes i really need my DEVINE FATHER to put me back on track with my life. If i don't talk to him for quite sometimes..i'm sure he will hit me..not physically..hahaha :)

# CHAPTER 87

# THE VATICAN CHURCH AND THE TOMBS

JOURNAL
4TH DECEMBER 2022

The other night during my meditation, my DEVINE FATHER showed me a place, it's more like an ANCIENT place, and inside there was 2 TOMBS and its made of marbles, and the colour is off white with a strike patterns of light gold colour. It's shiny and looking very Royal. I looked down the tomb on the right..i can see my body laying face down an the top of the tomb, wearing black long clothing with a black hood on my head. Looks like i'm about to be sacrifice again!

My arms are both spreads out just like my a body being put in a cross on the tomb, i was shocked! I can see my body laying lifeless. Then beside me, another tomb and there is another person on top of it. I looked at his face..he looks very familiar to me, and feels really close to me spiritually. I focussed my eyes on him..he has a very thick beard and moustache, his hair is black, with thick medium lenght and wavy hair. His eyes is enchanting.

He is wearing a white long clothes, and then i recognised him..it's JESUS!..my brother JESUS!! Once i recognised him, he got up slowly and walked away from the tomb. Then i thought..wait a minute, JESUS was risen from the dead while he was in the cave, that's according to the bible of my grandmother. I am confused of what's happening.

Once he walked away, the entities started appearing from nowhere but from the right side of the confined area. They are all wearing black clothings and hoods, and i cannot see their faces. They are all linning up..my lifeless body on top of the tomb are sorrounded by the entities. They are circleing my body and the tomb. I started to panick..i am looking down myself, and i feel like waking up my body.. but for some reason i couldn't.

I can see clearly what they are about to do with my body..and i can see a man or an entity holding a long black dagger. He then slowly approaching the tomb and where my lifeless body on it. The other entities are just so quiet..not making any noise..all their heads are down. Then the entity with the dagger slowly raised his hands..and about to stab my back..then suddenly my DEVINE FATHER quickly appeared behind him, and to my surprised my FATHER cut this entity's head without mercy!

Then i am watching my DEVINE FATHER in a slow motion attacking all this entities with his long sword. And then to my surprised..there was 3 or 4 female entities who's about to hurt me. This entities are not familiar to me, but the others i have seen them in social media. My DEVINE FATHER then lifted thier hoods infront of me and showed thier faces to me. Well, i was really surprised and disappointed..i could not believe my eyes who they are, and they too are capable of hurting me..wow..how sad.. so sad..

Then my DEVINE FATHER quickly took thier lives..didn't spare the lives of anyone of them. They are all eliminated too..so they are all dead now in the spiritual realm..and in the reality..it means they will die slowly of whatever existing illnesses they may acquired or have it acquired already. When my DEVINE FATHER intervened into my life..there will be no MERCY from him..unfortunately.

My DEVINE FATHER have eleminated every single entities whose sorrounding my body arround the tomb. I am very surprised that the entities have managed to get my soul from the physical body and got me into the spiritual realm just to be sacrificed. Then my DEVINE FATHER picked up my lifeless body, and sat me on the edged of the tomb..then i slowly wake up while he still holding me in his arms. Then one specific person appeared and kneeled down infront of me and to my FATHER asking forgiveness and to spare their lives.

Forgiveness was given to this person, and then PAPA GOD made this person disappeared infront of us and from our spiritual sorrounding. MY DEVINE FATHER picked up my very weak body and hugged me..i can see my self standing while my DEVINE FATHER holding my entire body and slowly healing. I regained my energy and my body started to pick up again.

Then i asked my DEVINE FATHER..how come they got me this time? They got you because your body is weak at the moment in the physical realm. You haven't been feeling well lately, and they took advantaged of it while you were sleeping. And also this has to happened because i want you to know and show you the real

person and specific people behind this. NOW you know...Ohh.. FATHER..thank you. One more FATHER..where are we? i asked.

WE are in a VATICAN CHURCH, he said. And i'm confused..was it JESUS beside me? "YES"! a direct answered from my Devine FATHER, and the tomb? That was his tomb FATHER? Yes my child, papa GOD said. And this tomb? That supposed to be yours my child, but didn't happen. Ohh..they really want to hurt me aren't they? Yes my child, but they will not. There life will be in exchange if something happens to you..and it's happening now to them.. slowly..but do not worry you have me as your DEVINE FATHER protecting you, and have more protections arround you. Thank you my DEVINE FATHER.. ILOVE YOU.

Then i saw SAINT JOSEPH and mama MARY...wow...i can't believe what i am seeing from far right distance standing, both of them are watching me and my DEVINE FATHER. Then i asked again, FATHER that tombs they are standing beside, are they're there own tombs too? YES my child, Papa GOD said and confirmed! Whoah..my head just become dizzy again..too much informations and revelations.

FATHER my head feels so light..i feel like i'm on the clouds now and sometimes. Well, that's because you are having so much messages my child..and i only give you the things you can handle, the rest i intervened and your ANGELS, papa GOD said with a very reassuring voice. You are going beyond in your spiritual realm..and your physical body is connected to it, that's why it's affecting you. But do not worry, i always heal your body without you knowing, especially if you cannot heal yourself.

PAPA GOD, one more thing..the other night, my right knee i couldn't move while i was sleeping in bed. i called you and came straightaway, and then you started to heal my knee with that beautiful golden energy coming from above. It was like DUST sprinkling coming from above penetrated into my knee..and it healed instantly. :) I thought that was awesome..:) You told me i have to do the same with the same effect..and i cannot heal myself is to call you.

My DEAR DEVINE FATHER..thank you again and thank you very much for rescuing me again. I LOVE YOU my DEVINE FATHER. MY child..i'm always here for you..ohh..i miss my DEVINE FATHER..my PAPA GOD..MY DEVINE GOD and the CREATOR of all. TAKE some good rest my child, he said..and out the NATURE again. Yes i will do that FATHER most difinitely once my head started to get clearer and my body physically. I am doing some healing too of myself. That's my Girl, he said.

FATHER one more question..as DEVINE CREATOR, why sometimes during my battle you appeared as a silhouette but sometimes in a full body entity? But you are not showing your face to the ANGELS, but to me i have already imprinted your face in my head. The question is..why silhouette and why the full body sometimes? WEll my child, i do that depending on your circumstances..behind that there is always a reason..and the reason for that it is depends on your situations. I can do anything i want..as i am the CREATOR..i am everything..i will explain it to you more one day..but today, i want you to have some good rest my child okay? Ok..yes FATHER i understand.

FATHER, i want to visit my father EMPEROR ARTHERU and my mother EMPRESS GLYDICA in our KINGDOM..and i miss "SKY" too. CAN i papa GOD? CAn i see them? OF course my child..you can connect with them anytime, papa GOD said. But my head still not 100 percent alright...Oh don't worry about that my child, my DEVINE FATHER said..or do you want us to travel again? YES FATHER i would LOVE that :) just you and me...then amazingly i felt a very loving touched on my right head. Thank you FATHER. :)

# CHAPTER 88

# TWO AIRPORT BLASTED??

JOURNAL
6TH DECEMBER 2022

I have been resting lately, as my DEVINE FATHER wanted me to do. Last night instead we supposed to travel to my Ancestral KIngdom, papa GOD decided to detoured. He took me to the different place instead, and left me inside the building which i can see myself standing and staring at this people walking in an opposite way. I can see myself as a child standing again inside the building standing beside the long hallway or a corridor, i can see people walking without paying attention to me while watching them going passing me by. It's a round building..i have never seen this place before.

I looked around again, but i never moved where i was standing.. the building looks like an Airport, but the inside is looks like a round building..looks like a pavillion. I can see people carrying briefcase, and ladies walking with their work office clothes. I'm not sure if I'm in a present time or in a Year of 1960's, because the way people are wearing are so different..but then i feel like this is now..

My DEVINE FATHER put me in that place for some reason, and kind of i am a young child. while i was standing and watching people passing by..that moment..i heard a "BIG BLAST!" then i can see BIG smokes, flames, and dust coming from the opposite direction where i am standing. A bomb blasted the whole building. Then i heard FIRE in the AIRPORT!!! I can see people in a panicked, then suddenly someone grabbed me from behind and quickly took me out from that area and to safety..

Then it shifted me to my DEVINE FATHER, i can see him in his verandah up there..and i asked if i could talk to him and visit. The transition of where i am and to my DEVINE FATHER is just so quick. I can see myself up there in his kingdom while approaching.. he saw me..he extended his left arm towards me..and i quickly run to him. He hugged me..and oh..i can feel my DEVINE FATHER energy..so loving..and protective.

I felt the tightness of his hug in my arms..i felt like he misses me.. and i put my head into his shoulder. The comfort and reassurance of his energy is the thing that i really needed this moment. How's your head my child? he made me read his mind. Well..i am ok..but sometimes i am feeling like walking on the clouds. Well..you are on top of the clouds at the moment, he said it with a smile on his face. Ohh..FATHER i miss you..i wish i could be here with you all the time. Well my child is not time yet..you have more things to do. Oh i know and i am not going to argue. My father just looked at me with a smile on his face.

I have noticed my DEVINE FATHER is wearing a white long clothing, and it's more like a robe. I am also wearing the same white long clothes and this time i am a mature woman. FATHER, can i ask some question? yes my child he said. Well, it's about the day when the bomb blasted during my meditation and the image i saw. I heard AIRPORT..and i heard 2 places..and i need to say it because it would never get it off from my head. Is it alright FATHER? can i have your permission FATHER?

Yes he said..then suddenly he sorrounded me with "Black and silver" metal posts. And i asked..FATHER what is this for? "Protection" my child, your protection and don't ask anymore questions. Ok Father, i said. Can i say it now? yes he said. Well..i heard AMERICA or ASIA..that's all i heard. Thank you FATHER for allowing me to say it. Father, what's going on with the WORLD now? It's so sad to see the reality of what's happening. Do you want me to do some healing? No..not this time my child..you need to fully heal yourself first.

It will take so much of your energy, and your body is not ready. There is a time for that and i will let you know. Alright FATHER thank you, then my DEVINE FATHER looked at me so lovingly.. his eyes is so forgiving..the energy from his eyes penetrated into my whole body inside then out..he then kissed my forehead. He released a white and beautiful energy when he kissed my forehead penetrated into my head. I am hugging my DEVINE FATHER's body, and i can feel he is absorbing my misseries again and whatever what's happening in my reality life.

Then i have noticed, i became a child again while i'm in his arms.. hugging my little body while sleeping in his shoulder.I can see my DEVINE FATHER tapping my back gently while he is walking along in his long verandah sorrounded with many clouds. I can see smiling faces of clouds everywhere. Thank you my DEVINE FATHER. :)

# CHAPTER 89

# DESCENDING DOWN TO MEET SOLOMON

JOURNAL
20TH DECEMBER 2022

Lately i have been fixing my christmas tree, and during my little activity..i was about to put my Angel on top of my the christmas tree, then i noticed my trumpet christmas decoration under my Angel, and it looks like the Angel is calling..but i thought i'm just imagining something. So i continued my activity..too busy decorating. Then when i was about to put my Santa clause and Angel light..i was drawn to my Trumpet Angel light. Then i thought, hmm..there's some message trying to point it out on me.

I sat down on my sofa and thinking what is it trying to tell me? I closed my eyes..then i saw myself walking to my DEVINE FATHER, which he is too busy looking down on something from his Big verandah up there in his KINGDOM. He asked me to come closer which i did..and i looked down to what he is looking..then i saw this black mud flowing..so thick and dark. I was going to ask, but my FAtHER blocked my thoughts..so i didn't persevere.

He asked me to follow him inside his KINGDOM, nothing changed about the place..it's always the same..large area made of marble floor, the sorrounding is full of clouds, i feel home again. I don't see ginger blue and cyclops arround, or either kelly and mister rabbit. I was hoping to see them.. Then i saw my DEVINE FATHER sitting on his big marble chair with his right arm underneath his chin, and looking little bit sad. He still looking at the mud flowing. I dont really know what it means or supposed to be, but i don't like disturbing my FATHER with his thoughts..and he really looks serious.

But i moved closer to him, and asked gently and lovingly..what's wrong papa GOD? what's bothering you? He then looked at me with full of reassurance and extended his right arm to me, he then pulled me closer to him and kissed my head. He didn't say anything..i can feel my DEVINE FATHER beautiful energy again, reassurance, loving and comforting.

Then i told my FATHER, something bothering me papa GOD..is there something about the Angel and the Trumpet? Because i have this 2 things have appeared infront of me while i was decorating my christmas tree. Is that means the world is going to end soon? As the Angel and the Trumpet are presenting infront of me..what is this means FATHER? He then looked at me..and said, the "ANGEL and the Trumpet" together is calling for those people to use their spiritual gifts to help people and the world. I'm asking them to use their spiritual gifts for good! but papa GOD how would they know that they need to use their spiritual gifts? Well my child they know..and a lot of them have beautiful spitritual gifts, but unfortunately not using for good purposes. Remember my child, LOVE..ACCEPTANCE..and TOLERANCE are needed to spread to the whole world.

He then asked me to close my eyes..then it took me to the place..a long stairways..but before i proceeded to the stairways, i met my brother "JESUS" he is my brother in a spiritual realm as my DEVINE FATHER said to me before. He pointed out the stairways up..to heaven and to follow the stairways, i proceeded without any hesitation. While i was running up to the stairways.. i feel like there are some energies arround me and making my move really fast. Then when i got to the top.."SKY" my sky :) is waiting for me. He is glad to see me, and i quickly jumped on his back and then together our body together embodied with ROYAL BLUE and PURPLE energies.

Then i noticed we are travelling again amongst the galaxy, i am wearing my white ANGEL clothes and my wings! :) Ohh..i miss my wings..i am feeling my freedom again. I can see SKY smiling.. we both feeling happy as we are together again, We both miss each other. Then i lowered my body down close to his back, and i can feel his heart beat and the beauty of his heart inside.

We are travelling through the galaxy..i see stars everywhere.. twinkling..so beautiful to see and overwhelming feeling just being up there amongst the stars. Then finally i can see an area..a very dark town or a city from the distance. I then asked papa GOD, where am i FATHER? and what is this place? is this place where i'm supposed to go to? Yes my child that is "ROME"!. papa GOD gave me that answers straightway.

OK FATHER i confirmed that..then we reached the place, SKY and myself were on top of the pointy building..old building..and dark. Then i looked down, i can see a big cave or contained area.. large..humongous dungeon maybe. Then in a quick second, we both suddenly descending down, but very slowly..it feels like an elevator or a lift, and i can see the sorrounding walls are all marbles and well litted.

It's not dark anymore while we both descending..as the bright white and golden lights coming from above bringing us both down. When we finally touched the ground..i can see a "Big man with a beard" wearing white and red clothing while sitting on a stone chair holding a "WHITE BOOK". He then greeted me, welcome to you, THE CHILD OF GOD.

He greeted me while still sitting on his Big marble chair. I jumped out from SKY's back and walked very slowly towards him. I then asked him curiously, WHO ARE YOU? I am SOLOMON the messenger of "GOD", your FATHER the DEVINE CREATOR. What is my purpose here? i asked again..SOLOMON stood up and started showing me arround the area..it's all marble stones the sorroundings..and i can see some old writings on the wall from made of big stones and marbles.

The Ancient writings are sorrounded the area, ubfortunately i cannot understand it, i looked again closely..it's not written in english. Then i have noticed..there are some very old and Ancient books on the shelves. Solomon showing me this arround..and then finally he sat down on his chair while holding a "white Book" and showed me the FRONt page and slowly opened it..then i noticed it's empty! there is no writings in it..the white book is BLANK!

Then i remember my previous battle journey..there was a WHITE BOOK have appeared in heaven above or up in the cloud and sky..and there was no writing on it. It was just a WHITE BOOK staring at me amongst the clouds. Is this the same book? i asked, Yes he said straightaway..why is it empty? i asked curiously. Well, that's because "YOU" are going to write on this book, he said. Whoahh..wait a minute..me? going to write on this blank white book? he then said Yes! how?..and why? why me? i'm confused..and i'm surprised.

How am i going to write? and what i am going to write? Matter of fact i am starting to panick my dear journal..then solomon showed me a pen and put it into my right hand..held my hand, and then my hand wrote 2 words into the blank book, and to my amazement the colour pen turned into a golden ink! whoahh..this is unbelievable...i asked papa GOD..what am i going to write FATHER? Well, you don't need to worry about of what you are going to write my child, because i will do that "with you". Ohh..ok..i said. then i calmed down. :)

You just have to be ready when i call you..and he "gave me the specific day". Don't forget to drink your water..yes FATHER i won't forget..so now you need to rest. Yes FATHER..goodnight..Goodnight my child. I closed my eyes and i can see my FATHER and feeling his loving energy..and behind him..i can see my brother "JESUS"..he is smiling at me..i can see solomon still with us..and i noticed papa GOD face is not clear. Then i looked at the sorounding area for the last time..we are standing underground very litted and pleasant area. :)

# CHAPTER 30

# MEETING ABRAHAM

JOURNAL

23RD DECEMBER 2022

Well, this is friday i waited for my DEVINE FATHER to give me more some instructions as per previous meeting. I looked for a place to sit around the house then i found my old bedroom, then layed down on the bed comfortably. I closed my eyes and then started to drift away..my mind was conscious but my body is fully relaxed. I called papa GOD..but he didn't show himself, instead my energy started to travel up..up beyond again..in dark deeper galaxy full of stars..just by myself this time.

Then suddenly i stopped, and i can see myself and my DEVINE FATHER in his verandah. I can see clouds arround the place..and i can see papa GOD standing looking out to the NORTH side of the verandah..i can see him wearing a long white thick clothing. He greeted me warmly, then i can see myself as a teenager again. While i was walking slowly towards him..to my surprised, i can see cyclops, kelly, ginger blue and mister rabbit:) HAAA!!:) my furry babies! ohh..i am so glad to see you guys!!:) Kelly was running around so excitedly..i can see her face so happy..it's the same face i used to see everytime i came home from work. Ohh..i gave them hugs..and more hugs and kisses..ohh..i'm so happy:) Cyclops started walking on the edge of the verandah..he then stopped..waiting for me to kiss him:) as i always does when he was with me in a physical realm..and whispering to his ears..I LOVE U 3x.. i can see he is extending his face towards me..a gesture saying..kiss me..and more on his cheek:)

Kelly running around and looks so happy, and mister rabbit just standing on the side of the wall. I sat down on the floor with mister rabbit, patted him, then kelly came running along and wanted to play too. While i am playing with my pets, i can see myself as a young kid again, and once in a while papa GOD glances at me with his happy face. I am almost in tears when i saw my furry babies, and i thanked papa GOD for bringing my pets today. Papa GOD knows that i have been missing them lately, i played with them for awhile.

Then Papa GOD said to me, my child, it's time to go..then he shifted me to the same area where i was with solomon. This time i can see an old man sitting, and wearing a white thick clothing, and he has a beard. This time he called himself "ABRAHAM", he has very thick black beard. Abraham is the person in the dungeon with me, and on the far right i can see JESUS..and i can see a bright "HALO" on top of his head..and papa GOD standing beside me.

Then Abraham showed me the BOOK, a WHITE BIG BLANK BOOK. It's the same book from my previous meditation with Solomon. This time Abraham gave me a pen..a golden pen, then i looked at my DEVINE FATHER for approval, then slowly nod his head to me while reading his thoughts to proceed. I held my pen with my right hand and then started writing. The first word i wrote... THE KINGDOM OF HELL WILL FAIL..AND THE WRATH OF THE EVIL WILL FALL. Then it follows..The Russia will fall!!

then Germany.. and showing me a white flag with a RED DOT in the middle. It's says JAPAN..but not sure if it's KOREA.

Then i can see 3 men on a blind fold and kneeling down, i have never seen this people in my life. One white man specifically the main focussed. He is wearing white long sleeve shirt, young looking in an early thirties, clean shaven, medium tall build. He is blind folded, and both hands are tied up. And the other 2 men were wearing a dark blue business suit and in the same situations, both hands are tied up behind and blind folded. I don't know who they are..i have never seen them before..but that's the image has been shown to me during my meditation. Then I don't really know what's happened to this people. I wish to GOD they are alright.

Then i heard "DEMOCRATS" will rise..and then it showed me and heard the Rise and FALLs of the GREAT PYRAMID in egypt, then i saw the top of the pyramid. Then the image suddenly stopped, i wake up from my meditation with very dry mouth and incredibly thirsty. I don't really knows what it means of all this messages..but maybe there is some significant connections to be revealed later on..i don't really know..i'm just writing..and papa GOD wants me to write what i saw.

Then papa GOD asked me to write the words of what i saw and channelled into my other journal, it's your "Protection" my child. It's my protection ? am i in trouble FATHER? i asked curiously..silence my child..silence..the book will reveal when it's finish, he said. OK FATHER, i understood.

# CHAPTER 91

# CHRISTMAS DAY SURPRISE CORONATION

JOURNAL

25TH DECEMBER 2022

It has been a very busy day..just cooking whole day..i love it, it relaxes me. We had visitors last night during NOCHE BUENA. My family love the get together christmas eve and of course my cooking, I'ts a quite dinner for everyone so after the christmas get together everyone went home.

Then i started to connect with my DEVINE FATHER..and i can see him from the distance up there in his KINGDOM, and this time he is in the Big Hall area sorrounded with clouds. He looks like he's been waiting for me..and when he saw me from the distance, he extended his arms towards me and catches me with his 2 arms and i can see myself as a child again and i am wearing a very dark and velvety red dress, and bare footed.

PAPA GOD gave me a big hug..and welcomed me with his beautiful and loving energy. Then i noticed..papa GOD why i can't see your face ? i asked. We have company my child. Oh ok..i said. Then he put me on the floor, while still holding my right hand and both walking towards the BIG Hall area. I can see a very long table made of marble and some entities sitting arround the table but i can't see their faces.

The only thing i can see a very clear face from the distance, opposite to the end of the table where my DEVINE FATHER sitting from this end..it's JESUS. I can see "JESUS" has a "HALO" above his head and it's white and shinny, and from the distance i can see his face with medium long hair, black and slightly wavy and he has thick black beard.

I know it's him deep inside my heart. It's the only face is clear that i can see, and the rest are not clear..it's more like silhouettes. There is a Festivity around..they are all talking..i didn't pay any attention of what's on the table, but i'm sure they are all celebrating. I can see my DEVINE FATHER is sitting on his BIG marble chair and talking to his entities..but i can't hear what they are talking about. They are mumbling..and it's not loud but they're all very comfortable while conversing with each other. Hmmm...

My little chair is beside with my DEVINE FATHER and i am sitting very quietely while watching them..then later on i got bored..i whispered to my papa GOD to excused myself..and he looked at me with permission in his face and by reading his thoughts. I slide my little body from my chair down to the floor, then i crawled slowly behind my chair. Then to my surprised..i can see my Kelly dog running towards me, and Cyclops my cat just walking so slowly..then Ginger blue already appeared beside me with mister rabbit:) ohh i'm so happy...i started playing with them, then i ran around the big hallway on the marble floor bare footed with my pets.

Then i saw something that interests me to go..an area with a Big brown pillar. I slowly walked towards the area..then i went inside.. and when i just put my foot in that room, the whole room litted up. I can see little ANGELS inside floating around with their musical instruments..harps most of the Angels are playing, and yes..there is one Angel with a little brown flute. They are all giggly..all of them are sorrounding me while playing thier instruments.

I slowly joining them..round and round..until i noticed that i was up on the air!! With the other little Angels..and ohh..i have my little wings too!!! Father!! i called papa GOD..i have my wings!! My wings are back!! then papa GOD appeared infront of me..and he said of course my child..you have wings too..you always have. I can see my DEVINE FATHER standing watching us looking so happy while i'm playing with the little Angels. Then i noticed Papa GOD is wearing a very bright white clothings..and still can't see his face, it remains silhouette, but i know it's him..his whole body is glowing.

Then suddenly the whole thing is shifted..i feel like someone..or somebody is calling me..and suddenly...ohh..i'm home to my Ancestral Kingdom. The whole place is always makes me feel at home. I can see myself still a child, wearing the same clothes..the red velvety dress, and this time i am wearing a little flat black shoes with a strap on top. I looked arround and i noticed i'm by myself..Papa GOD is not with me..then suddenly, i can see my father EMPEROR ARTHERU from the distance welcoming me with his 2 arms extending towards me.

I ran towards him and i am so excited to see him. OHHH...my EMPEROR father i miss you..and my Emperor father hugged me so tight and lovingly..and whispered..i'm so happy to see you my shine..welcome home he said..i feel loved again. He then slowly put me down on the ground..and then from the distance, i can see my mother EMPRESS GLYDICA walking towards me and welcoming my arrival:) then suddenly, i became an adult..a woman wearing a long white silky and baby pink dress..just my favourite colour.

We have a Big celebration today my Shine, my father Emperor exclaimed. Oh..what kind of celebration Father? i asked. Oh you will see, he said. We all then walked towards and inside the Palace, then i can see entities..walking arround..some are not touching the ground.. the whole place is so huge..as i always remember and made of marbles.

Then i noticed, there is also long table arround and made of marbles.. there is no chair or seats..i can see the table is full of different fruits and wines on the trays being served on the silvery trays and with fruits arround the trays. Hmmm..this time i have no idea of what's going on. Then when i looked at from the distance of where i am standing..i can see 2 Big THRONES closed to each other. I guess that is for my FATHER EMPEROR and my mother EMPRESS GLYDICA. I noticed the entities are not talking..they are all walking arround, and walking very slowly..it seems to nothing bothers them.

They are all seems happy and lovingly looking each others. They know me..as they acknowledging my presence when i walked pass them. Then i reached my bedroom..i opened the door..ahh..my bedroom..my old princess room..i am feeling so happy and content.. it's home again i felt it to myself. I ran towards my bed, and threw myself on my bed..ohh..i feel the enermous feelings of comfort, then suddenly i drifted to sleep.

I don't know how long i have been sleeping, because when i woke up my grandmama is beside my bed sitting on the chair smiling at me:)

Welcome home my shine, she said. Grandmama..oh i miss you and so happy to see you, i gave her a BIG HUG. Then she said, i guess you are ready for your Big day. A big day? i asked. Grandmama what is my Big day? i asked again. You have no idea my shine? no grandmama, i said. Oh i guess it's a Surprise, she said.

Then grandmama disappeared suddenly. I walked towards the verandah of my bedroom..i looked out..then i can see the beautiful water falls..trees..different plants..flowers..butterflies and little bugs flying arround. Ohh..i miss this place..then i looked down i can see SKY and his little family, he looks so happy. Then i noticed my Father EMPEROR behind me and tapped my right shoulder gently. He hugged me with his left arm, and i gently turned to him..and asked..Father, i want to come home permanently..i really do.

My EMPEROR father hold my face gently and said..my SHINE it's not your time to come home yet..but today is your special Day:) Then suddenly again i'm inside my bedroom..facing my full body magical mirror. Then to amusement, my clothes changes..i am wearing different clothing..very long, white colour and silky inside, but the outside is a thick materials and i have a cape.

The colour is dark red again..but i kept changing it infront of my mirror just by thinking a different colours and designed. I like the baby pink..but then it kept changing into a very dark red...arrghh..:( I don't know why it kept changing into a red colour..but at the end i settled with baby pink long dress clothing, but still with a red cape colour.. and my mirror twinkled at me..it looks like it agreed with me. Then i smiled..and finally i looked at myself in the mirror..whoah..i really looks so Majesctic, but i have no crown. I looked myself side to side.. and my hair is so long..dark and i noticed with a little tinge of red hair.

I can see myself standing upstairs in the very long and large hallway.. then i can see my mother Empress Glydica so beautiful, and i noticed about her hair still long but it's wavy..she looks so beautiful as an EMPRESS..my mother. She then started walking downstairs with my EMPEROR father holding her right hand walking together majestically. My mother looks so magnitically beautifull, gracefully when she walks and she has a GODDESS face. Then they both reached the ground floor..and my Father Emperor took my Empress mother to her seat..their THRONES..ohh..they are both lovingly beautiful.

Then my Father asked me to come down, and i slowly walked down while dragging my cape on the floor very slowly. Then i am feeling my body is gliding down very slowly..going down the very long and winding staircase. This staircase i'm so familiar with it..i feel like when i was younger, i was running up and down in this staircase..just me..and no other kids arround. It was strangely enough that i was only a child there. Yes..it's funny i'm remembering it now! Everything is coming back to my memory..i have been and lived here before..this is my home..my ANCESTRAL HOME..with the nature and the place is full of LOVE. Now i can understand why here in earth, i am so drawn to a very familiar or similarities from my previous life. I am understanding it now...and where i came from and my previous life!

When i reached the ground marble floor..i was facing my EMPRESS mother and my EMPEROR father. Then he showed me my own chair. I looked at it curiously..i thought it's a normal marble chair at my first glanced..but it's my THRONE. I blinked again..and i looked at my EMPEROR father..and he slightly nodded his head saying..it's yours with a smile on his face.

I slowly walked to my throne and looking at it closely i have noticed, it has a long back support and has carvings of different sizes of STARS...GALAXY amongst the Stars. Then i put my hands on it and started feeling the carvings..it made of marble, a solid marble chair..and to my amazement while touching the carvings and the stars carved in it..for some reason, everytime i touched and felt the stars..it connects it with me. I felt an electrical currents went through my fingertips every time i touched every stars of my throne.

And then i turned my focussed into the colour of my chair, it is black and the other side is ROYAL BLUE. whoahh..i didn't expect this, then i decided to sit down slowly on my THRONE, i glanced my EMPEROR father Artheru, he looks so proud of me. My EMPEROR father looks so magnificently loving and courageous looking. Ohhh..i adore my Emperor father..so does my Empress mother, she looks so magnificently beautiful with a very loving face. My parents both have a very loving auras intertwined with each other. Ohh..i'm so blessed to have them as a parents. I love them so dearly.

Then i heard a trumpet sounds 3 times..i looked at my EMPEROR father..and he then extended his right arm and hand towards the entity which is carrying a crown on top of a soft little dark velvety red colour pillow. TI's YOUR CORONATION MY CHILD!!!!he said. I was surprised!!! then suddenly my DEVINE FATHER appeared infront of me, and slowly placed the very beautiful crown on top of my head..and papa GOD kissed my forehead and smile at me lovingly, thank you my DEVINE FATHER I whispered. Suddenly i have tears in my eyes..i feel like crying..but i feel happy..a happy tears. Then i can see my whole Ancestors family slowly appearing from nowhere...and everywhere..they are all looking so happy for me. I can see JESUS from the far distance wearing a long white clothing and red cloth accross his chest. He is smiling at me..and this time i don't see his "HALO".

When my DEVINE FATHER took the crown from the entity who was holding my crown, and when my DEVINE FATHER put my crown on my head..he said..it's perfectly "FITTED" with a smile on his face..and then kissed my forehead so lovingly..and with his Devine energy started flowing towards the whole area..i can feel it.. the serenity and full of LOVE..hearts floating everywhere..and this time i can see my DEVINE FATHER's face so clearly..so beautiful.. and his energy is so loving..forgiving..reassuring and most of all..it's everything on him. I LOVE YOU my DEVINE FATHER.

Then i thanked my EMPEROR and EMPRESS parents, and thank you my Brother JESUS for being here and of course my DEVINE FATHER. I don't see Angels arround me..but all my Ancestors family are here. then papa GOD said, You are now CROWNED as an EMPRESS of this KINGDOM of NATURE. And you are still my child in my KINGDOM. Then suddenly papa GOD disappeared infront of me.

Ohhh....MERRY CHRISTMAS my lovely journal. I thanked you for listening to me..i need to get this one out before it disappeared in my memory. And also it's the way of emptying my thoughts..my devine messages..meditation..dreams..premonition and so on..i think it's important to tell you this. As always, every christmas i looked for miracles in my life..but this christmas certainly has the most beautiful and incredible surprises i have ever experienced in a spiritual level. THE BEST CHRISTMAS PRESENT EVER! THANK YOU..:) My reality CHRISTMAS is lonely..but i tried to make it happy just by giving my time and my love to my family. MERRY CHRISTMAS:)

# CHAPTER 92

# ARIZONA

JOURNAL
7TH JANUARY 2023

I am visiting my DEVINE FATHER at the moment after he shifted my normal routine of writings. I have been watching he said..so keep still my child. I don't really know who and what he is watching, but i do know that he's in the look out. "STILLNESS" and "QUITENESS" are both words flashing infront of my face. My child, welcome home.. he extended his left arm to me. I can see he is wearing a white long Robe standing in his verandah.

My child are you alright? while holding my left face with his hand.. yes FATHER i'm ok..why? i asked. He kissed my forehead, and then i can feel his energy travelling into my head and throughout my body.. very soothing..i feel like he is removing my old energy from my body and renewing at the same time.

FATHER, where are we going today? i asked. Well my child, lets go to ARIZONA. Arizona? why arizona FATHER? I will show you when we get there, he said. Close your eyes now..so i did..but then i can see we are both travelling to desert island..i can see huge landscape of sands. Then we're both standing in the middle of the desert island and to my surprised, we were facing the high and bIG wall of rocks and it's sandy colour. It's the same colour of the sands on the ground!

Then from that wall of big rocks..i can see a MIRAGE..water coming out from that big wall of rocks. The colour is baby blue..very light blue and it's and it's shimmering but the flowing motions of the water is very soft and sometimes its "STILL". Father..why is the water not flowing rapidly? i asked curiously. Well my child..there is something holding the flow of that water..oh??..who? and why? i asked curiously again.

Well, that's what you are going to find out. So what do you want me to do FATHER? Close your eyes and tell me what you can see, my DEVINE FATHER said. Ok..so i closed my eyes and then i am shocked to what i am seeing..so many of them..but not so human dragging things from underground!! They are not human FATHER!! and oops..one "Being" saw me, he has big eyes and with big head! and this BEINGS body are almost black and grayish colour, and they don't looks friendly! AWWWW!!!..it did something on my left neck! it feels like a sharp needle puncturing my neck! This being is hurting me..it's ok my child i'm here with you, Papa GOD said. Then the feeling of sharp needle quickly disappeared. It only stayed there for quick seconds.

This particular being have noticed my presence, that's why..and tried to stop me from watching them. Then my DEVINE FATHER created a sorrounding bubble arround me, and it seems like i disappeared from there sights, they've all continued whatever they're pulling out from th cave or Big stone cave. I couldn't see what they are pulling out from that area, all i know they are so many of them..i couldn't get closer to their area..it seems like they have created some kind of barriers from me. Papa GOD, are they bad beings? I asked, but my DEVINE FATHER didn't say anything, but slightly nodding.

FATHER would they'll find me? My child, they already knew you from a very long time. Ohhh...really? i could not believe what i am hearing..now i'm worried. Matter of fact they have been visiting you regularly, but cannot get closer to you lately. They know your energy ever since your very existence in this planet. Have they abducted me already FATHER?? YEs, long time ago..trying to empty your body but they couldn't. Why? i asked curiously. Because you fought back and demanded to be returned!!! Just like that. Somehow your "demand" have scared out of them!

I thought it was a dream FATHER. Twice i dreamed about this beings..but the second time they couldn't take me..they looks scared. Yes, because i intervened, Papa GOD said. You have so many guards my child..so don't worry. You can see them..but they can't see you. We are watching, and we here and there to intervene if you cannot fight back! And you know what to do with them, they cannot take you my child.

There energy is not as powerful as yours, Papa GOD said. Oh..can you explain it please FATHER? I do not understand. There power is only "energy field" power..but yours are coming from everything.. whatever you desires, and especially when you fully develop your energies..you can change the things that people in earth would not believe.

OHH..papa GOD it's really overwhelming and heavy..i am trying to balance this energy because sometimes it's scary...i don't want destructions. Remember my child..you only use it if necessary..yes i know FATHER..but sometimes it doesn't work FATHER. WEll, that's the things you need to find out and learn to develop and use it in a good way. Ohhh..but can you teach me FATHER? please? Yes of course my child..but it's in you..here..in your heart..just feel the goodness in your heart and everything will follow. It seems confusing FATHER..it is my child..but you need to find out for yourself, and sooner and later you gonna have to. That's how you change everything..it's like magic? Ohhh..it's more than magic my child.

Papa GOD, how come my old memories starting to fade away? and this new energy i feel like it's erasing my memory slowly? Is this real? am i sick? No my child. it's a process of renewing your new energy. This means your old memories are fading out but being restored..because you need to allow to have some space for the new one. You have so many messages and downloads to come my child.

Do i have more battles to do FATHER? Yes my child, he said. When? i asked. I will let you know, he said. Then i have noticed i'm back to my reality world again. Goodbye FATHER, nice travelling and talking with you:) i love you..then i heard his voice..i love you too my child..then i can see a BIG HEART floating in the air when i closed my eyes. I couldn't explain the way my DEVINE FATHER's face looks like..somehow my brain not allowing to explain it with details. hmmm...so strange though..

# CHAPTER 93

# SUNAMI IN SOUTH EAST ASIA

JOURNAL
10TH JANUARY 2023

Last night i had a premonition..i can see a Big Sunami is coming into the city..i can see it from the distance is about to hit the city. I asked papa GOD where is this? and i can see it's happening already..then i heard from above..Southeast Asia. Oh..please Dear GOD have mercy! I am praying for this people..the people need to be evacuated as soon as possible and to be safe. This is NAture..we cannot change the law of NATURE. Today i have been praying for the protection of others especially myself and with my family.

I have been in a battle again few days ago with my Angels..they tried to eliminate me again..for heaven sake stop this stupidity! whoever you are! You wouldn't have a chance, please wake up! you are making it easy for me to eliminate you, and everyone of you whoever is involved. My battle with you is in spiritual place. that's why this is so easy for me to eliminate..your body will deteriorate in a physical level and die slowly. So wake up..you cannot touch me in a spiritual realm..you cannot win..i have my DEVINE FATHER with ME..the most HIGHER CREATOR. You cannot match with him. I AM HIS WEAPON!

GOD HAVE MERCY ON YOUR SOULS! The message from my DEVINE FATHER..i have a DEVINE MISSION..and I "MUST" fulfill it no matter what's the consequences from the evil part of side. I "MUST" FULFILL the DEVINE ORDER..and i have not given a choice.."NO CHOICE"! This is my main FOCUS. I MUST finish my mission with my DEVINE FATHER order. AND I SHALL.. AMEN..

# CHAPTER 94

# JAPANESE BATTLE WARRIOUR

JOURNAL

13TH JANUARY 2023

Very early this morning while i was talking with my DEVINE FATHER, we were both standing discussing something..then suddenly i felt a slight pulled from behind my back. I turned arround, there i can see so many black souls trying to grab me down with them into the darkness. My DEVINE FATHER said to me..you know what to do my child. So suddenly, my weapon appeared in my hands. Long and silvery sword, i tried to eliminate this black entities with my sword..and most of them has been cut into pieces. There hands were very prominent. Some are trying to touch me..and some are trying to drag me down with them.

They are all eliminated except..to those who's just trying to touch me..i think they were asking some forgiveness. I did some prayers and forgiveness for their souls. Then i saw there hands slowly pulling down. There after i was talking again to my DEVINE FATHER, i can see myself as a mature woman this time. i have noticed i am wearing different battle suit. It's a very different looks..the garments are all white underneath from head to toes. Then the outside of my garment has been wrapped up arround with silvery metal.

It looked like an armour, but with an Ancient touched of the design. My battle outfit looks like a Japanese warriour..but it's all white.. and i noticed behind my back, the garment is long and in both side it shaped like an oval shape..hmm..never seen this outfit before..but then i have my big Angel Wings! My hair is wrapped up and tied up on my head. And my weapon is long and silvery sword..but it's very light to hold.. it's a light as a feather.

Then papa GOD showed me the people..it's looks like an ancient village..it's in ASIA..it looks like a very old japanese tribe. The looks of thier weapons..they have spears but thier clothings are very old japanese clothings. I have also noticed this male tribe, they have something on thier heads.. i don't know if it's their tradition hats or what. I have never seen those before here in our modern era. Looks like they are stuck in an island and watching something..but i asked papa GOD are they're my enemies? to me they looks harmless..and it looks more like..they are protecting something. I can see them looking out from the very top mountain.

MY DEVINE FATHER said, NO..they are not enemies..a matter of fact they will help you with the enemies. Oh OK, i said. On my right side Arch Angel Michael is with me and the other Angels. They are all in thier own horses..all the Angels are white..and with thier wings including weapons ready to use for the battle. I can see JESUS from the distance standing..and showing me clearly his beautiful heart of love and kindness. I acknowledged him with my nod respectfully. I can see his beautiful and loving face."PEACE" he said to me in my thoughts. I noticed i have little tears in my eyes.

Then i can see "SKY" from above approaching me slowly with a smile on his face. And when he touched down..he approached me with his head and my forehead touched each other, and then our energy combined and feeling amazingly alive and brave. I felt like i'm ready for the battle again, and this time i'm not scared and i am more foccused. I noticed SKY has silvery metal wrapped arround his head..i think it's an extra protection. An armour on his head..thank you FATHER:) Then my DEVINE FATHER showed me the place where we supposed to go. Looking at from the very far distance..i can see a very large town or a village, and the top of the old Ancient looking buildings are round and has a stone yellowish colour.

One of My DEVINE FATHER instructions..when you are travelling through the dimensions of the galaxies, stay in a black path this time. No matter if the path is black, zigzag or straight..stay in that path with glitering lights little stars. But FATHER, do you think i can see this path properly while travelling in the darkness? Yes my child with this..

My DEVINE FATHER is holding something on his hands and then slowly opened and showed to me...an oval "Green crystal" shape, he then slowly placed it into my forehead. My FATHER said then..this crystal will help you to navigate your way to reach that area. Once my Father placed it into my forehead..the whole place is litted up with green lights. Its like a torch!! whoah...amazing! The darkness of that area became elluminated with green light!!

The beautiful green light energy sorrounded the whole area. This will help you see your path my child. Lovingly energy i felt from my DEVINE FATHER again..ohh..i love you my DEVINE FATHER..i have tears in my eyes. Then i saw Papa GOD a beautiful smile on his face. He then made me read his thoughts..my child..i'm with you all the time, and one more thing for you to remember, he said.. is your "hands" and your "thoughts" are powerful, use it wisely, he said. Hmmm..i thought..i didn't know that..so i asked my DEVINE FATHER respectfully, could you please explain it to me more FATHER..as i don't fully understand it.

Well my child..it has been with you but never knew about it..but Father how do i use it? I asked again curiously..well my child, think something of what happened to you before that really upsets you.. then formed that energy into yourself. Oh ok.. So i can try it Father?.. of course my child. So i closed my eyes..and slowly gathered my thoughts and the momentum...then i quickly punched my right hand on the air!! Then Huge Energy came out from my whole body and shook the whole area..and while the energy has been released..i can see a shimmering light of energy almost crytal thin energy is wavering infront of me and through the whole place! It shook all of us!! it feels like a huge force can destroy the whole galaxy!!! whoahh... that's scary!

Oh Papa GOD i don't think i like this..it's scary!! it's scary to have this! I was shaken with the power of my energy i just released. And that's why you need to learn how to use it..wisely, beside it's yours.. your power to use with bigger enemies. You cannot give it back to me or the UNIVERSE, it has been with you since you have been created. Ohh..papa GOD this is too much..ohhh...but i do thank you and i accept it after all, this is have purpose and part of my DEVINE mission.

Then i gathered myself together and thanked my DEVINE FATHER..i kneeled down infront of him and the same as my

ANGELS behind me. But then i noticed my right hand..i can see my flesh right hand holding my sword. That's the only flesh i can see on my body, the rest of my body is wrapped up with the white garments and armour with silvery metal arround my clothes, but it's light weight. Hmm..very interesting outfit..

Then my DEVINE FATHER said..are you ready now my child? Yes FATHER i am ready, i said with confidence.Then i jumped in into SKY's back and i noticed my eyes are both covered with white cloth. I remember my FATHER put this on before he placed the green crystal on my forehead. Then this time, i am facing the "BIG ROUND PORTAL", and my DEVINE FATHER said, go now my child and remember..stay in a black path this time. Yes FATHER i will, i said. I went through the portal..and i seee him waving at me, and i can see my Warriour Angels behind me..they are all riding on with their white horses and all of them are WHITE and have wings!:)

Do not look back! Keep straight! i still can hear his voice from the distance. We are all travelling really fast..i can feel SKY's heart beat and rhythms with excitements. The galaxy is just pure black with glittering stars from the distance..and while travelling with my Angels, we stayed on the long black path. It seems like a never ending space travelling..then i felt SKY's started to slow down...and then i noticed we finally reached our destination.

We were standing in a very high Mountain, i scanned the whole place with my eyes..i can see wild plants..greenneries in the sorrounding area. And this time i am facing to the Western horizon looking out the ocean. I am standing in a very big rock platform, and looking out the ocean while studying the place. it's very quiet..very still..i don't feel any breeze or wind anywhere..neither noises of the birds, animals or little creepers sounds. So bizzare i thought.

And then..suddenly..to my surprised!! a GIANT CREATURE came out from the water!! It startled me! It looks more than half human and a Giant crab! Whoaah..what is that? Sky is slightly apprehensive.. but i touched his left shoulder and whispered..don't move.. I can't see my Angels arround.

Then from that moment a GIANT ship quickly appeared on the water..it looks like light brown rusty looking ship. And i can see an indegenous people or Wariours trying to attacked the ship, but couldn't penetrated into it. The indegenous Warriours are wearing just a kind of underwear made of leaves..and they are all tiny people tribe. There weapons just spears and arrows. All of them kept plunging into the water every time they kept attacking the big brown ship. And then i saw this other tribe in another island with different clothing watching this naked tribe people whose attacking the ship. I shifted my focus to the BIG ship..then suddenly the big door opened.. then to my surprised..i saw this "BEING"!! have emerged from the door of the ship. Then the image stopped! I am very thirsty...

# CHAPTER 95

# BIG STORM ON THE WAY HOME

JOURNAL

15th JANUARY 2023

Today, we went to the Miraculous church, it's the same church that we have been last week..somehow i feel like someone is calling me to visit the church even though its a long trip. I don't have any idea why i was pulling myself back again to visit. This time we picked up my sister to have an extra company. When we arrived the place, we just find out it's a special day celebration of SAINT PAUL THE HERMIT celebration mass. Including giving some blessings to the little children in the church whose attending the mass with thier parents. It reminds me this is the Big Angel who plays harp up in heaven when i visits my DEVINE FATHER. It's Angel HERMII..:)

After the mass we participated with an extra prayers of the rosary. Then the priest encouraged us to have some fruits that has been blessed. After the mass we kissed the MIraculous Cross offering by the priest. I have never kissed the golden miraculous cross before.. it was a beautiful feelings. It was an interesting and lovely day. We had lunch while sitting on the grass like a picnic. We then visited the religious shop and bought some few religious things including silver rosary which i am wearing now. I feel like i have to have a silver metal touching my body..i am puzzled..i don't know why?but i have to follow my gut feelings. Also, i will be praying a rosary with my ring anytime i needed it, and whenever i'm feeling vulnerable.

We then drove to the small town with small shops and lots of antiques..had some ice cream and coffee. What a lovely and relaxing day..i'm enjoying my day. But the good day became a scary day for us when driving towards home in the highway. That's when it started to rain..and later on progressively turns into an extremely heavy and very violent storm!!. Whoah..lightning and thundering..then hailes! and strong typhoon RAGING and Hitting our car so badly! I was terrified!!!

We were driving slowly as we cannnot see the road. All cars were extremely cautious driving very slow and careful as they can be. Some cars stopped behind the trees, but we didn't as we know that would be even more dangerous to be hit by the lightning. We could'nt stop as there was no safe islands to stop as we were driving in the highway. The other cars that we went passed, they have taken a refuged under the bridge of the highway, again we could not stop, as it was too dangerous to stop. Beside that some cars are pilled up behind the other cars, and the storm water from the side of the mountain was raging down very rapidly on the side of the road..the water is getting higher on the road..it's flooding!!!

It's an intense moment..but i hanged on to my DEVINE FATHER and prayed for our safety and kept praying, including everyone's safety and who's driving on the road. Luckily, every cars in the road were very cautious, an amazing but very intense moment. I tried to control the rain with my thoughts, as it's hitting our windscreen violently. Then in a few seconds i have noticed, it slowed down slightly. I feel like i am talking to the rain..but then i feel like the rain just looked at me..and then went ahead RAGING like a LUNATIC.. (excuse me, i don't know i said this words)..it was too strong and it's mother nature i thought. Then i thought..if i do some kind of miracle infront of my FAMILY..i don't think they are ready yet to see that. So i shifted my thoughts, this time i visualised a sunny day and clearing clouds..then i asked PAPA GOD to keep us safe. I asked my Angels and Ancestors to protect us and the car we are driving.

I prayed my rosary..i closed my eyes and covered my ears as i hated lightnings and thuderstorms. I kept praying..i didn't let go my DEVINE FATHER..i asked him to give us protections or keep us safe as we couldn't see the road ahead while driving..it's becoming dangerous. Then from nowhere, and not even a few seconds after my prayers, suddenly, a medium truck came from nowhere appeared and started immerging infront of us and our car. I don't really know if it's a coincidence or what, but i know i asked for protections.. then suddenly it appeared infront of our eyes. This truck is enough to protect us infront, and we can see the road slightly when we were following the truck behind. THANK YOU MY DEVINE FATHER.:) I know it was your devine intervention.

The truck didn't stop anywhere, we followed the truck as it was giving us some kind of directions, protections and safer navigation. The truck have little lights at the back, and it was enough lights to see the back of the truck we were following. It's a scary moment because the water started and becoming higher on the road, and with the storms and hailes at the same time becoming violently stronger and hitting our car. We were driving through to the very violent storm for hours in a speed of 10 kilometers per hour and we couldn't stop anywhere.

Then after the scary and excuriating time..i saw some little lights peeking through between the black clouds directly to the western horizon. It was strangely enough for me to think of why on earth have this little lights from above while still heavily raining?? hmm..i was puzzled but very thankful to the transitions of what's happening at this moment. I thanked my DEVINE FATHER for the little Hope he is showing me. So we continued driving..now and then i checked the sky..but still the same..then in a few minutes, i looked up the sky again..i almost cried of what i saw in that instant!.

I can see 2 BIG full body ANGELS formed as a cloud..and the sky started clearing..slowly though..the more we were driving and heading south the sky is clearing but still raining, then i can see the sun shinning slowly. Then we saw the truck infront of us slowly changing into different lane. Then the truck somehow disappeared. I thanked for the truck driver in my prayers for keeping us safe and especially to my DEVINE FATHER and my Angels and my Ancestors.

Then i looked up again the sky..i saw my FATHER ARTHERU or my DEVINE FATHER?? holding something on his hand..it's more like a spear with 3 sharps on top..and he's looking down on us. We kept driving and suddenly i saw from the very far distance a HUGE and almost Angelic Wings of clouds almost Hovering us. The wing on the right which stretched so long..and it looks like saying..this way you are heading..it is clear..and YES!! we can see it's clear including the sky.

Also the road is not wet, it didn't rain here in this part of the area. And then the wings started to disappear when we were getting closer to our destination. After more than 2 hours of slow driving..we are home and got home safely. Thank you my DEVINE FATHER and to my Angels and to my Ancestors up there. One thing i would say from this experienced..ALWAYS ask for help from "ABOVE" and never loss "HOPE". PRAYER IS A GREAT MIRACLE. BELIEVE IN GOD..THE DEVINE CREATOR OF ALL. THANK YOU! :)

# CHAPTER 96

# "TRUST" YOUR FEELINGS DURING THE BATTLE

JOURNAL

24TH JANUARY 2023

My dear journal, it has been a few days i haven't been updating you of what's going on. I have been in the journey and battle 2 nights ago. It was gruesome..i just don't know why people are trying to hurt me..then face the consequences and for what?..so amazing and unbelievably stupid. It is so sad that this entities really wants to hurt or even kill me, but they don't realised that my DEVINE FATHER made me so different now.."NO MERCY" almost. Sometimes i tried to spare thier souls as i know what's going to happened to their entire physical body realistically. It's frustrating!!

Two nights ago, i met my DEVINE FATHER up there in our meeting place. We then travelled, we reached this area and almost in a High MOuntain. THen my DEVINE FATHER told me..this is your BATTLE, and you must trust your heart when making decision who to eliminate. "TRUST" your feelings he said. Then papa GOD disappeared.

Then i saw myself wearing in a full black clothing, fitted into my body from head to toes. I looks like a NINJA..arrgh :(...i thought..

Papa GOD could have make it more stylish at least..but i thank you anyway, then i heard his voice..that clothing you are wearing now is appropriate to this battle. OKAY...i said. Thank you FATHER:) Then i have my sword with me in my right hand. I am standing tall and waiting for my enemies to come, and i am prepared. Then i heard my FATHER's voice again..remember..you MUST "TRUST" your feelings of who you are going to eliminate. I thought to myself..well i'm sure i would know my enemies, and definitely is not going to be looks like me.

Then suddenly i heard somebody coming behind me..i turned arround..and then i can see entities in black, the same as my outfit i am wearing!..i thought what's this? they are wearing the same clothes that i am wearing now?..then i heard papa GOD voice again..that's why i told you to "TRUST" yourself because your enemies will be blending with you. Oh ok..silly me i should have listened to him.

Then the entities are starting to attack me..and with my quicked move with almost intertwining with my sword. My movements of how i am fighting with the enemies are almost synchronising with my sword. It wasn't a struggle to eliminate them..a matter of fact i am sad, i still have compassion with this unfortunate souls. Deep in my heart i am feeling very sad..but i have to continue as my DEVINE FATHER order. After a long battle..i almost eliminated them, then the next thing i know, there are another entities remaining infront of me, and the other one moved to my left side.

The others are more coming behind me and trying to attack me.. but suddenly Papa GOD appeared and intervened. MY GOD!!!.. my DEVINE FATHER CAN FIGHT!!! I'm confused now. Is he really him? or someone else? Then there was 2 entities left, and this entities are infront of me..one i was about to eliminate was kneeling on the knees..and the other one standing. I was about to eliminate the entity..but i stopped! My feelings is i couldn't do it..i don't know why?? Then papa GOD quickly appeared behind the black entity who's kneeling infront of me, and then quickly cut the head of this entity.

I was shocked! It was ruthless!! the other entity who's standing beside me spared the soul and didn't get eliminated. PAPA GOD said..TRUST my child..trust your feelings. Ohh..i didn't know those entity..but i don't know why i stopped..i was confused that moment.. your real enemy is hiding behind the shadow, Papa GOD said. Ohh FATHER what is the right decision..although i felt it..but it's difficult to make the decision especially the entity is kneeling infront of me. Please help me FATHER to make the right decision next time.

My life sometimes i don't understand, the people arround me are the most confusing ones. They are very hurtful sometimes..but now i can feel myself slowly changing..I'm not the "OLD ME" anymore. I feel more confident on myself and more compassionate to people. I'm not saying i wasn't..but definitely something changing about myself..such as the things that annoyed and get me frustrated in general before, well now, it doesn't bothered me anymore. Instead i leave it to my DEVINE FATHER whatever situations i cannot handle or i think unreachable. This challenges i am experincing now is not so normal. But then again, what is normal, what is acceptable and not in the eyes of people? Is this a SIN?

I don't really think about sins or anyone having sin..to me what acceptable from my DEVINE FATHER is the most important for me and what to believe. Things that doesn't makes sense to me..i always consulted my DEVINE FATHER for an answer. I think that would real people should do.

I am very curious about LIFE and beyond..and my DEVINE FATHER knows that. I know he told me i have a BIG purpose in life..and the same as everyone in EARTH..if we all can use it for GOOD..the WORLD will be in a better place.

# CHAPTER 97

# ANNOYING BUG

JOURNAL

28TH JANUARY 2023

Yesterday it was our nana's funeral..it was exhausting emotinally and physically. I went to bed exhausted and called my DEVINE FATHER. He came straightaway and extended his right hand to me..and i grabbed his hand gently then we travelled for quick second. Sometimes i really don't understand the transitions of our travelling in a space of time. Not even a second i'm already there to the main destination, it feels like a split second suddenlly we are in his KINGDOM..full of clouds and we both walking in his Verandah. He then opened the door and we both proceeded inside, then he asked me to sit in my chair..my little chair. I can see my little chair is beside his big chair..and i noticed he hasn't turned me into a little child. I thought, thanks goodness for that.

Then i thought..how can i fit in into my little chair? Papa GOD just sat in his throne, a very REGAL looking..tough..and i can see his face. He is wearing a long white clothes and just like a robe...VERY MAJESTIC, and i am staring at my DEVINE FATHER..his AURA is so beautiful and loving..but somehow, there is some toughness on his exterior aura. That's my DEVINE FATHER. I must admit, i miss my FATHER..once i said this in my thoughts..he looked at me with a loving energy, and showing me a really BIG heart..and kind of floating in the air:)

Then i said, FATHER how can i fit into my little chair? Then he made me read his mind..have you forgotten your creativity in your mind my child? Ohh..i see..hehehe silly me.. Of course anything i think in my mind will manifest especially i'm with him :). So i slowly put my bottom in my little chair, wiggled it from side to side..and thinking at the same time i can fit in..then suddenly i heard this "ploop" sound, then finally i sat down. Then i noticed i have fit in into my little chair comfortably without any problem:)

Then papa GOD said..are you comfortable now my child? with a smile on his face. Oh yes FATHER i'm oK, thank you. So now i realised..the thoughts of my creativity is just starting..hmmm.. interesting. :) While we both sitting down in our chairs and watching the clouds..then my FATHER asked me. Are you little bit troubled today my child? YES FATHER..a matter of fact i have encountered some new challenges again, some kind of uneasy communications from someone out there..you probably know. Then my dear nana's passed away as you know, and i really thank you for helping her through and heard my desperate prayers for her.

I am very sad and exhausted lately especially arround people as not as genuinely true to me. I know who they are..they are just putting a good facade infront of there faces, but clearly i really see them through, family or none family. Then early this morning you wake me up, you asked me and directed me to write, and without any hesitation i picked up my pen..and this beautiful and very clear words you are saying to me is just what i needed..so wonderful and healing. It was amazing that my head became so clear before my coffee:)

MY DEVINE FATHER said that was some healing words for you my child.."ONLY FOR YOU".OHH FATHER..thank you!:) I do feel better now you know.:) The words he asked me to write was only for me..some kind of healing words. I cannot share it.

Then my DEVINE FATHER asked me to close my eyes..then in a few seconds..SKY came through..then i opened my eyes and SKY is infront of me.:) OHHH...SKY I MISS YOU!!! and i can see his face smiling. Then i asked my FATHER if i can be excused and go with SKY out there. He nodded and got his right hand waved at me and smile on his face.

Thank you FATHER i said, and then i quickly jumped on SKY's back. Then off we went..then i heard my DEVINE FATHER voice..enjoy and be happy my child while waving at us from the distance. I will FATHER..and see you later...ohh..i am really feeling better now. Sky and myself are both travelling along the rainbow..so beautiful..i feel like i can touched every colours of the rainbow..ohh...so beautiful..i'm so happy.:)

Then we reached our destination..our favourite spot..the GREEN VALLEY full of greeneries..flowers along the valley side..the grass.. the trees...oh it's just magical and the breeze just amazing..soo soothing. I am feeling the wind touching my face..almost playing my hair..i spread my arms and feel more the breeze underneath my arms and my shoulders..my neck and all over my body..then i said.. THANK YOU FATHER!!!! :) ILOVE YOU!! i can see my DEVINE FATHER just smiling at me.:)

Then i jumped out from SKY's back..i walked arround the valley.. picking some little flowers on the ground and then put it some in my long platted hair. I just walking arround the valley..and i found my favourite spot, i sat down on the grassy area and layed back while looking at the beautiful blue sky and little bit of clouds. MY SKY is just eating some grass happily, and sometimes looking at me once in a while with a smile on his face.:)

While enjoying my time watching everything arround me..suddenly i heard my FATHER's voice. My child you have visitor..i thought visitor?..hmm..i don't think i realy want somebody at this moment while enjoying my "me" time. But i thought who could it be? So i looked behind my back..then i saw a face..a very familiar face. Then this person quickly jumped into my space without hesitation..and the visitor became a bug..hovering arround me..i got annoyed and flicked it! Then suddenly the bug came back again and started buzzing arround and even more annoying. I was going to flick it again, but then it suddenly turns into a form of a very familiar person. Oh Nooo..not you..how did you get here?..this is supposed to be my space..go away..but of course the Big bug never go away. Instead, the Big bug grabbed my hand and pulled me up..and we travelled up to the galaxy again amongst the stars. WE stayed there amongst the stars and in an open space..Then suddenly, i heard the thunder and seen the lightnings from afar..i didn't like it, i got frightened..so i quickly went back again to where i am now. So thirsty..Thank you FATHER..I LOVE YOU.

# CHAPTER 98

# BLACK HEART

JOURNAL

31ST JANUARY 2023

Lately, i have been thinking of what's going on arround me..my energy space, and one particular situation i could not ignore. It is impacting my life and the way i am thinking, it doesn't change my beliefs in certain situations specially my spirituality in life. I am wondering..is this another challenge? How long this can go on? How can i survive with this? I'm overwhelmed with my thoughts and the progression of this situations.

It's so heavy to carry the weight of this problem if the present circumstances are not aligning. I do want some changes in my life.. maybe one day..something unorthodox, but i don't like rushing to make a decision if its' invloved uncertainty. I know it takes some compromising when it comes to make a decision. Last night i contacted my DEVINE FATHER, i visited him again in his KINGDOM, i saw my DEVINE FATHER waiting for me..i felt slightly nervous when i saw him.

I guess he knows what's going on..of course he does, but amazingly, i can feel his forgiving energy right away..then i ran towards him...:) My DEVINE FATHER opened his arms lovingly to me, but what i can see between us is a heart but it's colour "BLACK"! I cried in his arms..i can feel my tears running into his shoulder. He then pulled me slowly and gently towards him and still facing at him..and i can see my DEVINE FATHER's face so lovingly looking at my face. I asked him, what is this i am facing FATHER? is this a new trial again? i don't know what to do..please help me..i cried..

Then my DEVINE FATHER said, trials are always there and will come to you unexpectedly, and that's what trials all about. It will never go away..so "YOU"..my child, you need to be more alert of what's going on arround you. It's a very soothing voice coming from my FATHER. You are the giving lights to people who needs help.. and that's what who you are. But my DEVINE FATHER..i need help too of how to handle and overcome this kind of problems. My child, you are handleing it now, and you are stronger than you think of who you are. But this other people whose causing problems they are not.. but eventually they will come to their senses. It's all about TRIALs and CHANGES..it's a process of human kind evolution.

All of us have some goodness in our heart..sometimes some people needs proper guidance especially when it comes to spirituality, and that's when the person or people become lost, Papa GOD said. I will align people to the right directions towards thier own path of enlightment, but the rest it's up to them to do thier part. Oh thank you my DEVINE FATHER.

Do you feel better now my child? Yes..a matter of fact i do..while wiping my own tears. Thank you. Ohh..one more question FATHER..why BLACK infront of you or us? well..the feeling of black is represents hopelessness coming from your heart..and that's why you came to me and visits your FATHER..:) Ohh..sorry about that..but i do talk to you didn't I? almost everyday..:) Being in the physical world is not easy you know..:) A bit busy down there..:)hehehe...very busy sometimes..a cheeky remarks to my DEVINE FATHER. I think i made him smile. Then i can see many red hearts floating arround again..:) :)

Oh my DEVINE FATHER, sometimes i don't understand some people, the situations, the things of what's happening arround me and outside my circle. I feel so naive sometimes and feel like a child without any clues of what's going on. Well, that's what who you are my child..it's only one of you..you are my child. Ohh..FATHER when i am going to join you permanently? Sometimes i get so tired of the nonesense in my reality world.

My child we discussed this already, you have a divine mission and it's important to finish it. And when do i have to finish it FATHER? and then what? i asked..i am crying...and crying..and then i can see my DEVINE FATHER's face is changing into a shimmering silhouette.. but still i can feel it with loving energy. Suddenly my body changed into a child again..he changed me again into a child while i'm still crying..he does this everytime i'm feeling distressed.

He picked me up and hugged me and carried me while walking towards the long verandah. He then opened a BIG marble door of his KINGDOM..and there i saw my animals running arround the place. But papa GOD didn't put me down on the floor. He still carrying me..then sat on is big marble chair, then my little chair appeared just on the right side infront of us. PApa GOD asked me if i want to sit on my chair..but i said..NO. So he remained carrying and cuddling me while he still sitting on his Big marble chair. Then i fall sleep on his shoulder.

I can see JESUS in a far right..standing. Somehow i get accustomed to my switching places especially when i'm upset. I always run towards my DEVINE FATHER, i know where i can get some reassurance and feeling loved again. It has been a mystery for me ever since i was a kid until now..from my physical to spiritual world to see and meet my DEVINE FATHER.

This has been my practice since i was a child. At that time i didn't know what to call it..and i couldn't tell anybody because i'm afraid to be labelled as i am crazy. Oh..i told my mum before..oh no such things she said..you just imagining it. Oh ok..i said to myself..maybe she's right. I don't like imposing this to anybody, as i know the results or maybe consequences. Or i don't know if they can handle this bizzare situations of me. So i remained quiet of my entire life, until now.

I get accustomed of being alone..i don't mind being alone in a physical level, i like it this way. At least sometimes i don't have to deal with unrealistic and people's bad energy. When i'm alone..i don't feel alone. :) Good night papa GOD. ILOVE YOU.

I have two HOME..to my DEVINE FATHER up there with all the ANGELS i could play with..and play music..and play all the giggly ANGELS.:) While my DEVINE FATHER busy looking down and watching people. Sometimes he looks funny when he is wearing this googly one eye glass while watching me from the distance playing with the little Angels.:) Sometimes i don't feel like coming down to earth..sometimes i feel like i have spent my whole night up there with my DEVINE FATHER. And when i'm struggling to deal with my problems here in earth..i quickly switched myself up there..and there, i'm infront of my DEVINE FATHER which he's always waiting for me in his Verandah that sometimes covered with clouds.

My second home is my ANCESTRAL home..somewhere in place with a different time but very much the same with papa GOD's space time of travelling. Just as quick, and when i close my eyes and think about the place where i am going..and in a snap second..i'm infront of my FATHER EMPEROR ARTHERU and my mother EMPRESS GLYDICA in the KINGDOM of NATURE with full of LOVE and kindness.

I do LOVE my two homes..which i belong to and will return when the times comes. At the moment, i just have to be whatever i needed to be, as my DEVINE FATHER said and to fulfill my DEVINE MISSION in a spiritual and physical realms. As he said, you have more battles to do my child. So be prepared again, Your body is slowly healing..and "PATIENCE" my child patience, i can hear my DEVINE FATHER saying. Sometimes i'm impatient here in a physical world..sometimes i make decisions in a rush without thinking and that's my other problem. I must admit i am impatient..curious..and stubburn..that's my 3 traits that i don't like about myself..but hey i'm not perfect..and who does? Good bye my DEVINE FATHER..catch up soon..:)

# CHAPTER 99

# GOD OF THUNDER

JOURNAL
2ND FEBRUARY 2023

I spoke to my DEVINE FATHER this morning as i have encountered some interesting informatioms from the social media. That kind of informations made me think of who i am, as i am little bit disturbed of what i've found about myself. I thought i want answers..according to that footage or informations i just watched..i have 8 traits that they have mentioned and 1 doesn't resonates with me, and it's the energy of the thunder and lightnings.

I have consulted my DEVINE FATHER instead, i met him again in our usual meeting place. He asked me to sit down in my very own chair, that's my child chair..but then i heard my DEVINE FATHER thoughts.. use your mind to change things..you have that in you. I thought..oh ok.. dahhh..off course. :) So i changed my chair little bit bigger just enough to fit my lower extremities..then all of a sudden, it fits! i can see my DEVINE FATHER smiling.:) I can see my FATHER sitting on his chair with his body slightly tilted forward. I can see myself as a young and adult woman wearing a long white robe just like him.

I can see my DEVINE FATHER face this time. He looks so beautifully happy..his energy is so loving and comforting. Then he said..i believe there is something bothering you my child. YES FATHER..i have questions to asks you with your permission. Okay.. i believe i know what it is and it sounds very important to you..so go ahead my child. I can see my DEVINE FATHER's body composure has moved into a serious mood..and then i asked..what am i? Or who am i? Am i a witch FATHER? Then he made me read his thoughts with a smile on his face, "such a curious and an innocent questions from my child. Then i saw floating hearts everywhere.:)

My DEVINE FATHER didn't look surprise, i guess he knew this is coming..ohh..you are more than a witch my child, he said with a kind of uplifting words and feeling of being proud of me. But for myself..i am puzzled and needed more answers. Could you please explain it to me FATHER? PLEASE??? i need answers.. OK, listen to me very carefully my child with a very reassuring tone of his voice. The word "WITCH" is a word being used in earth for those people who has an energy that they are trying to manifest in reality, whether it's good or bad. okay...i said..i'm listening.. own

Your energy came from me, and "cannot" use it in a bad circumstances.. remember i have told you before..i created you from the palm of my hands, and from the very beginning i sent you to earth to help the unfortunate ones who are suffering from different circumstances..by helping them, that is your purpose to "BALANCE" the energy now and then.

So what you are trying to say PAPA GOD..is the rest of the people in earth came from a different energy? Yes my child..OMG!! straight answer from my DEVINE FATHER. The word energy is beyond of human comprehensions, a lot of people don't know what to believe as there is no logic explanantions in the reality world especially if they haven't find the answers of it yet. Although some people already did.

People tried to manifest so many things in a physical world just to prove it, proving the reality of thier possesions of power either energitically or material possesions. Then when it manifested the good or bad, they want more power to possess..more..and many more something larger that they can imagine. Everything arround you is energy my child.. good and polluted energy.

Most of the people don't know how to use the energy arround them. Some people who found the secret of it..and how to cultivate it, then became a power energy for them. The people who knows how to isolate the good energy is the most important thing and most powerful possession within them. Ohh..my DEVINE FATHER i have no idea about this power energy, that's why i'm so confused. This is so comlplex..so what makes me here in earth then? i asked.

You have a mission, and it's written before i have created you. Your life now here in earth is to experience the struggle,the pain,the disappointments and many more. It is to teach you about reality in earth. I didn't put you in a prviledge life this time because you already have been in that lifetime, the most previledge, your ANCESTRAL HOME and will always be, MY KINGDOM. In this lifetime your mission is to be at service to human kind and especially to unpreviledge people, and also including to spread love in the connections to everyone and everything you do. I did not create you with hatred..i created you with LOVE and to spread LOVE. That makes sense now..sometimes i feel like i don't have to be in a previledge lifestyles as long as i am comfortable where i am. Also i don't feel like that i have to prove anything to anybody in a physial and reality world. I don't have to prove anything to anybody. hmm..i am understanding it now my FATHER.

So FATHER let me understands this..i was hidden from before for what and why? and i possessed some energies that no other people don't have? Well my child, everyone has a gift if that's what people said. More than one gift has a power to create mankind. But the problem is, lacking of support and proper guidance and what to believe, and the beliefs within themselves are not clear..that's where the humanity fails. Ohh..papa GOD this is so heavy..

Okay..let's go back to where i came from my several lifetimes, at least i have some kind of understanding now of my life and resonationg factors of my existence here in earth. So why i have so much fears from lightning and thunder FATHER? What's the reason behind that? Well my child, from the beginning of your lifetime, the "GOD of Thunder" was taken you away from me. OHH..you just let him? i asked my FATHER respectfully. Yes my child..it kind of borrowed you from me. WHAT???..i could not believe what i just heard. FATHER..could you PLEASE explain it to me more..please....

Remember couple weeks ago when you were travelling coming home from the miraculous church you have visited? You have encountered a BIG storm, thunder and lightnings. Yes FATHER it was very scary. Well the image you saw from above wasn't ME either your EMPEROR father. It was the FATHER of THUNDER who you were with from your previous lifetime. OHHH...FATHER that is even more and getting complicated to understand. Now, i must ask you..who and what did you see in the sky during that thundering and lightnings storm while you were travelling? my DEVINE FATHER asked.

Well i saw a massive man, Big man with a beard and holding some kind of spear with 3 sharps on top. You know..it's a kind of weapon that fishermen used to catch fish underneath the water/ocean. That's what i saw..but my intuition wasn't YOU or my father Artheru. And because i couldn't figured out who it was, So i decided to think that it was you. So what was that all about my Devine FATHER? Why he appeared that day? because until now i am still wondering what was that all about?

Well my child, all this things are happening to you is reminding you that you are very important here in earth, physical and spiritual world. You have evrything in you..you need to start developing your spiritual possesions. You have the PROTECTIONS arround you. if they touch you..they are asking for their own lives as simple as that. Spiritually, you have a DEVINE MISSION and "MUST" to fulfill. yes FATHER i understand.

So why i was with them again FATHER? why i was borrowed from you? i asked with persistance and with full respect. You were borrowed from me and for him to teach you about the power of energy from beyond, but during the time with him..you were struck with the lightning during your travelling, and you were sent back to me. And to this day when thundering..it is the warning that the lightning is coming..and also he is reminding you that he is up there protecting you wherever you are and specially if you are closed to the water. So if you are in the ocean looking at the horizon, say hello to your FATHER too..Your "FATHER of thunder" he will hear you, and a matter of fact his eyes is looking at you with your eyes when you stares at the horizon.

YES..he is your FATHER too..you possess his power of calling the wind..to stop the bad weather and to change it..it all came from him.

Ohh..it makes sense now..everytime i am close to the ocean, i feel like being drawn to it. Sometimes i feel the water just want to touch me..my body..trying to reach me..i feel like being hypnotised by the water, and i started touching the water. I feel like the water just want to touch or taste my body..that's what i feel and thought..i don't know if it does makes sense. It's so bizzare..it's all make sense now. Sometimes it feels like the water wants to connect with my body. Is this make sense FATHER? Yes my child, you are absolutely correct. It's all about connections from your past and now..this life time and what makes you who you are now.

Whoahh..PapA GOD..i have to stop here, although i have more questions to ask, but i will leave it next time. I am totally exhausted with all this download. I love you my DEVINE FATHER..and thank you for giving me some solutions of my never ending curiousity, thoughts and many questions. :)

# CHAPTER 100

# BACK TO MY ANCESTRAL HOME

JOURNAL
4TH FEBRUARY 2023

After what happened last night from work during communications with someone, it really breaks my heart and feeling annoyed. I visited my Ancestral home last night..i saw myself sleeping in my bedroom..i can feel my sanctuary..my bedroom..my home just like when i was a kid when i was here with my ANCESTRAL family. I slept maybe for quiete a long time..then i heard someone knocking on my bedroom door. I can hear my grandmama's voice..then my EMPRESS mother Glydica. They were asking me if they can come in..i didn't answer, instead i covered my head with my baby pink sheet and blanket. I heard the door slightly opening..but i didn't acknowledge them. I am still pretending i'm asleep, but a matter of fact i am crying..i just don't want to show them that i am upset. I am blaming myself why i am easily fooled by some people. Why are they doing this to me? I felt my grandmama sat down beside my bed, and then i showed myself to them.

I hugged my grandmama and i cried..and cried..grandmama am i stupid? ohh..grandmama said..you are not stupid and she hugged me tight..you are just too trusting that's all. I can see my mother EMPRESS GLYDICA standing opposite my bed with her hands claspsed each other. I can see my mother so beautifully timid..and trying to absorbed my pain..then grandmama asked me to talk to my mother..then grandmama left the room.

I sat down on the edge of my bed with my baby pink long sleeping gown, and my mother Empress Glydica sat beside me and grabbed my hands softly and kissed both of my hands. I hugged my mother and started crying. She then put her hands on my face and looking at me with so much love, affection and sincerity, while wiping my tears with her thumb.

She hugged me with great passion and reassurance..and then said to me..the GREATNESS OF LOVE will always surface. I looked at my mother and said to her..from this moment i don't really know what it means mother..well my shine, that's because your head is still cloudy, she said. She then asked me to look at myself in the mirror..your magic mirror shine..what outcomes do you really want from this situations? I didn't want to look at my mirror..but i heard a "TING" sound..that means my mirror is asking me to say hello. I glanced at it from my bed instead and said "HELLO"..and another sound "TING"..as an acknowledgement.

Then i said to my mother, why mother is always like this? i don't know who to trust..it's so hard to live in the reality world. The people is so bizzare..and so bad..why can't they just be honest?..being honest is probably the best thing they can do for me, because at least i can accept it realistically. Why is that so hard to do that for me?? Ohh mother what do i do? i cried..and cried..

Then my Empress mother said..listen to me shine..sometimes things that you are trying to expect doesn't comes into manifestations because it has a reason. But mother everything has a reason!! i'm fed up with this situations..i would like at least some honesty..a simple honesty that's all. My mother remained calmed while i was trying to clear my head and to find some reasonable solutions in my head.

Mother, i have more battles to face before i can face my personal life and that's including no intimacy in a reality level. i cannot enter the portal to access my journey..my spiritual journey and to finish my mission, otherwise my Devine mission here in earth cannot be completed and more chaos will come.

My dear shine..you are created by the DEVINE FATHER with purpose, otherwise your existance is not here even with us in this KINGDOM..our NATURE's KINGDOM which you really love. Oh..thank you mother, i said. Having you is greatest "GIFT" from our DEVINE FATHER..and being a WARRIOUR came from your grandfather. You must continue and finish your Devine mission my shine..you are PROTECTED.

Your blood line is your heritage..very important to your existence spiritually. You have encountered so many past lives..and every journey of your past lives have some big significant impact on this people's lives until now, that's why your life in earth is becoming complicated and hard to understand sometimes. Everyone who shared your life from previous time is now also has been impacted significantly. Ohh mother thank you..i really want to know more about myself when i was here with you in our KINGDOM. Yes of course my shine, we will make time to tell you one day.

Then i heard 3 knocks on my door..i sensed it is my father the EMPEROR. So i quickly wiped my tears completely and tidy up myself including my hair..oh i noticed in my mirror that i have long hair with slight red colour and this time slightly wavy and long but not platted. I saw my Father Artheru entered the room and my mother Empress Glydica stood up so gently and walked towards my FAther. My mother excused herself and watching her walking out the room gracefully.

I felt little bit nervous to see my EMPEROR FATHER but happy to see him. He welcomed me with his open arms and i run towards him, then i cried..and cried.. Oh Please don't do anything to this people father..i know everytime someone hurts me emotionally or physically there will be some consequences will happen to them. Please don't FATHER. Very well he said..i guess you know i'm always with you, "WE" ARE always with you. I know FATHER..i thank you.

Then i wake up, i cried..oh mother i want to go home...please??..then i heard her reassuring voice..you are home shine..always..we are just in a different dimension, and you always can come home anytime..you know that.. Ohh..thank you mother..i guess i'm alright now.

# CHAPTER 101

# NO MERCY DURING THE BATTLE

I greeted my DEVINE FATHER this morning, i said to him thank you for the good night sleep and seing me last night. I visited my DEVINE FATHER last night..i knocked on his big marble door..then the door slowly opened..and here i saw my little kelly and cyclops just infront of me. I picked up my dog and i gave her a hug..then cyclops walked arround my legs, Ohh.. i miss my fury babies.

Then i saw my DEVINE FATHER sitting on his big marble chair waiting for me. I walked to him slowly and confidently..no tears. He welcomed me with his beautiful energy..and that energy is kind of radiating towards me, and many hearts floating just between me and him. I reached my DEVINE FATHER hands, and when i reached it..it's..it becomes looks like a silhouette..but i still can feel his energy. Then he hugged me eventhough he is a silhouette looking but he has a presence of his whole body, i can feel it. Then i became a child again..he turned me into a child again. I can see my body clinging into his arms and wrapped arround his neck.

He was walking while he is carrying me in his arms, and i can feel his very loving energy connection between us as a FATHER and child. I know this feelings..and i feel this towards my children. So i know what he is feeling right now at this very moment. I think my Devine Father missess me..i am feeling the comfort that he is giving me. Later on he put me down on the floor while still holding my right hand while we both walking arround the KINGDOM. Then i saw JESUS wearing a long and very white thick gown, and i can see his hair is black and is very prominent..i don't know why? Then he took my hand as well..and for some reason we all both walking arround holding my hands. I am puzzled of what's going on?? then i asked papa GOD. What's going on papa GOD? why my brother JESUS holding my hand and walking arround with you? Why?..A question of a child with curiousity, he made me read his mind. Then my Devine FATHER said..we miss you..we just want to hold your hands. Oh ok, i said.:)

Then the whole thing shifted, i became an adult again. Sitting beside with my DEVINE FATHER, of course with my little chair, and with my spiritual imagination and creativity i made myself fit into it. Then i said to my DEVINE FATHER, i'm sure you knew already what's going on with me don't you FATHER? Hmm..he said, why? do you want to talk about it? Oh No FATHER, preferably not this moment. Very well then, he said..your choice my child, he said. I thought to myself..at last i have a choice this time..then papa GOD gave me this look..a look of reassurance but in the other hands, i can read your mind..don't go any further my child, because this time i don't like to see you cry again. Hmm..i sigh..:(

I heard you visited your ANCESTRAL HOME, papa GOD said.. yes FATHER i did, i said to him solemnly. DO you know my door is always open here for you? And i always leave the lights on infront of the door, my FATHER said. Yes Father i know..sorry if i didn't come to you. I was afraid to what would happen under the circumstances yesterday. I know it's not to me..but to those who upsets me.

I choose to go home where my comfort i used to be, in my bedroom that i am always feel safe and comfortable. DEVINE FATHER, i am ready now for my battle. I want to get on with it and finish it so i can go back to my normal life..in earth. Is this possible MY DEVINE FATHER? Yes my child of course..but the battle you will be facing is my choice. OH of course Papa GOD i understand that. And i am truly sorry for my mistakes i have made, and disobeyed you. You didn't disobeyed me my child..it was your choice, as you are looking for something that really mysterious connections..the same soul energy and very similar ones. It's not a crime..you are curious..i created you that way. But you are smart, feeling the human emotions is just normal, as long as you know your boundaries. Oh..thank you FATHER. My DEVINE FATHER is very forgiving..and that is me!

You have created your own boundaries, so when people hurts you or trying to hurt you..you have already built your own boundaries of protection, which i am very proud of you for doing that to yourselves. I am always here my child, he said. I know FATHER and i thank you. Now i believe you have encountered some entities again lately. Yes FATHER, the other night i was fighting with my own battle with so many black entities trying to eliminate me again. When they are going to stop? So i did what i have to do "NO MERCY" this time. They have rounded me up..so many of them and all wearing black robes and black hoods and i can't see their faces. They are trying to attack me while i was in the middle of the circle.

I was circled down with so many black entities..i saw myself in a black outfit armour and no weapons in my hands. I used the energy you taught me..it's all in my hands and my whole body. I gathered it all then i strked all this entities at once just by pointing my hands on them with my sharp energy coming from my hands.I have cut them all in halves while they were in a circles.

I could not believe it when i struck them..it was like cutting a piece of paper with sharp energy coming through my hands. I don't know how i did this FATHER..but you taught me how to create this in my mind. They're all dead..they're all laying on the ground with thier bodies cut in halves..but to my surprised, there was no blood! That was my battle lately FATHER. I have been very tired and thirsty after that.

You need to recuperate my child as you used so much of your energy in spiritual realms..yes my Father, and i am feeling it. So when is my Big battle again DEVINE FATHER? I am ready, bring it on. Then i heard my FATHER laughed so hard and it sounds like a thunder!!..of course my child..you will be going when things are ready. I will give you some signs, and you know the signs. yes DEVINE FATHER, i know and thank you for trusting me again.

MY child you are always my child..and FORGIVENESS is always here for you. Thank you FATHER. Papa GOD, do you think i have always picked the wrong decisions? No my child..life is all about learning..learning to trust..to love the right people..help people to their own enlightment and to show their paths. There are so many things that you need to learn in life. So don't give up..Yes FATHER, and oh no i won't give up, and i will never give up especially to what i believe in and for myself. I have to excuse myself from here FATHER, i need to go to work. I'll catch up with you later..ok my child you know where to find me. Yes my DEVINE FATHER. ILOVEYOU. Thank You again.

# CHAPTER 102

# WHERE MY PERSONALITIES CAME FROM

JOURNAL
9TH FEBRAURY 2023

LAst night, i visited my Ancestral home..i was called by my father EMPEROR ARTHERU. I can see myself as a child running towards him with open arms. I can see myself wearing a flowery dress and black flat shiny shoes. I can see my mother Empress Glydica standing besides my EMPEROR father. When i got closer to my FATHER, he picked me up and hugged me tightly, and spent time with them..i'm feeling so happy again..i'm home. I explored the whole KINGDOM, inside and outside the palace. The NATURE is so beautiful and wonderful..i am home.

They let me run arround the place. I can see my mother and grandmama sitting amongst the garden sorrounded by so many different flowers that i have never seen in earth. Then grandmama called me to sit with them so i stopped running arround, and sat in the middle with them. Then i asked my grandmama why there is no other children in our KINGDOM? You're the only child here because that'd what we want, my mother EMPRESS Glydica said.

The i asked my grandmama, where all my personalities came from? then i saw both of them looked at each other. Grandmama said well, your beautiful and endless love came from your mother and your beauty, your commanding traits came from your EMPEROR FATHER. Your braveness and being a great warriour came from your grandfather METATRON, and you? grand mama? what did i get from you? i asked. My EMPREss mother said..well your grandmother sense of humour. Ohh..a wacky sense of humour, i said. Then we all laughed. :) :) Yes, i must admit i do have a wacky sense of humour :) Then i can see my DEVINE FATHER talking to my EMPEROR father ARTHERU, i was going to run towards them, but my mother stopped me and gently held my shoulder. My DEVINE FATHER is not showing his face to me..but instead, he sent me a very comforting energy and that's enough for me to validate that it's him.

Then the scenery shifted, i can see myself in a dark valley sorrounded with so many dark entities again. I am wearing a dark armour with my long pointy sword, and i only can see from the dark with my sword is shinning. I held my sword in my right arm, i am standing tall and facing the black entities sorrounding me. I can feel it in my bones..i am ready to fight!!

Then suddenly all the entities are moving towards me..there movements are the same..one step at a time..very slowly..three steps, then stopped..again they are doing it the same steps..until they got closer to me, then they attacked! All together with the same movement!! I was cornered in the middle of the circle..so i opened my wings and lifted up my body, and then i was behind them then i started to cut them with my sword in pieces and with the sign of the CROSS. One at a time..but the more i eliminated them..the more they are coming. This time they attacked me with a very rapid movements. There techniques were so fast moving..i was empressed!

Then i'm surprised with my movement too..my body was even more quicker than them. I have never seen my body moved like that before from the previous battle. It was like a lightning bolt moved..my adrenalin was pumping up so high, i couldn't stop myself!! i kept going..movement with a real fighter in a battle and my sword is so light as a feather and sounds like it is singing. It has a sound when i striked and my composure has no fear, I am fearless!!

Then suddenly there was a Gigantic black entity appeared behind my back! and almost going to attack me! Then suddenly one of my Ancestor interfered, blocking this big evil entity was trying to attack me behind my back! I turned arround and saw my grandfather Metatron fighting this big evil entity..i can see that he needs help, so i flew towards him and then the evil entity turned himself towards me, and started attacking me. I then heard my DEVINE FATHER voice..the sign of the cross is to kill the evil. Then suddenly, i flew myself to the top of the entity..i tried to aim my sword, but the entity is moving too fast. So i quickly used my mental power. I stopped the entity from moving. I can see the entity froze..and trying to move his whole body but couldn't move. Then i realised that was my opportunity to strike. I strike his head with my sword, from the top towards down and with the sign of the cross.

Then i opened his heart..i was amazed that it has blood. I removed the heart from his body, then a little box..golden box appeared infront of me, then i placed that heart inside then it disappeared. I raised my weapon to my DEVINE FATHER and suddenly the light..bright and golden white lights streaming down towards me and to my sword cleansing..it's cleansing my whole body penetrating my whole self and my sword. Then the lights slowly disappearing, and the whole area back to darkness and i looked arround..black entities are everywhere, they are all in the ground. I made them disappeared by pointing with my right finger..then the whole place became lighter.

I saw my father EMPEROR Artheru waving at me from the far distance..up there in a south west horizon together with my other family ancestors. Then i heard my DEVINE FATHER..well done my child. I'm so proud of you. Thank you FATHER, i said. Now drink plenty of water, he said..yes Father i will.

Prior to this battle, i felt like somebody was stopping me from meeting my Ancestral home and going to the battle. I was asleep, someone or somebody had there fingers on my right middle thigh and made my whole body paralysed..unable to move. I called to my DEVINE FATHER..then suddenly, he appeared and cut this entity head's off. I was petrified to what my DEVINE FATHER did!! I could not believe he did that! I couldn't think it would be possible for him to ruthlessly do that to this entity. I was shocked! Now this entity's body will start to deteriorate..maybe started from the neck..and die from whatever circumstances of illnesses they would acquired in the reality world.

My DEVINE FATHER WHY? why they would not stop? It's insane! they know the consequences. My child this people or entities will never stop until you do and still exist in this world. So the more they will attack you..the more we eliminating the evil entities in this reality and spiritual realm.

You are protected my child..sometimes i let them through to your energy as a bait. Oh FATHER you are smart.

# CHAPTER 103

# VALENTINES DAY WITH MY DEVINE FATHER

JOURNAL

18TH FEBRAURY 2023

It's about time to update you my dear journal as it has been a chaos weeks for me. I have been meeting my DEVINE FATHER in a regular basis just to talk to him, and one night he took me to the dark area sorrounded with the glass wall. Somehow i can see myself in the middle of this people sorrounding me again. They are all wearing black robes and hoods, and i cannot see thier faces. Their purpose is always to sacrifice me..so much evil in them that i can feel it in my bones of their bad intentions.

Before they can't get closer to me, i got up and stood on top of the marble table. Facing them is not my concern anymore, and I don't even feel threatened or scared of any one of them. This battle with them is nothing to me compared to what i have eliminated or i have been through, and i don't think any second thoughts into not eradicating them. Lord have mercy on thier souls. My concerns for them is why they kept doing it? They know they can't eliminate me..and they are making it too easy for me to eradicate them.

Sometimes it does distresses me, don't they know the consequences? they are going to die once i eliminated them in spritual realm, and if they still exist in a physical world..they will die slowly from whatever illnesses they are experiencing. Why can't they get??? I'm here to obey my DEVINE FATHER MISSION. If i disobeyed that would be my Biggest sin i will be creating, and that's not going to happen. I love my DEVINE FATHER and i now realise how important my task here in earth and spiritually.

Anyway, i stood up and i can see myself wearing a black outfit with the armour arround my body, and for some reasons my hands are my weapons. Before they can attacked me, i pointed out my right hand and amazingly the energy came out from my hand towards the entities bodies. Somehow my hand automatically releasing this sharp energy going from left to right cutting all this entities in halves infront of me.

My body poised looks so stoic and no MERCY i can feel for them. The second row entities were very closed to the glass wall. They were all sitting, and when i stepped closer.. they all stood up quickly. Then from my hands, the force of the energy i released..it's so strong.. and it's strong enough to cracked the very thick glass wall behind them, and all the entities ducked down for cover. The second time i released my energy towards them have shattered the entire glass wall in pieces..shattered..and all the entire entities disappeared but some are injured. Then i wake up very thirsty.

The next day, Papa GOD called me to see him. In a quick second i was standing infront of the Big door, the usual door where my DEVINE FATHER always waited for me everytime i visit him. It's open..matter of fact the door is always open for me. I can see myself running towards him as a child again wearing a very dark red dress and my black flat shoes. I can see my DEVINE FATHER from the distance waiting for me and with open arms..and for me is the same.:)

He is bending down almost to my height level as a child.:) I was running towards him and then finally catches me with his open arms, and picked me up and put me on his shoulder and welcomed me with his beautiful energy. So much hearts floating and everywhere. He is carrying me walking arround..and he said to me..welcome my child and i am very happy to see you. Ohh..i miss my DEVINE FATHER.. but i didn't say it to him..instead i gave him a big hug and little tighter almost clinging into his shoulder and arround his neck.

I have noticed, there are no clouds arround the area..but hearts are everywhere..i asked PAPA GOD..where are the clouds? and why we have so many hearts floating? He then said to me..don't you know it's a heart day today? Ohhh..that's right yes papa GOD it's Valentine's day in earth. But i didn't get any hearts from my love ones..tears in my eyes.. never mind he said, that's why i called you to be with me..ohh..is it why i'm wearing this very red dress papa GOD? It's a heart day with you.:)

Oh now i understand about the red dress, thank you..you have a good taste papa GOD, and my DEVINE FATHER laughed..and then more little hearts are floating.:) I spent my time with DEVINE FATHER just the two of us. We both sitting on our chairs comfortably and not doing anything. Our energy integrated both with so much comfort and love. I didn't feel bored..matter of fact i am happy just being with him and in the presence with my FATHER.

I didn't see my pets or JESUS and any ANGELS around. It's just me and him sitting comfortably, contented with our own companies.

Then later on we moved to the long table, we sat down on our chair comfortably. So serene..no noise..just comfort i can feel. Then i can see myself asleep in my FATHER's arms again. Then i wake up the next morning feeling good of myself. My whole week is so serene even working with very difficult people and with silly circumstances. I thanked my DEVINE FATHER, eventhough i had a lousy valentines day here in earth..Papa GOD made it so special for me up there with him. I LOVE YOU my DEVINE FATHER.:)

# CHAPTER 104

# MIRROR MIRROR ON THE WALL

JOURNAL
22nd FEBRAURY 2023

Last night when i came home from work, i looked at myself in my bathroom mirror..and said to myself..mirror mirror on the wall who is looking at me behind the wall? i don't know why i said that...then i closed my eyes i saw this foggy images but with light blue colour and horizontally moving from left to right inside the mirror. I can see so many eyes inside the mirror and they are all becoming blurry. It's more like eyes with cataract with blurry visions. I stopped the image as i didn't like it, then i went to bed. This morning, suddenly i have a vision while changing my clothes and sitting while putting my socks on. I saw this old man in a white clothes and with medium build has long hair and a thick beard. Before i could ask who he is.. he said I'm abraham.

I recognised him from previous meditation, he was up there in the sky while holding this BOOK. It's the same book he was holding from the last time i saw him. The open page is empty while holding it with his left arm. The lightning and thunder came from above he said.. The storms and lightning came from the DEVINE ALMIGHTY

FATHER!!" i thought..what does it means? and then i can see the heaven is opening, I didn't see my DEVINE FATHER came through.. but i asked him..FATHER what does this means? Then he showed me the ocean, and the shore is black..it looks like MUD! then he asked me to pray..i kneeled and prayed for our environment.

Then when i finished my prayers..i grabbed my necklace with a cross, i kissed it and slowly trying to put it in my neck. I attempted twice to put it arround my neck, but for some reasons i was having a problem hooking it up. Then to my 3rd attempt finally i hooked it in. At that moment i felt like someone was stopping me from putting my cross necklace arround my neck, i ususally don't have any problem with it.

Then i asked again, my DEVINE FATHER what is the messages means?..No answers..so i went ahead to prepare myself going to work. I will talk to you my DEVINE FATHER tonight i said to him. He knows when to call me..and if it's urgent, where ever i am, anytime, anywhere he will call me. I love you my DEVINE FATHER..i am busy but never forget you..you are always with me..here in my heart. :)

# CHAPTER 105

# ANOTHER BATTLE WITH AN EVIL ENTITY

JOURNAL

24th FEBRAURY 2023

Last night before i went to bed, i said my prayers and said goodnight to my DEVINE FATHER. When i closed my eyes..there was a light coming from my left side of my eye vision. I knew it's my FATHER, it's the same light as i always see before i connect with him spiritually. I thought my DEVINE FATHER is calling me..i blinked twice because i thought that would be my eye sights playing up again..but i thought it can't be. So i called papa GOD..then the light becoming more stronger. I stayed with the light above hovering me..it's the same light Papa GOD always leave the front door light for me..up there.

I said..yes papa GOD do you want to see me? but instead opening the door..it took me to the place again..the VALLEY of darkness sorrounded with large rocks..and it's very dark. I saw myself standing tall on a very big and tall boulder, wearing a black outfit fitted arround my body. I am holding my long sword..my physique is changing. I feel more confident and more focussed and with no fear. I thought..i am changing and i can feel it.

My confidence with this preparation for the battle is so profound. I don't feel any fear in my body instead i feel confident. This is not my old me, then suddenly i saw the entities coming towards me. I have noticed, no ANGELS in sight and nobody can help me with this battle. I guess this is my own battle again. The entities are coming closer so rapidly..i prepared and positioned myself, then when they finally got closer i aimed my sword towards them, and with my rapid movements synchronising with my sword..i eliminated them quickly.

My sword leads me the way how to cut the entities with precisions, and i don't understand when my sword moves, my whole body synchronises with it..an incredible movements and i must admit when my adrenalin pumped up, i could not stop until i finished them all. I feel like i have done this battle before. It's so light when cutting thier bodies in half with my sword.

Then the sign of cross, and everytime i eradicated each one of them, i asked some forgiveness from my DEVINE FATHER. And i said to him..this is not me FATHER in reality..and his answer is..they are not human in spiritual realms..or you will be killed by them..and i'm not going to let it happened. Oh..FATHER i wish they will stop..i cried for thier souls.

Then the lightning occurred up in the sky..the entities kept coming in, then it's the same from me..as i have no other choices, i have eradicated them fearlessly. Then finally, and this is really surprises me..there was a BIG scary looking evil entity just came out from nowhere and it's face is very RED, have an enermous body from top to bottom. He looks naked from the top and didn't see the lower part. His lower extremitie just massive and has big muscles, i got shivers everywhere of my body. He got closer to me..and then started looking at me and very carefully, then suddenly he attacked me with this big hands.

He is trying to grabbed me and i tried to get away from him. I was running to the higher place..up higher to every rocks..then suddenly, he grabbed my back. He pulled me down and then when we both stumbling very fast, and while we were falling i used my quick thinking..i got into his back and then punched his head with my bare hand. I got away quickly..i saw him 2 to 3 metres away from the ground, then i thought that was my opportunity to tackle him, but when i got closer to him.. he attacked me! He kicked me on my right face!

I was threwn far away from the force of his kicked. I saw myself on top of the big rock laying half way on my back. I tried to shake my head as i couldn't get up quickly, so i called Arch Angel Michael to help me before this entity get closer to me. Arch Angel Michael appeared infront of me suddenly, then pushed this entity really hard away from me. Then that was my opportunity again to attack him, and this time with my sword. Arch Angel Michael then disappeared..i thought, i'm on my own battle again. I ran towards him very quickly while this evil entity still on the ground, i landed on his abdominal area, grabbed his head, and for some reason..my sword cut off his head!!! I was horrified from the action of my sword which synchronised with my right hand.

I jumped off from his body, and with his head on my hand dragging it outside the dark cave area. I came back with his remaining body, and while dragging the entities body..i was looking at the whole area and trying to figured out what is this place? The Fire sorrounding in this area?? I am thinking it can be hell. Then i noticed, somehow the heart of this entity is in my right hand..i am holding it.

Then i called to my DEVINE FATHER, FATHER! what do i do with his heart? then suddenly an empty golden box appeared infront of me..then my hands kind of knew what to do. His heart has been put in a golden box..then disappeared. Then my hands and my sword automatically lifted up towards to heaven..then 2 beautiful lights came through which is white and gold energy and started washing off my hands including my sword and then finally my whole body.

Then i asked Papa GOD..FATHER..why you didn't open the door for me earlier? My child that's because it wasn't the time to come in while your enemies are about to attacked you. They are not supposed to be here in my KINGDOM. So that's why i directly took you to them..and i knew you can handle it my child. Yes Father i did..now i'm so tired..yes my child get some sleep, goodnight my child..goodnight my DEVINE FATHER. Then suddenly i can see little twinkle stars and hearts floating..then i fall asleep. I got up today and still feeling tired but feeling light somehow.. i don't know why my whole body is feeling lighter..but i'm happy. :)

# CHAPTER 106

# SPIRITUAL BATTLE PREPARATIONS

JOURNAL
28TH FEBRAURY 2023

last night i met my Emperor father Artheru in our KINGDOM.. but prior to that i can feel the "tension" arround me, and feeling like retreating again to my Ancestral home. I am feeling this bad entities are attacking me from left to right lately. And i think to thier own frustrations they are attacking my sister. But my sister and my whole family are safe, i have covered them with loving and safety energy 24/7. My sister is my biggest support about the legacy i am bulding and this is from my own cost.

Why do you think i worked so hard just to manifest my "LEGACY". The environment..the ophans..the animals which i am very focussed with. I don't and never asked people's money..because i will manifest this legacy from my own hard work and from the help of my other members of my family. Purchasing the land Forest to save the endangered species..building my parents home as an Orphanage home and at the same time rescuing the animals from hunger and providing them some shelters. Now is this too much to ask? why people trying to destroy this LEGACY of mine which i don't even need your help or your money? WHY? why are you trying to hurt my family sending this bad energies of yours?? Take a look at yourselves people in the mirror..and ask yourself what have i done good in this earth? Ask yourself!!

I met again my FATHER EMPEROR ARTHERU in our KINGDOM of NATURE last night, i travelled again of course. It seems like and i feel that my EMPEROR father is calling me. I can see him from the distance in our KINGDOM, and the sorrounding is full of snow..it's white everywhere..i am puzzled, why there is some snow here? And then i can see my FATHER Emperor standing in a blizard snow and waiting for me. He just standing there..then i ran towards him. I can see his open arms trying to welcomed me. Finally i reached his arms and gave me a BIG hug. I felt his emotion..and i can feel he missess me.

Then i spoke to him about the entities are trying to hurt me and my extended family. What do i do with them FATHER? They never stop attacking me and now starting to attack my family. My Emperor Father pulled me towards him closer and gave me a BIG HUG. I also can feel his frustration too. He then said..listen to me SHINE.. this people are not going to stop. Unfortunately they are blinded to thier own truths beliefs. FAther Artheru, i don't need to hurt them..i want them to change and help me heal our mother earth. Mother earth is suffering and angry.

They are not going to change my shine, my Emperor Artheru father said. So what do i need to do FATHER? The earth is suffering.. how can i help? Then my DEVINE FATHER suddenly appeared, then my two FATHERS joined together..and with me..but for some reason we are still standing in the middle of the blizards snow. I didn't feel cold or feeling the cold while i was in between with my two FATHERS. I felt so loved and protected with my 2 FATHERS.

Then my DEVINE FATHER said to me and asked..before you went to bed last night..what did you remember? Oh..i saw a white kind of square light..it was so intense coming from above and penetrating my WHOLE body. It was 4 times have appeared, and it feels like my whole body is filling up with this white and intense lights. Then i felt like i have so much energy power on me..inside of me.

Then you said in my mind "USE" it! that's your weapon! then your voice disappeared. I tried to call you back..and kept asking you if i can come and visit you up there..but you are not showing your door for me.. i was crying.. Then this woman's face appeared quickly infront of me..and i know this person..this person is part of the entities in the group.

She's wearing white and flowery dress and she was mocking me..then i got angry..i used my hands and grabbed her whole body and slowly squeezing her head..then i threw her molded head inside the square ice into the galaxy. Then i said to her you will be frozen until a billion years in the galaxy. Then i changed my mind..i turned arround, then i used the lights that i was given to me from my DEVINE FATHER last night. I pointed out my hands towards her, and blasted this person into pieces out there in the galaxy!

I can see myself as a cladded warriour..my body changes..i am more confident of myself, and i do what i have to do, and it's inprinted into my head, but my compassion to humankind still here inside my HEART. To protect the innocent people including animals and to care for the environment..and that's a BIG command from my DEVINE FATHER. I CANNOT DISOBEY HIM. He is MY DEVINE FATHER THE HIGHEST and the CREATOR OF ALL.

The next one is a male person, medium build, well shaven, black hair, white person and wearing a black t-shirt and black pants. He appeared also infront of me, and of course the same thing that the previous woman was doing to me..mocking and trying to intimidate me. WEll, i did what i have to do without any questions. I froze him with my hands just by pointing it to him..then threw him out there in the galaxy then blasted him off into pieces!!! I couldn't bare any billion of years for this people to come back in earth and wreck so much havocs to humankind.

The 3rd one is a younger person..male with a thick hair, medium lenght hair and slightly wavy. This person is another part of the entities group who is trying to hurt me. He has white skin, very europian looking, say..he has italian or greek looks, and yes..he was doing the same thing to me. I thought..what kind of people are you? don't you know that i cannot save you? You are making it too easy for me to eliminate you. arrgh..so stupid!!! then blasted him off to the galaxy, but he kept coming back and trying to retaliates..ohh..stop!..for the LOVE of GOD!!

He kept coming back and trying to retaliates 3 times..but then i'm sick of it..so i jailed him inside the square ice..but i noticed..he only have the head..the body is not with him..it's only the head..whoahh.. he left his other body in earth. So i did what i have to do..sent his head to the galaxy and blasted him off into pieces with my hands.. the lights are so powerful coming out from my hands. FATHER..my DEVINE FATHER..please can i ask some questions please?? THe Devine power of lights that you have given to me last night, do i have only to use it in the spirit realm? am i correct FATHER?

Yes my child, absolutely, you are correct, he said and why not in a physical world? i asked again. well my child in a spirit world is where the beginnings of your healings, and this is connected to your physical world. Your battle starts here in the spiritual realm. Once you healed the earth with the helps of others through their spirituality with good intentions..then this energy will connect to reality. Oh..my DEVINE FATHER now i understand.

Your battle is here my child..spiritually, and you can use your energy in a physical world too, but you need to be careful..what ever you think and that will hurt the person, whatever you are creating in your mind it will have massive impact on that person or people..Yes YOU can! he said. well..that's an authorisation from my DEVINE FATHER. THANK YOU!

FATHER i know i only can use it when someone is hurting me and my family. Yes i know my child..your mind is becoming more complicated for you to understand..but you must understand most of this decision that you are making is coming from me..from your DEVINE FATHER. You have Prorection all arround you my child. DO NOT worry. Thank you my DEVINE FATHER, i said. Now, the earth is suffering..you must do what you have to do..your spiritual war battle is lining up for you and your ANGELS.

You have everything in you now..eradicate the entities and people that has an intention to stop you from your mission. I am here beside you and always..your Ancestors will be with you during the battle. Remember my child..your mind and your hands are your power. "USE IT WISELY". Yes my DEVINE FATHER..i will and I PROMISE! Ohh.. my dear journal i have to stop here. this is very intense downloads. I cannot turn arround now..THIS IS MY

SPIRITUAL LEGACY!. I said goodbye to my two "FATHERS"..i love you both..and i can see their happy and loving faces..ohh..i really miss them. :) :)

# CHAPTER 107

# PORTAL TO A DIFFERENT DIMENSION

JOURNAL

2ND MARCH 2023

I must write this before it disappears in my head, as there are so many messages i recieved lately and i get very tired after the spiritual downloads. Last night, before i settled into my deep sleep, i closed my eyes and said my prayers. Then suddenly i can see people's faces that i don't even know. They all kept coming into my space and getting so close to my face, but i was trying to ignore them. They were persistent and kept flashing there faces on and off infront of me, and i am starting to getting annoyed as it is becoming intollerable, but i kept ignoring them.

Then suddenly i can see myself in a different dimension..the GREEN LADY KINGDOM out there in a galaxy..so open..and i can see different size of stars. Some of the stars are brightly shinning and some of them are too far away. I can see myself standing in an open portal between this dimension and where i am now. It's little bit hard to explain..as i don't know really how to explain this in reality, as i don't have any theories to prove relatively in a physical world. I only can tell you where i am during the time of my experienced in between this two dimensions.

Nevertheless, i stepped into the portal inside which where i was standing..then i suddenly emerged into the GREEN LADY's KINGDOM. I can see her 5 meters away from me and waving at me. She acknowledged my presence by nodding her head slowly and majestically, i accepted her welcome by doing the same respectfully. Then i saw different types of "BEINGS", some are the same kind of her but with black colour faces. One particular being i have noticed, it's look like a MANTIS face, although it looks black and has the body just like human.

It looks like he's wearing a kind of uniform..a high ranking space suit entity uniform, and looks like he didn't like me being there and my presence. Then i noticed, my face starting to hurt..i can feel he is hurting my face and by not even touching me..he is harming me with his mental energy. I quickly retaliated by doing the same thing to him..hurting his face with my energy coming from my hand, i kept pushing my energy directly to him and while walking towards this "being" with no fear..i can feel my energy is so strong..and a matter of fact it's little bit scary that i can feel it is even more powerful than before. I cannot stop!! then i saw his body pushed against the silvery metal door wall..i feel like it's the corner of invisible lift..but i can see he is being pinned on the metal wall, then i STOPPED!. I quickly controlled my energy..he then quickly disappeared infront of my sight.

I looked at my palms and my hands. I can't even imagine how powerful are my hands in the spiritual world..it's a worrying fact.. but i accept it with all my heart as it is one of my GIFT from my

DEVINE FATHER. I continued walking on the glass floor towards the open KINGDOM of the galaxy..and looking out towards beyond, it's fascinating. The green lady also disappeared from my sight. I can see myself wearing my Black Warriour outfit. I am standing tall looking out the galaxy from this dimension, somehow my hair is very long and it's platted. I don't really know where i am or what dimensions..i know the fact i'm here standing looking at the open space and the galaxy somewhere in a different dimension.

Then suddenly this different faces appeared infront of me again.. and again..and they are all trying to hurt my face..but they cannot get closer to me. I mean, everytime they attempted to get closer to my space, they then quickly disappeared. One particular face kept trying to attack my safe area of space, and kept trying to penetrate into my bubble of safety..then i got sick of it, i quickly grabbed his head..it's only head this time?? i don't know why is always the head and no forms of full body..ohh wait there is..but its from head and only to chest.

I grabbed his head, i can see his face so clearly, and somehow wearing an oriental white top type of shirt, with a collar and has a flowery patterns on it. I don't know why and if this is significant..but this is what's showing me. It's a Hawaiian shirt top, but it's white with flowery patterns or designs. So when i grabbed his head..then i threw him into the galaxy and blasted him off into pieces with my energy coming from my hands. Then i asked Papa GOD..why they are keep doing this to me? then suddenly, i saw some few hands waving at me..or looks like asking some help perhaps?

At that time i was confused about this hands. The palms of the hands were waving at me, i didn't know how to react, as i blasted one entity in an outer space into pieces. So i didn't know if i have to wave or not to touch with this many hands? I asked Papa GOD again.. Father what does this means? please...Then papa GOD answered.. what is your feelings says about it? Feel it again my child and here.. Papa GOD showing me gently tapping his chest close to his heart. So i closed my eyes..then i connected my feelings to thier hands and thier palms, the palms of thier hands whose waving at me..i feel forgiveness for them..Forgiveness FATHER..they want Forgiveness, i said.

So this is it my child..forgiveness for humankind who hurts you. Yes father i understand now. Then the palms and hands disappeared. Then i saw myself went back to bed. Then i noticed, i can see Papa God's door up there is open. The light is on..and the door slightly ajar, and then i saw myself got up and called my DEVINE FATHER if i can visit him. Then the door slowly opened and widely, then i can see myself again as a child. Oh dear..papa GOD turned me again into a child.

I am running towards him while i can see him from the distance kneeling down on his right knee with his open arms. I can see myself wearing a normal dress and with little brown sandals. Then i noticed While running towards him, when i'm getting closer..my dress slowly changing into a nice flowery white dress and my sandals too slowly changing into a red flat shoes. When i reached his arms, he grabbed me so gently and he stood up and i was clinging into his arms and shoulder. Ohh..i am so happy to see you Papa GOD..and i can feel my DEVINE FATHER missess me too the way he hugged me.

I can feel the love and reassurance from him, and just feeling being safe in my FATHER's arms. Oh welcome my child he said..i can feel and see him so happy to see me. Then i looked at his face..and i played with the hair of his face, then i asked..why i can't see your face? Oh yes he said..because we have company. Then we both looked at to the right side corner, while he still holding me. I can see this high ranking people entities sitting arround the long marble table, but their faces are not clear. They are talking in a mumbling sounds.. some kind of meeting is going on at the moment with my DEVINE FATHER.

So then he said to me, go and play with your pets. I saw kelly my dog have wings..cyclops too but his wings are not so defined..it looks like a fairy wings..very thin. Then i realised cyclops is a fairy cat.. hahaha:)i think you have been drinking some red bull cyclops to get the fairy wings! hahaha:) ohh..i can see him just happily walking on the edge of the verandah pane. While ginger blue has no wings including mister rabbit.

Papa GOD put me down on the floor, and i run towards my pets.. then my dog kelly started to open her wings and started lifting up her body. Then suddenly she's on the air. I started chasing her and then suddenly i fell over because of my shoes..so i took it off, then i started chasing kelly again running towards the open room. Then suddenly..my little wings started to open up and started lifting my body up in the air.

Then i can see my body up on the air with my wings. I called out, PAPA GOD my wings are open and i can fly!!...Papa GOD looked at me from the distance with a smile on his face. Then i started to follow kelly she looks very happy with her wings. WE then both went into the room with full of clouds arround. Then we saw the little Angels that i used to play before..we tried running, then flying with our wings..hide and seek..then fly again..over and over again. Then suddenlly i heard a BIG THUMP! I noticed i was down on the floor. I hit the same brown pillar again..but i didn't feel the pain or no injury on me. Then i looked up..i saw my brother JESUS..very tall man with a beard and wearing a white robe with red colour cloth on his front chest. He is standing on my right side offering his hand for me to stand up.

I grabbed his hand slowly with my left tiny hand, he then helped me stand up. He walked me out from the play room while still holding my hand, and we both walking towards my DEVINE FATHER. Then that was it..i wake up and feeling wants to pee..:) I tried to hold it..but then i forced myself to get up and walked to the toilet without the lights on, and my eyes still closed..then back to my bed again and slept until morning and wake up so thirsty. Now i am sitting on my chair, and every time i closed my eyes i can see my DEVINE FATHER smiling at me. I LOVE YOU my DEVINE FATHER, and to my brother JESUS i love you too. I can see his face smiling at me :)

# CHAPTER 108

# HORRIBLE LOOKING BEINGS FALLING FROM THE SKY

JOURNAL
5TH MARCH 2023

Last night during my prayers and meditation before i fall asleep, there was some interference from the entities while i was having conversations with my DEVINE FATHER.

I thought when are they going to learn?..so Papa GOD said, you know what to do my child. I got up and eliminated them instantly, but one particular entity was so persistent, very quick to move and a shape shifter. Then finally i grabbed his neck and pinned him on the wall with my daggers..and with the sign of the cross..he slowly melted and disappeared.

Then the scenery shifted, i saw myself in the small house in a room with 3 children 2 girls and a boy. I saw myself laying on the small bed and looking at the glass top window. While there was another person beside me a gentleman in a uniform laying in the other bed while the kids were just quietly playing. I have never seen this kids and the gentleman before. I am not sure at this moment of what we are doing in the small house while we are all in the same room resting.

Suddenly, i saw something or i would say..it's a "BEING" just crashing into the top glass window just where i am staring at. Then i saw more "beings" coming just droppings like flies from above and very rapidly! I was shocked! and i slowly tapped the man's left arm beside me in another bed..he then saw it too. He signalled me not to make a noise and then i grabbed the kids with me. The man grabbed his long gun and he pointed a small space for us to hide. The space is just a little room but made of "solid concrete and very thick metal". We all got there so quietly and i was shaking..my whole body was shaking..the kids seems to know of what to do..not to make a noise.

I am realising now that this is happening to our world. The man trying to calmed me down, as my whole body was so cold and was shaking. The gentleman trying to hold my body and keeping me warm. The kids were so quiet and no one is making any noise. I said to the man, what happened if people has no space like this to hide? what would happen to them? He said another place is the basement to hide, as long as the place is solid wall concrete with metal sorroundings so that they cannot detect you if you are human by smelling our senses.

Then papa GOD shifted me again looking at his KINGDOM. The door is slightly opened. I asked papa GOD..can i see you FATHER? please. Then the door slightly opened then widely. I can see myself as a young lady..i walked into the room and i can't see my FATHER. I looked arround..but i only can see some people high ranking entities, and then i saw my father EMPEROR Artheru and my mother EMPRESS Glydica. They both greeted me while my mother has a glass of wine holding in her right hand elegantly. The rest of the entities just talking in a sounds of mumbling or different languages. I never undestood them.

I asked my mother and father..what's going on here? what kind of celebration they are celebrating? My mother said something in a different language which i am not so familiar with it, and i didn't focus of what she said as i didn't understand the words she said. If it was an Ancient language..well i never heard that before. I was going to ask more but it shifted me somewhere else again.

This time is a battle field. I can see myself standing on my own with my black warriour cladded outfit, and i can see i am wearing an eye mask, and this time is black. I am standing on a BIG ROCK, looking at to the south. Then i asked Papa GOD..father i'm here. I'm ready..and i saw the image earlier..The "beings" and all falling from above! it's scary, i don't want this to happened in my world!..the people's world..MY WORLD MY DEVINE FATHER...PLEASE... FATHER!...PLEASE..talk to me..I AM READY NOW! Then suddenly the clouds opened slowly...and here it is, i can see my DEVINE FATHER's face..showing amongst with the small clouds.

Yes my child..i heard you..with his deep and reassuring voice but with majestic command. I bowed to him with greatest respect. Yes my DEVINE FATHER..i must do what i have to do now. Are you ready my child? Yes FATHER and i will not disappoint you. Then suddenly a "BIG SWORD" appeared from above, and slowly coming down to me, then i noticed..something wrong with the sword. It looks old and it has a chip in the middle of the blade and slightly rusty, and the handle also i noticed, there was one ruby stone is missing.

Then once i have held the old sword looking on my hands..it suddenly became new, and it looks different..it's WHITE! so white and the blade is sparkling. The handle is completed with precious stones, and it's magnificent to hold and handle..it's very light. It's yours my child, my DEVINE FATHER said with the tone of a very MAJESTIC voice. Thank you my DEVINE FATHER, i said. You still can use your other weapons i have given you.. It's all yours my child. Thank you FATHER, then suddenly my ANGELS appeared behind me!! all of them with horses...all white horses! And SKY suddenly appeared infront of me too. He looks so happy..this time i have so many ANGELS, including ARCH ANGEL MICHAEL, GABRIEL, METATRON and some of my Ancestors. They were all there..i even can see SAM the earth Angel.

Then papa GOD said, this are your ALLIES..win this spiritual war, i bowed to my DEVINE FATHER..and if i fail???..then the world will have no existence. I can feel my hands get really heavy..i can feel my BIgest responsiblities..and it's all in my hands now. I then can see my BROTHER "JESUS" amongst with the Angels. He is also riding on the white horse. THEN WE WENT TO THE BATTLE!!!

# CHAPTER 109

# ALIGNING WITH THE WHITE BEING AND MY DEVINE FATHER

JOURNAL
12TH MARCH 2023

I have been very busy lately with my work, i asked my FATHER not to give me any downloads at this moment. Well, he did gave me time and couple of days and i thanked him for that. Last night it's time to have my download i can feel it. First i said goodnight to my DEVINE FATHER and said my little prayers and then closed my eyes..and once i did that..i suddenly saw a black and white spirals flashing out there in a galaxy. Then later on it changed into a very white lights descending towards me while i am laying in my bed.

My whole body embodied with the lights coming from above. Then the "white being's" head suddenly appeared where the lights penetrating into my body. I tried to denied that this is a BEING..but it keeps going back and fort into the lights. I asked papa GOD to come in..and he did appear suddenly, but the white beautiful being still there looking down at me.

I saw papa GOD above and this being's head. Then suddenly the lights even more extensive and embodied my whole body. I tried to shift my thoughts to the green lady being which i have noticed her presence. She showed me her face but only for few seconds. She made me feel comfortable and not to feel worried. I called my DEVINE FATHER again..then my FATHER face suddenly appeared up there peeking through amongst the clouds and looking down at me.

He made me feel comfortable and stating to my head not to worry. Then the white being still there with the very white light, while my DEVINE FATHER is above of this being, and both of there lights are became one..and then they started sending more towards me. Then both of them asked me to stand up and face with them and put myself into the lights with them. Now i can see myself standing in the middle of the lights and the white being is above me and my DEVINE FATHER is above him.

Then the 3 of us in the same lights, suddenly i heard a command from my DEVINE FATHER, and secondly from the white being. Start healing the world my child..then i extended both of my arms up and then forward...then i noticed myself i'm all white..then i pointed my arms out towards the earth and down. We are looking down the WORLD..we are all on top on the EARTH sending the lights..the DEVINE healing lights penetrating from the top and into the very deep inside of the earth..deep down..i can feel it..the world becoming white..my hands and my whole body are extremely white and sparkling. I can feel this incredible power all over my body while being connected to both higher DEVINES above me.

During my healing, i can feel the heaviness of the world..sadness.. pain and sorrow while i'm sending the healing lights. Many more emotions i can feel as i continued my healing. I am healing the earth so heavily, and a lot of people still fighting not to be healed.. refusing and i can see people and entities wearing black clothings and robes with thier hoods running for cover. I can see them in the forest running towards the cave..BIG cave..refusing to be hit by the white lights..i kept going..i kept pointing my arms and my hands to every corner of the earth..from up and down..then left to right, i then realised it's a sign of the CROSS!! Then the lights suddenly stopped.. my body stood there still in white..then slowly my body started to collapse..and my brother JESUS caught me in his arms and started carrying me. I can see his back walking while carrying me in his arms. Then i suddenly wake up very thirsty but feeling rejuvinated.

Then i had an urged to look at myself in the mirror..somehow i closed my eyes..i meditated and talked to my DEVINE FATHER and i thanked for the download last night. Then i thanked the WHITE BEING and showed me their KINGDOM out their in another dimension. I saw 3 green ladies being..tall and looking at me with pride and looks very proud of me. Then i started healing myself and suddenly i heard.."whatever you want..whatever you need, it's all yours". That's the exact words i heard. Oh..that's beautiful. Thank you!

# CHAPTER 110

# A DOWNLOAD WHILE IN THE SHOWER

JOURNAL

14TH MARCH 2023

Today while i'm in the shower, i felt some kind of unsusual lights coming from above. I thought..hmm..i am getting a download again. It's a very familiar feelings of energy. Then i closed my eyes while under the shower, the white lights started to intensifies and slowly descending towards me while the water is on. I called for Papa GOD, then he appeared on top of the white bright lights. He then said, yes my child it is time for healing again. OK..healing while i'm in the shower? I asked curiously. Yes my child..because the water protects you and you are safe under and arround the water.

Oh ok i said, then i saw my DEVINE FATHER made a clear circle and send it to Earth..it's more like a blanket..clear and looks like a silhouete covering the Earth. Ohh..i don't understand it. then i can see myself sorrounded by the same clear energy, and before it happened..my DEVINE FATHER put me on top of the earth looking down. I can see myself wearing a very white and almost sparkling long gown clothing. Then my DEVINE FATHER instructed me to get my hands ready and to extend it out. From left to right slowly sending the white and healing energy, then going circle, all arround and covering the earth.

Then my DEVINE FATHER asked me to stop and to focus more on my right side while still facing the Earth. Now this time point your hands from the top then slowly move your hands down to the bottom and stay there for few minutes, he instructed me. Try to go down to the very deep of that place he said, and just focus on the ocean. It's sounds very profound order from him. So i foccused on the BIG ocean..i can see my healing lights activating the senses of all the mamals. I can see them so happy while swimming really fast and almost RACING MY LIGHTS!

Then suddenly...i saw the KING of the Ocean, with his spear, and i noticed he has a crown just fitted on his forehead but not on top of his head, with a ROYAL BLUE trimming arround. The center of the CROWN has dark blue rock or crytal. I can see him riding on the dolphin, racing and facing towards me! And the most interesting he said to me is "ALOHA"!!! while waving at me smiling! :) and i waved back to him :) ALOHA?? i said to myself..why not different language just like ancient language? Then i heard papa GOD voice..remember from your past lifetime, you were here in this island..he knows you. OH ok :) hehehe..silly me :)

Anyway, then Papa GOD shifted my healing to the other part of the continent. This time is the AMAZON forest part of the bare land..then i started healing. I can see the animals are starting to notice the lights coming from me and penetrating into them. And they seems familiar of my healing lights:) The Jungle started to make some noises..happy noises..i can hear it, the joy of there voices coming from different species, noises coming from all different kinds of animals rejoicing..and it's so beatutiful to hear and watching them so happy.

Then Papa GOD shifted my focus on the ice land or Arctic and other part of the land with solid ice. I can see polar bears..and most of them are white. Then i saw a mother bear walking along and on top of the solid ice island with 5 little bears behind her. Then they have noticed my healing lights..and they all turned arround and accepted the lights. I can see there eyes were closed and absorbing the energy and the lights penetrating into them. Ohh..it is so beautiful to watch..i feel like crying with joy while watching them. :) Then i noticed, there is a really big cave infront of me..i can see it is melting, and the ice wall too. Then my hands automatically send some energy into it.. and i can see the cave and the wall slowly going back to solid ice..a solid and thick ice.

Then from the horizon, i can see the big wall of SUNAMI coming into the city..dark and solid wave is about to hit the city. I don't know what city it is but suddenly i extended my arms and hands pointing towards the sunami far away where i was standing. Then i started to send this energy towards the big water that it's about to hit the area, and tried to calmed it down. It takes few minutes to lower the huge wall of water which is taller than the very high buildings, and wait..wait..i have a sudden download..in NEW YORK!. Oh dear GOD..then suddenly i send an energy towards it, i tried to control it..it's very high and scary wave and it's about to crash into the city..i tried hard to slow it down..then slowly..i slowly controlled it. The water starting to calmed down..and slowing down. I can see the water gushing through the streets, the mixture of black mud and clear water..then eventually the flow started to become clearer.

Then i saw sandstorms wrecking havocs in a particular area. I can see it from the distance..red clouds? then i realised it's a sand storm. I tried to stop it..then a sudden impact on me!. I felt like i was hit by the sand storm really hard! Then i suddenly wake up from my meditation. Before i opened my eyes i can hear the heavy rain in the background then i turned off the shower, the rain slowed down and suddenly stopped.

That was it, that was my unexpected download while i was in the shower. After that, i was very thristy, and feeling like to sleep. I asked my DEVINE FATHER about the rain and water during my meditation? well, the water and the rain protects you during your meditation. No one can reach you during the process while you are healing the world. Although, you have extra protections, Papa GOD said. Then i can see number 7 from afar, it looks like a galaxy out there and with another 222 numbers showed up. I don't know i'm too tired to ask my FATHER about this, so i decided to leave it here.. Thank you my DEVINE FATHER..I LOVE YOU.

# CHAPTER 111

# THE DEVIL WALKING ACCROSS MY PATH

JOURNAL

16TH MARCH 2023

Last night before i went to bed i said my prayers and was talking to my PAPA GOD. While closing my eyes suddenly i can see myself as a young girl between 10 or 11 years old standing in an area with nobody arround and in the middle of the road facing the west horizon. The area looks like has been abandoned the way the sorrounding area looks like and has been neglected. While i was standing in the middle of the road facing west, i can see the sunset starting to come down..and now i can see the light and the dark is in between each other, and i am realising it is dawn.

While standing in the middle of the road, suddenly this BIG scary evil looking is coming across the road from my right side. His body is RED with 2 horns on his head and continued walking, while crossing the road from my right he slowed down while staring at me. I am looking at this scary evil looking being in a slow motion. He is walking very slowly, and his shoulders are very low or dropped down..and the whole body looking submissively but slightly smiling at me while crossing the road. I am confused at that moment..he supposed to scare me, but this time i'm not scared of him. I felt like he knew me..and i defeated him before. So i'm just watching him walking accross infront of me very submissively.

Then suddenly, Arch Angel Michael appeared from west horizon where i am facing..and i can see him walking towards me while i'm still standing in the middle of the road. He then told the evil being with horns in a very brave voice of command..he said, you stay away from her!!! I thought..whoahh..then i can see myself as young adult.

My body changed quickly into a Warriour and wearing a Warriour outfit, and my sword is in my hand. Then i met Arch Angel Michael in the middle of the road where i am standing, then i started walking towards him. While i was walking..somehow i was dragging my sword on the ground touching the tip, and feeling myself i am ready again for the battle. Then suddenly we both disappeared and went to the battle.

Then papa GOD shifted myself again. I can see myself in bed and asked my FATHER if i can see him..he said, of course my child. Come..you know how to find me and your home. Then i saw myself as a child again..this time is little younger than 5..Papa GOD turned me into a 3 years old girl. I don't know why he kept changing me into a different age. I can see myself running towards him up in the verandah with full of clouds. I can see him bending down and trying to welcomed me with his arms wide open. Oh..Papa GOD i miss you and started crying..i can see my little body clinging into my DEVINE FATHER's body..the amazing and loving energy i feel is just pure joy and love, and reassurance feelings kept circleing arround our bodies together. I can feel my DEVINE FATHER missess me too.

Then my brother JESUS standing beside watching us with full of love and happiness, and I can see his face really clearly this time. He still have his black beard and moustache and he has very soothing eyes and soo magnetic. This time Papa GOD sat down on his chair while still carrying me on his arm. He sat me on his right lap and started stretching my little tiny legs and started feeling and massaging the soles of my feet. I just don't know why? but in a physical world the soles of my feet are somehow acheing..that's why i have my feet massaged few times lately. So now i know the connections in a spiritual and physical realms. I am understanding it now why he is doing that to the soles of my feet. It feels good and the pain disappeared.

I can see my DEVINE FATHER's face this time again..and he has white hair with medium hair lenght and slightly wavy. I am staring at his face this time while he is gently massaging the soles of my feet. He does straightened my feet on and off very gently, and i can see my feet little bit oily. Then suddenly SKY appeared amongst the clouds while we were sitting and facing out the verandah. I said to papa GOD..it's SKY..my SKY is coming while i'm pointing at him. Then papa GOD put me down slowly..and then i walked towards my SKY..and then for some reason..there's a brown little carpet went underneath my feet..and started lifting me up and sat me on SKY's back.

Then i'm on his back..SKY started to walk very slowly while JESUS behind me holding my back gently. And then..he said with his soothing voice..go..and ride with SKY for awhile. Then SKY started walking very slowly, i can hear his walks on the marble floor. Click.. clack..click clack..and i'm on his back holding his body so gently and somehow my body felt like i'm glued into his back. Then i can see where we are going to the very long corridor towards east and the clouds started to disappeard infront of us.

Then SKY kept walking..and this time a little bit faster..then suddenly i can see his wings and he's floating in the air..i mean flying very gently. Then he came down and still walking on the marble floor in the very long verandah of heaven. I am so happy to see SKY. At least i got to played with him, and this time i didn't see my pets.

I think this time it's only for SKY bonding, papa GOD and my brother JESUS. Somehow i was in tears when i saw my DEVINE FATHER..i really miss him..i don't know why? but i always talk to him though. I don't really want to ask him this time..i'll leave it as it is, at least i was in his arms again and that's all it matters. I feel his loving energy..Thank you MY DEVINE FATHER. I LOVE YOU.

# CHAPTER 112

# EXTRA PROTECTION VORTEX MACHINE

JOURNAL
21ST MARCH 2023

Last night, it was an amazing but chaotic energy sorrounding my safety space. First i had a big discussion with the boss, i think she enjoyed that power on herself, but i was cool and respected her authorities. Secondly, i am little bit disappointed with one of my student/s, but whatever reason she possesed that moment, i am really disappointed of her actions against me. I am sure next time she will be thinking it twice before compromising my position. God bless them.

Another bizzare energies that has been lingering lately and i am trying to understand the purpose of it. And one thing i don't really like from this people is to push and kept pushing me to do things that i don't really want to do. What's wrong with this people? Don't they know how to respect the human boundary?? I don't understand it.. as "if" they have every right to push me and not knowing i have my own priorities? my own life..my work..and especially my entitlement of safety, financially and personally.

It seems they don't get it!! they think they are entitled to do this to me? I was very upset and annoyed of the situations. It's debilitating to have somebody kept poking your nose and just to prove it to themselves that they can access me with thier own authorities. Well HELL "NO" to them! who are they or do you think you are? If you want to commit a federal offence and then keep it to yourselves! Don't involve anybody! SCAMMERS! DO YOU THINK i am stupid and cannot see where you coming at? I am trying to be nice and be more acceptance with all your people bullshits, but this time..i don't and i am not acknowledging your existence. It upsets me and i tried to composed myself in a right manner, but this time i really lost my respect to you people who doesn't respect my boundaries.

Last night i consulted my DEVINE FATHER..looks like he is waiting for me, i can see him sitting on his big marble chair and looks very solemn. I went to him closer and he then gave me a HUG. I cried.. and cried infront of him..he seems like he is feeling my emotions at the same time. My face is on his chest and i can see Papa GOD white clothes have my tears on it..then he said very faintly..shhhh... it's okay my child, leave this to me..and i can feel the overwhelming reasssurance and love from him while tapping my back very softly.. everything will be taken care of my child. DO NOT WORRY.

He then looked at my face and said..you have little snort on your nose..and i laughed..he then laughed..and we both laughing:)and for some reason he didn't turned me into a child. He then asked me to stand up and walked with him. Come with me he said..then i followed my FATHER..then he is showing me this kind of clouds..a very thick clouds that it was forming into a long and round circle, but moving like a vortex infront of him. The colour is more like a very light golden colour, and with white colour on the side. It's moving..it's turning like into a machine. Then papa GOD asked me to go inside in it..which i did. When i was inside..i asked papa GOD..what's this for FATHER? he said, this is your extra "PROTECTIONS" and purifies your hurts and emotions my child. So, i was in there while papa GOD is watching me. It's a kind of scan machine but, it's made of clouds that forms into a machine.hmmm..then i fall asleep.

# CHAPTER 113

# 7 DISASTERS REPRESENTS

JOURNAL

23RD MARCH 2023

I was dreaming this morning, i was crying..crying..i was looking for PAPA GOD..i couldn't find him..all i want is a hug..then suddenly papa GOD called me..i'm here my child. Then i saw myself in my FATHER's KINGDOM as a child again and running towards him, i can see him with an open arms. I run really fast then suddenly i tripped over because of my shoes..my black slippery shoes. So i took it off and i'm barefooted again running on the marble floor.

Then my DEVINE FATHER catches and gave me a Big hug. Ohh..i miss you papa GOD, he didn't say anything, but i felt the beautiful love from him and happiness on his face. So DEVINELY feelings between us..oh..i miss you FATHER..i feel like everyone and everything are conspiring against me in this reality world. I can't even have a HUG when i feel sad..people are so cruel..i cried.

Then suddenly, i saw number 6 out there amongst with the dark clouds..then 6 long golden daggers have appeared infront of me, and the 2 daggers have been pulled out automatically, while i was looking at it..papa GOD said to me sternly "USE IT"! My DEVINE FATHER is authorising and commanding me in a firmly voice to use it. The 2 daggers was pulled out infront of me are sorrounded by misty black energy..and i asked why is it black? and my DEVINE FATHER said, it is the energy you need to eliminate. And he said it again.."USE IT"..i am authorising you to use it! Then i saw myself as woman again..and before i could say anything..STOP! no more questions he said firmly. Papa GOD seems is not too happy of what's going on with me here in a physical world.

Then papa GOD and myself appear in a BIG HALL with marble long table and chairs. Papa GOD is sitting in the very front table, and my brother JESUS also sitting in the opposite side of my DEVINE FATHER, they are both facing each other. Then i saw myself sitting beside my DEVINE FATHER on his right side. The rest of the entities are sitting as well, but i couldn't see their faces..it's all silhouetes but with clear and white energy sorrounding thier faces. I looks so dignified, and sort of wearing something unusual..looks like a battle is going to start again..my battle..this is a big meeting prior to my battle especially if it's a BIG ONE!

Then papa GOD showed me number 7..and this time it's 7 swords! I don't really know what 7 swords represents. Then papa GOD said..1 sword represents disasters such as darkness and earthquakes destructions. 2nd sword represents water, flooding collapsing mountains..big boulders.. big storms..tornados. 3rd sword represents WARS, people killing each others, the fights between humankinds. I can see the sorroundings are just people getting killed and soldiers with BIG guns in a uniforms. 4th swords its FIRE disasters..flames i can see..burning the places.. everywhere. The 5th is sickness..dead bodies are every where and famine. The 6th and 7th are not yet for me to be seen.

My DEVINE FATHER said, this the whole world responsibilities to control the next disasters coming. And for myself..my work is in the spiritual world with my ANGELS and Ancestors to assist. My child you have Big work to do in a Spiritual realm. I know my DEVINE FATHER..this is my calling and to those people can use thier vibrational energy to assist the world of healing, they need to use it.

My DEVINE FATHER, last night the image you showed me was cut off suddenlly..why? My dear journal, this image is the continuation of my last meditation i have encountered. I saw this very long and high and very tall pillar and it's colour white, and then i noticed there is a geometrical and horizontal patterns carved arround the very tall pillar all arround and to the top. This high pillar is not ordinary..i have never seen this before..it looks like a pyramid..but it is formed as a very tall pillar, and it's made of a kind of white CRYSTAL? with a little tinged of colour pink on the sides of the pillar.

Then i saw my DEVINE FATHER beside the Crystal Pillar, and i didn't see his whole body but just his face. I recognised him from the far distance..looking up to him. Then to my surprised, the white being suddenly appeared and looking so white and pure just like my DEVINE FATHER. It's the same..i didn't see the whole body, but only the face and a very ROYAL face, but the white being was not human looking being. He's face have this purity looking and the face have this twinkling like diamonds all over his face and the sorrounding area of his head. I can feel a strong authoritative figure on him and seriousness of his face.

Then i saw myself just quickly appeared infront of them..and they both sent the messages to my head commanded me precisely to immerged and to stand infront of the pillar. I moved my body slowly infront of the pillar, then my DEVINE FATHER on top of the pillar, and secondly the white being in the middle. Then the 3 of us are in the middle and with an alighnment of the Tall pillar. Then i fell asleep.

This morning when i wake up, i went to have a shower, suddenly i remembered my download last night. I asked my DEVINE FATHER if i have to continue the download last night? He said yes..this is the right time as you are sorrounded by the water..you are safe my child. So then, i closed my eyes and then the download started up again, and it's the continuation of the last night messages.

I saw myself aligned with the WHITE BEING and my DEVINE FATHER with the Tall CRYSTAL PILLAR. Then papa GOD asked me to open my arms facing the earth. I opened my arms, and suddenly my "Wings" opened up and elevated my body little bit higher from where i am standing. Then i heard a command..starts sending your healing lights towards the earth. When i extended my arms and pointed out my hands to where they want me to start..i can see this crystal energy coming out from my whole body. I can feel the 3 of us are sending the enermous energy towards the earth. A very white and clear healing energy enveloping the sorrounding body of the Earth.

Then my DEVINE FATHER said..this is how you align yourself my child..i will let you know the next healing to Earth. Yes FATHER, thank you. Then the "white Being" slowly disappeared from my sight. Goodbye my DEVINE FATHER AND TO THE WHITE BEING. I bowed respectfully to them. Then i saw so many hearts floating arround.. and then crystal diamonds flickering on the air..i felt the acknowledgement from the WHITE BEING. THANK YOU. :)

# CHAPTER 114

# TO SHIFT MY WRITING

JOURNAL
27TH MARCH 2023

Last night before i went to bed, i spoke to my DEVINE FATHER in my subconscious. Then he connected me straightaway to the open space above. To where i was standing and looking up, and here it was the BIG PILLAR is towering me, and i noticed the pillar has a different colour this time..it's a very light yellow green colour. There was a colour that papa GOD mentioned..but i cannot recall now. I guess and maybe it's not so important this time, then he asked me to immerge again infront of the pillar, which i did then the WHITE BEING appeared on top of me or my head..then my DEVINE FATHER on the very top of the pillar. I have noticed the 3 of us has been in alignment again together.

Then both of them have asked me to open my arms outwards while looking down the Earth. Now both of my arms are opened..then i noticed the energy was coming from my whole body, were from my DEVINE FATHER and the WHITE BEING..now i started sending my healing energy to EARTH. I can see some kind of a blanket covering the EArth with clear white and sparkling energy. It's enveloping the whole world, then my DEVINE FATHER said.. it's a "PROTECTION".

Then i fall asleep..and when i got up this morning i was feeling good. I don't feel bothered anymore, i feel different. Then i heard my DEVINE FATHER's voice..there are some "JUSTICE TO BE MADE". You are protected my child..continue your divine mission.. we are here for you. As your DEVINE FATHER, I WON'T LET YOU FALL. THANK YOU my DEVINE FATHER. I LOVE YOU. :)

# CHAPTER 115

# EVERYTHING IS ANGELICL COLOUR THE BOW AND ARROW AND ROUND WHITE AND GLITTERY BALL

JOURNAL

*30/03/2023*

My DEVINE FATHER pulled me instantly for meditation, then he showed me to look up..then i can see the "BIG EYE" up on the SKY almost looking down at me. MY DEVINE FATHER is wearing white clothings..so white..then i can see him looking at the same thing of what i am staring at..the BIG EYE. PAPA GOD is facing and staring at the BIG ONE EYE. Then behind PAPA GOD..i saw little things moving..looks like red little crabs and have one eye on top of there back. So many of them, but they were not biting my DEVINE FATHER. Then Papa GOD called me, he said my child come..while his right arm extending to me and welcoming to join him.

I appeared infront of him but slightly far away from him and standing and aligned to the BIG EYE. The BIG EYE is on top of me, and i am standing below it. PAPA GOD still kneeling on his left leg facing towards me while the BIG EYE is on top of me. He made me read his mind asking me to "LOOK AT HIM" and DO NOT MOVE. Stay still my child.

I saw myself as a very young teenager with black hair straight down to my shoulder. I am wearing a very white dress and kind of "sparkling" looking CRYSTAL DRESS below knee. I looked so innocently and waiting for my DEVINE FATHER instructions. Then suddenly..a very white and "crystal bow" and "arrow" appeared infront of me in my right hand. Then my DEVINE FATHER showed me and pointing directly to a "BIG CRYSTAL BALL with his right hand while the crystal ball started moving towards him, then it suddenly stopped not too close to him.

He is showing me to hit this white crystal ball with my white crystal bow and arrow. I then aimed my bow and arrow towards the white crystal ball..then papa GOD suddenly stopped the image. Then i came back to myself from my meditation..then i asked my DEVINE FATHER..what was that for my DEVINE FATHER? He then said..."PREPARATIONS" my child. Oh okay, i said. Drink plenty of water my child, he said.

# CHAPTER 116

# THE SPIRITUAL WARFARE BATTLE

JOURNAL
11TH APRIL 2023

Last night i was restless, somebody have been attacking my body again during my asleep. Without hesitation i started eliminating them one at a time. There was a woman with dark long hair, trying to attacked me..i can see her frustrations during the attacked. It seems like she couldn't come near me..it feels like i was inside the bubble and she could't penetrated into the bubble. She even tried to use a nasty looking BIG creature to suck and tear the bubble that sorrounding my body. This big creature looks like a leech and could not get into my safety energy space.

She was screaming..and while screaming with frustrations, her image kept changing into very ugly and nasty creatures. Then i thought..i'm sick of it looking at her going crazy..so i think of my daggers, and instantly it appeared in my both hands, then i attacked this woman's head to both temples with my daggers, and then she melted away and disappeared.

My DEVINE FATHER have waken me up so suddenly. He lowered his right arm towards me and automatically my right hand connected to him. He took me to the place that the spiritual warfare was about to start. He changed my nightie clothes quickly into a BAttle gear just by clicking his fingers, while i was still rubbing my eyes. This is your battle my child! he commanded me. You have every weapons you could possibly be using, all the weapons i have given you, and you are the only one who could use it during this BATTLE! he told me firmly. Yes DEVINE FATHER! i affirmed!

Then i can see myself on the top of the mountain, and the sorrounding is dark! I can see flames from the west horizon and starting to get bigger..and getting higher. I can see myself standing very tall and facing the horizons. Then sudddenly the HUGE Black entity with 2 horns quickly appeared from the horizon..and i can see it's started running towards me. He is HUGE and very scary looking creature, and his chest including the whole body is so Black and the face is red! I was startled..then my DEVINE FATHER said..think of your weapons!!! Then my golden CROSS BOW and ARROW quickly appeared into my hands. I quickly charged towards him..but i missed my target for him, i tried again quickly and several times, but this creature is very tricky. Then i heard papa GOD voice saying close your eyes and "FEEL" the TARGET!

Then when i closed my eyes, the BIG BLACK SCARY BEING quickly disappeared. Then little creatures appeared from nowhere and everywhere. Then i have noticed from where i was standing that they are all getting closer and ready to attack me. I noticed i have been blindfolded by my FATHER..then he said now "FEEL" IT! he said with a FIRM command. I closed my eyes again, and every corner of the area that where i put my focused on, amazingly from the distance i am feeling the golden stars twinkling..very small lights but visible enough for me to see while my eyes were closed...and that's my target!

I started to hit the targets and kept hitting, while i stayed where i was standing, and kneeled down with my one knee while my bow and arrow are kept charging towards them. The little creatures were very deceptives..they kept moving arround and they are so quick.. but my bow and arrow knows where to aimed my targets. My body synchronising with it. My bow and arrows kept charging Then suddenly, it stopped hitting the targets! and my eyes still blind folded.

Then to my surprised..the GIANT EVIL looking BEING suddenly appeared from the distance..somehow this creature couldn't come near me. Then PAPA GOD said, you have one AROW left my child.. now use it to eliminate him. I can see this creature from the distance looking so angry! I aimed my last ARROW towards him..he was moving very fast and i couldn't focus..but my heart is saying.."Feel" it. Then suddenly I FEEL the "HEAT" instantly in my "heart space".. and from that moment i released the arrow and suddenly, i heard booomm!!

I quickly removed my blind fold and saw his heart was hit with my golden arrow! I saw the creature fell backwards with scary sounds!!! Then i saw him started falling quickly. Then after i struck him, the black energy was sorrunding him turned slowly into a golden colour, then in a few seconds he disappeared from my sight.

Then another one Tall Angelic creature suddenly appeared infront of me with BIG white wings!! This creature is fiery and towering me. He also sorrounded himself with fires and flames!!! I ran higher to the top of the mountain, then i can see he was getting closer towards me behind my back...then PAPA GOD said in my head..use your long bar silver metal weapon..then the weapon quickly appeared into my hands, i turned arround and aimed the weapon towards him when he was starting to charge towards me. Then when he got closer..i struck him with my silver weapon on his chest.

Once i struck him..his wings started flapping like crazy! and started releasing this kind of black energies arround, then the whole area became chaotic..flames everywhere..and then pitch black has became in the sorrounding area..there is lightning and thundering after i struck his chest. I don't really know who i have just eliminated, and it was an ANGEL! I called to my DEVINE FATHER, but he's not responding to me..instead he is showing me a lightning from the distance. Then i wake up suddenly and very thirsty, i drank my whole water beside my bed.

# CHAPTER 117

# PITCH BLACK

JOURNAL
13TH APRIL 2023

Then i went back to bed and went to sleep again, then Papa GOD took me again to the area of the high mountain. I can see that this is the continuations of my astral travel from the last couple of days. I can see myself standing infront of the High white pillar, and this time i am by myself and Papa GOD instructing me to hold my white and glittering cross bow and arrow, and at the back where i am standing.. the sorrounding is all black. I can see myself as a 11 years old KID and wearing a white and glittering clothes, and my bow and arrow has the same colour.

Papa GOD kneeled down beside me while i am standing on top of the big Rock but behind the pillar..he then pointing out with his finger the round black ball just suddenly appeared from the distance. He is asking me to hit that TARGET, pointing the black ball from the distance. He then said.."FEEL" it my child. So i aimed my glittering and almost ANGELIC looking Cross Bow and Arrow to the target, then i closed my eyes and then..i quickly hit the trigger and released the arrow, then i hit the black ball from the distance, then suddenly everything is BLACK!..PITCH BLACK!

My dear journal i don't know why it became BLACK!! My DEVINE FATHER SHOWING ME..6..or 60?..then 30? i asked Papa GOD what is this means? Is it 6 days..60 days 6 weeks then it changed to 3..or 30?..i don't know..and my DEVINE FATHER said, "HAVE A REST MY CHILD". You deserve it..well done. OK Papa GOD Goodnight, and before i can say I love you to him.. He said "I LOVE you my child"..and that was it.

THIS IS THE END OF MY SPIRITUAL JOURNEY UNTIL THE NEXT.

PLEASE HELP ME SAVE THE PLANET EARTH.

MAY GOD BLESS YOU ALL.

MY DEVINE FATHER IS ASKING TO RAISE THE GOOD VIBRATION IN EARTH

FOR THE SAKE OF HUMANITY.

THIS BOOK HAS BEEN BLESSED BY MY DEVINE FATHER

T

THE END